The **SEL** SOLUTION

Integrate Social and Emotional Learning into Your Curriculum and Build a Caring Climate for All

Jonathan C. Erwin

free spirit
PUBLISHING®

Library of Congress Cataloging-in-Publication Data

Names: Erwin, Jonathan C., 1954–

Title: The SEL solution : integrate social and emotional learning into your curriculum and build a caring climate for all / written by Jonathan C. Erwin.

Description: Minneapolis, MN : Free Spirit Publishing, [2019] | Includes bibliographical references and index.

Identifiers: LCCN 2018061371 | ISBN 9781631984372 (pbk.) | ISBN 9781631984396 (epub) | ISBN 1631984373 (pbk.) | ISBN 9781631984389 (web pdf)

Subjects: LCSH: Affective education. | Social learning. | Academic achievement.

Classification: LCC LB1072 .E78 2019 | DDC 370.15/34—dc23 LC record available at https://lccn.loc.gov/2018061371

Free Spirit Publishing does not have control over or assume responsibility for author or third-party websites and their content. At the time of this book's publication, all facts and figures cited within are the most current available. All telephone numbers, addresses, and website URLs are accurate and active; all publications, organizations, websites, and other resources exist as described in this book; and all have been verified as of April 2019. If you find an error or believe that a resource listed here is not as described, please contact Free Spirit Publishing.

Edited by Eric Braun

Cover and interior design by Emily Dyer

10 9 8 7 6 5 4 3 2 1

Printed in the United States of America

Free Spirit Publishing Inc.
6325 Sandburg Road, Suite 100
Minneapolis, MN 55427-3674
(612) 338-2068
help4kids@freespirit.com
freespirit.com

FSC
www.fsc.org
MIX
Paper from
responsible sources
FSC® C005010

Free Spirit offers competitive pricing.

Contact edsales@freespirit.com for pricing information on multiple quantity purchases.

Dedication

This book is dedicated to my loving children,
Nathan David Erwin and Laena Maryn Erwin.

Acknowledgments

First and foremost, I would like to express my gratitude to world-renowned educator and psychiatrist, the late Dr. William Glasser. His work in the fields of psychology and education continues to empower people to be better teachers, managers, and parents, and to achieve their full potential as people. I am also thankful to the William Glasser Institute (WGI) for giving me permission to use Glasser's Choice Theory as the philosophical and psychological foundation of this book. Specifically, thank you to Kim Olver, the executive director of the WGI; Bob Hoglund, the president of the WGI-US advisory board; and all the WGI faculty members and friends who helped me apply Glasser's ideas over the last 25 years, including special thanks to Nancy Buck, Cathy Curtis, Ellen Gelinas, Bob Hoglund, Carleen Glasser, Judy Hatswell, Al Katz, Lynn Sumida, and Bob Sullo.

Next, I'd like to thank Marjorie Lisovskis and the whole Free Spirit Publishing team for the opportunity to publish with such a high-quality organization, with special thanks to my tireless editor, Eric Braun, for his time, effort, and all his excellent questions and suggestions throughout the editing process.

Third, I'd like to thank all the students I've had the honor to teach and learn from over the last 30 years, not only the K–12 students, but also the thousands of teachers and school administrators who have attended my seminars and workshops. I'd like to thank my family and friends for your encouragement, patience, and honest feedback during the years it took to complete the manuscript.

Fourth, my deep appreciation goes to the following people who reviewed my manuscript during development: Lauren Grader-Fox, Bradley Evans, and Kristen Bivens.

And, finally, I'd like to acknowledge that that my wonderful children, Nathan David and Laena Maryn Erwin, are the inspiration behind *The SEL Solution*.

Contents

List of Reproducible Forms

Page numbers listed below refer to thumbnail previews. See page 191 for instructions on how to download the reproducible forms.

Introduction

Beginning this book with an analogy may belie its practical nature. But as a former middle and high school English teacher, I love analogies. And actually, analogies are very practical: They are a wonderful teaching tool, helping people see clearly that which otherwise may be obscure.

Here's the analogy: Educating students is like growing a garden.

Imagine an empty lot, one that we want to transform into a lush flower garden. As those responsible for this garden, we might begin by hiring a well-respected landscape architect to create a design for it, just as in education we spend billions paying teams of experts to create federal, state, and local curricula. Once we have our design, we might then hire a knowledgeable landscaper to plant, fertilize, water, weed, and nurture our new garden. Similarly, in schools we hire the best teaching candidates, expecting them to use the most effective instructional and classroom management practices available, resulting in our students learning and growing to their potential.

In time, we will evaluate our garden in terms of how we originally envisioned it. Based on our evaluation, we may need to make adjustments— moving a plant into a sunnier spot, watering more or less frequently, and so on. In schools, educators use a wide variety of assessments to evaluate our students' learning: formal, informal, formative, summative, standardized, teacher-created, and more. As in the gardening scenario, the results of the assessment may call for adjustments or improvements. In such cases, we may reexamine and revise our curriculum, our instructional

or classroom management practices, and/or the assessment tool, hoping for better scores on the next assessment.

Common sense would tell us that these three elements—planning (curriculum development), planting and nurturing (instructing and managing), and assessing and adjusting—would be everything we need to create a beautiful garden or educate our students.

There is a fourth element, however, which seems so obvious that we may not even consider it: the climate in which we attempt to grow our garden. For example, if a landscape architect from the American Southwest doesn't consider the climate of a garden planted in a southern Quebec province—many of the flowers and fruit trees he plants won't survive the harsh winters. His design will fail. No amount of tending will make a difference.

Similarly, if we don't attend to the climate in which our students are "planted," we, as educators, will also fail—no matter how well-designed the curriculum or how effective the teaching is.

Of course, some plants can thrive in a wide variety of climates, just like many students can learn and thrive in almost any learning environment. However, many plants thrive only within a limited range of temperature, rainfall, and other climate factors, and many students require specific school climate conditions in order to reach their "growing" or learning potential.

If we don't consider the climate in which our students and educators are striving to meet education standards, we are doomed to repeat the pattern of examining and revising our curriculum, instruction, and/or the assessments while continuing to achieve the same unsatisfactory results. Doing the same thing over and over and expecting different results: Isn't that the definition of insanity?

Here is where the garden analogy breaks down: We can't control the physical climate in which we garden. It's impossible to turn an arctic tundra into the tropics. However, we *can* have a profound positive impact on the climate in which we educate our children. Through intentionally focusing on improving and maintaining a positive school climate, we can create a learning environment in which all students can thrive.

This book shows you how.

Why School Climate Matters in an Era of Standards and Assessments

Educational policies in the United States and Canada, and those in many other countries throughout the world, seem to focus on one main goal: global economic competition. In the United States, especially, education seems to be driven by the economic and political objective to be number one to an extent not seen since the Cold War—particularly since the Sputnik launch in 1957 and the subsequent emphasis on science and mathematics. Today, however, more is involved. Nations are concerned with attaining or maintaining their economic status in a highly globalized, complex, dynamic, volatile, and ever-shrinking world.

This drive to be first in the global marketplace has had a profound effect on educational policy and practices over the years. The call to "Raise the standards!" has been the battle cry since the 1980s, with educators in the United States now grappling with more demanding student learning standards (such as Common Core State Standards, or CCSS). We have been introduced to dozens of learning and teaching models, from Madeline C. Hunter's elements of instruction to collaborative learning to brain-based learning to differentiated

instruction to response to intervention (RTI)— and on and on.

Likewise, educators have learned about many assessment models, including authentic assessment; curriculum-based assessment; and mastery, competence, or proficiency-based education. And, of course, today's educators are well aware of assessments designed to evaluate how students and teachers are performing in terms of meeting the CCSS. Even with the passing of the Every Student Succeeds Act (ESSA), with its intent to diminish excessive use of testing, the focus remains on testing and accountability that impacts educators and students every day.

The Impact of Current Trends on Administrators and Educators

For educators, federal and state mandates and the focus on achievement test scores can be overwhelming. Administrators are concerned with finding dollars in the budget to comply with the ever-increasing unfunded state and federal mandates. They express frustration with the number of teacher observations required while continuing to effectively address the daily crises, parent communication, stacks of paperwork, student discipline, and other responsibilities piled high on their professional plates. The bottom line is stress for most, *dis*tress for many.

Being under this kind of pressure and scrutiny is too much for many teachers, who are choosing to leave the profession. New teacher retention has reached what some call a crisis. The stresses of teaching, and subsequently of high teacher turnover, take a tremendous toll: first, on those thousands of young people who have invested money and time toward achieving a teaching degree that they are not likely to use; second, on already inadequate school district budgets in terms of taxpayer dollars spent on advertising, hiring, and training new teachers; third, and most importantly, on students who are assigned to novice teachers or long-term substitutes. The students in these classrooms often lose a sense of continuity and the benefits of learning from seasoned professionals.

The Impact of Current Trends on Students

Kids come to school stressed. An American Psychological Association survey reported that adolescents are, on average, at least as stressed as the adults around them, sometimes more.[1] During the school year, their stress level increases significantly.

It isn't hard to understand why. The pressure and distress that administrators and teachers feel can trickle down to students. As more time is focused on mathematics and English language arts, less time is dedicated to art, music, history, science, STEM, physical education, experiential learning, team-building activities, and play. Many students' homework load can interfere with important free time at home and sometimes with family plans and activities, creating more stress. Test preparation often results in sedentary learning—students working independently at their desks on reading, writing, and computation—with little opportunity to talk or exercise.

The tests themselves, of course, are stressful. But more stressful is the anticipation of them. Children lose sleep and many teachers regularly "stress" the importance of these assessments and spend class time on little else but test preparation.

So much for the proverbial carefree childhood; today's kids are stressed! And many—those who set almost impossible goals for themselves, or who struggle because of economic, family, social, emotional, or learning challenges—are *dis*tressed! More students than ever report having issues with anxiety, depression, and anger.[2]

Of course, not all students are distressed. The majority of students can deal with the stress and seem reasonably able to manage their emotions and behavior. But many of these kids, if you ask them, will tell you that school is not on their top 10 lists of places to be.

The Default Climate

Due to all these pressures, the current climate of many schools is in what I call the default mode.

The default climate is often characterized by stress, anger, mistrust, fear, resentment, boredom, and us-vs.-them thinking (state vs. district; teachers vs. administrators; central office vs. site-based leaders; teachers vs. students; parents vs. school officials). Worse, many people experience feelings of powerlessness or helplessness. When people feel helpless and out-of-control, they tend to exert as much control over things (and other people) as they can. This often leads to controlling behaviors such as blaming, complaining, criticizing, threatening, bullying, labeling, name-calling, punishing, and bribing (rewarding to achieve compliance). These behaviors tend to erode relationships, trust, and a sense of shared purpose and increase a sense of isolation and fear.

Who wants to, or even can, work or learn in this kind of default climate? It's no wonder that research connects the characteristics of the default climate with increased meanness and bullying, lower graduation and attendance rates, and—critically—compromised learning and achievement.

Every School Can Do Better

Perhaps you don't recognize your school in these grim descriptions. Maybe your school is doing okay, or even pretty well, in terms of climate and achievement. Or maybe you're a teacher looking to create a more positive classroom environment without the benefit of a whole-school approach. The truth is, every school—and every classroom, team, club, or group—can improve its climate, and thus its achievement.

Components of a Positive School Climate

So what makes a positive school climate? According to the National School Climate Center's "School Climate Research Summary," virtually all researchers suggest five essential areas of focus: safety, relationships, teaching and learning, the institutional environment, and school climate, the processes of school improvement.[3]

---

[1] American Psychological Association, 2014.
[2] Ibid.

[3] Thapa, A., et al., 2012.

Safety

A positive school climate is one in which everyone feels a sense of physical and emotional safety. It is one free of threats, violence, meanness, bullying, and relational aggression. Students and adults are encouraged to take risks without fear of embarrassment or being labeled a failure. Additionally, there is a sense of order in the school and classroom, characterized by predictable, consistent procedures, routines, and fair, consistent discipline.

Relationships

All stakeholders in the school community—parents, teachers, students, school leaders, and support staff—share a sense of acceptance, mutual respect, and shared core values such as empathy. Roles and responsibilities are clear, social support is available, and rather than a strict social hierarchy, there is a sense of positive interdependence as all stakeholders work toward a common mission.

Teaching and Learning

In a positive school climate, the emphasis is on student engagement. Students understand the usefulness of the information and skills they are required to learn and are taught in ways that actively engage them. Additionally, social-emotional learning is integrated into the core curriculum.

The Institutional Environment

The physical structure of the school is safe, clean, uncluttered, and aesthetically pleasing. All people have adequate resources (textbooks, technology, space, and so on) to do their jobs. The hallways and classrooms are designed to provide students and adults with a warm, friendly, inviting atmosphere.

School Climate, the Process of School Improvement

Studies suggest that the most effective school improvement programs are those that are incorporated directly into the curriculum and addressed by the school community as a whole. When we treat school improvement with the same intensity and gravity as academic subjects, climate improves.

Student Voice

The National School Climate Center does not mention student voice, but in my work with schools, empowering students and providing them with a voice in improving their school is vital to climate improvement. Just as most businesses and corporations invite customer feedback to improve their products and services, providing our "customers"—the students—with opportunities to have a voice in their educational experience can have a significant impact on school climate, particularly in terms of adult-student relationships.

In fact, listening to students may be the most effective way for educators to show that they care about students. Research on teacher-student relationships links greater opportunity for students to have a voice with a greater likelihood for positive relationships. That can lead to greater academic success.[4] Students feel more connected to their school when they are given opportunities to participate in processes such as the making of rules and organizing of school events.

Benefits of a Positive School Climate

By placing an emphasis on developing a positive school climate, we can make significant strides toward addressing some of the most important concerns in education today:

- Reducing discipline issues including meanness and bullying
- Increasing the graduation and attendance rates
- Improving student learning and achievement

Reducing Discipline Issues Including Meanness and Bullying

Bullying has been and continues to be an enduring issue in schools everywhere. The Youth Voice Project surveyed over 13,000 students in grades 5–12 from schools all over the United States. Their findings:[5]

- 1 in 4 students reported being excluded or emotionally hurt by another student on a regular basis.
- 1 in 10 students reported being physically victimized on a regular basis.

---

[4] Barile, J.P., et al., 2012.
[5] Davis, S., & Nixon, C., 2010.

- 48 percent reported being regularly exposed (as victim or witness) to relational aggression (seeing or hearing rumor-spreading, exclusion, or students working together to be mean to someone).

- 54 percent reported being regularly exposed to name-calling or threatening comments.

Yet, despite the media coverage and public attention that bullying receives, despite the anti-bullying and anti-discrimination school legislation enacted in many states, and despite the hundreds of anti-bullying programs being used, what schools are currently doing still does not seem to be enough.

Improving school climate can help. One of the most important aspects of creating a positive school environment involves building positive relationships. The degree to which students feel accepted and connected at school has a profound impact on reducing meanness and bullying. Research shows that students' sense of connectedness is a powerful predictor of and/or is associated with:

- preventing school violence

- reducing conduct problems

- reducing aggression and violence

And while it's important to base school improvement initiatives on research, it's also common sense that if students like and accept each other, they're far less likely to engage in mean, aggressive, or violent behavior.

Increasing Graduation and Attendance Rates

Dropout rates in the United States continue to be problematic. In 2012, there was an 81 percent U.S. national graduation rate, below that of most developed countries.

In an article entitled "Understanding Why Students Drop Out of High School, According to Their Own Reports,"[6] the researchers examined seven studies conducted over the last 50 years on the reasons students cited for dropping out of high school. The reasons for dropping out fell into three categories: 1) Push Factors involve "adverse situations within the school environment," 2) Pull Factors involve factors within the student that divert him from attending to school, things like

financial worries, family problems, pregnancy, marriage, out-of-school employment, and 3) Falling Out Factors, which occur when a student does not show significant academic progress in schoolwork and becomes apathetic or even disillusioned with school and eventually leaves.

The authors conclude that, while in the past pull factors were most prevalent, the most recent studies find that push factors are most frequently cited by students. The reasons students reported for dropping out frequently included:

- not liking school

- not getting along with teachers

- not feeling like they belong, or not getting along with other students

- fearing for their safety

- feeling unable to satisfy academic requirements

These factors all relate to school climate. We, as educators, may not be able to directly influence what the authors call pull factors, but we can be deliberate about creating a school climate and culture that addresses push factors.

Improving Student Learning and Achievement

From my perspective, district administrators, school leaders, and teachers are working as hard as they can and in many districts are doing so in the face of significant budget cuts, which often result in staff and program cuts, larger class sizes, and fewer resources. To meet standards, many schools have extended the school day and/or year and cut back on music, art, library, and physical education classes to make more time for reading and math instruction. Some have gone so far as to eliminate recess in elementary grades.

Educators are doing all this to raise achievement. But there is a better way. A large and growing number of studies show a strong link between school climate and academic achievement. Through an extensive analysis of educational, social, and cognitive psychology, researchers have found that school climate is one of four variables (including student engagement, learning strategies, and socio-familial influences) directly linked to academic achievement at the K–12 level. Another

---

[6] Doll, J.J., et al, 2013.

study linked higher scores on standardized tests with healthy learning environments.[7]

In 2011, the Collaborative for Academic, Social, and Emotional Learning (CASEL) conducted a meta-analysis of research on the benefits of social-emotional learning. That meta-analysis—which is a core element of this book—shows that in schools that included SEL as part of the universal curriculum, among other important outcomes, students' achievement scores increased by an average of 11 percentile points.[8]

Six years later, CASEL conducted another meta-analysis, this time on the long-term impact of SEL, finding that achievement for "students exposed to SEL programs was an average of 13 percentile points higher than their non-SEL peers, based on the eight studies that measured academic performance."[9] In addition, the study showed that behavior problems, emotional distress, and drug abuse were significantly lower for students exposed to SEL programs and that students exposed to SEL had more positive attitudes toward themselves, others, and school.

Benefits of SEL

CASEL reports that students who attend schools that integrate SEL into the curriculum demonstrate improved social and emotional skills; report improved attitudes toward teachers, other students, and school in general; demonstrate more pro-social behavior; and experience a sense of connectedness, acceptance, respect, and mutual trust.

The implications of the research are clear: Being intentional about creating and maintaining a positive school climate can have a profound and positive impact on student learning and achievement.

Additional Benefits

A positive school climate is also associated with other important benefits. Studies have shown that approximately 30 percent of high school students engage in multiple high-risk behaviors (such as substance use, sex, violence, depression, attempted suicide) that interfere with school performance and jeopardize their potential for life success.[10] The National School Climate Center reports that positive and sustained school climate is associated with and/or predictive of not only effective risk prevention and health promotion efforts,[11] but also positive youth development and student motivation to learn.[12]

And importantly, while the emphasis so far has been on how positive school climate benefits students, it is also shown to have positive benefits for teachers. Research shows that it improves teacher practice and leads to higher job satisfaction.[13]

So, in summary, a positive school climate helps improve achievement and improves the happiness of students and educators—that's you.

About *The SEL Solution*

Who This Book Is For

The SEL Solution is designed for anyone in a school or district who has the desire to create a positive working and learning environment in their school(s) or classroom(s)—an environment that will inspire and sustain members of the school community as they work together toward the common goal of professional and academic success for all. This book is most effective when used as the basis for a whole-school approach to climate improvement involving all stakeholders, led by a climate improvement team composed of administrators, teachers, student support staff (social worker, counselor), parents, and student representatives. However, it contains valuable insights and practical strategies for all these readers, even if they are not part of a school-wide climate program. You can use ideas and strategies in this book to improve the climate and culture of an individual classroom, a sports team, a musical organization, the cast of a play, or any extracurricular club or organization.

Some of the initiatives and practices explained in this book are school-wide in scope. Some are designed for specific settings—the classroom, the principal's office, various meetings, discipline settings, and so on. Many of the approaches and structures can be used by all community members

[7] Lee, J., and Shute, V.J., 2010; and MacNeil. A.J., et al, 2009.
[8] Durlak, J.A., et al, 2011.
[9] Taylor, R.D., et al, 2017, p. 1170.

[10] Dryfoos, J.G., 1997; and Eaton, D.K., et al, 2008.
[11] Cohen, J., and Geist, V.K., 2010.
[12] Eccles, J.S., et al, 1993; and Goodenow, C., and Grady, K.E., 1993.
[13] Cohen, J., and Geist, V.K., 2010.

(the process for positive change, for example, on pages 167–177). Others are designed for specific roles, such as school leaders, teachers, school counselors, coaches, club advisors, and parent-teacher organization leaders. No matter your role, it can be helpful to read all these sections.

Most of the strategies in *The SEL Solution* work in elementary, middle, and high school settings, but some are specific to particular developmental levels. While the majority of the classroom strategies are designed primarily for students in third grade and above, many can be used just as explained or modified to be used with students as young as kindergarten. See pages 9–10 for a detailed explanation of the structure of the book, which can help you focus on the chapters most relevant to you.

A Note on Audience and Style

To avoid confusion, and to provide consistency in point of view, I have written this book with all educators in mind as the audience. When addressing a more specific audience (classroom teachers or school principals, for example), that audience is clearly identified, as is the developmental level the strategies are designed for.

When referring to people, I have used plural pronouns whenever possible. When unable to avoid single third-person references, I alternate between *he/his* and *she/her*.

In short, whether you are a school superintendent seeking ways of improving the graduation rate; a school principal hoping to improve academic achievement; a school counselor wanting to decrease bullying behavior; a coach looking to improve team cohesion; a PTO member trying to improve the sense of emotional safety at school; or a teacher seeking to create a better learning environment in the classroom, this book is for you!

How to Use This Book

The SEL Solution is designed to be practical and flexible. It can be used as a school-wide manual for climate improvement, implementing strategies and processes in a chapter-by-chapter process. It might also be used as a reference to help expand a climate improvement initiative already in place, implementing, for example, the student leadership chapter or the touchstone process. (Read about the touchstone starting on page 34.)

Many of the activities are intended for a school-wide setting, but many can be used in (or modified for) an individual classroom, where a teacher might use this book as a grab bag of strategies to build and sustain a positive classroom environment. Central office and school leaders may want to use some of the strategies with their staff to improve relationships, reduce stress, and improve communication. (Adult interactions in schools can have a significant impact on climate.) See Chapter 1: Getting Started for more information about approaching your climate solution.

However you choose to use this book, you will soon find that the process of creating a more human and more humane learning and working environment for everyone is a joyful experience.

The Story Behind This Book

During my preservice training to become a secondary English teacher, the courses I took provided me with a solid foundation in English literature, a rich array of instructional strategies, and a fairly traditional approach to behavior management. I don't recall even hearing the terms *school climate* or *classroom climate*.

In my first year as a teacher, working mostly with seventh- and eighth-grade students, I did my best to implement all that I'd learned in undergraduate school. I even tried not to smile until Thanksgiving, as the old teaching adage suggests, but caught myself smiling as soon as the first student came in my classroom. At that moment, I remember thinking, "Maybe I'm not cut out for this profession. I want to smile and I want my students to like me, not just respect my authority."

Nonetheless, I forged ahead with my instruction and the traditional approach to behavior management, which included clear, simple rules, incentives for positive behavior, and consequences for breaking the rules.

The results were also fairly traditional: a bell curve in terms of student performance and (as in most middle school classrooms) fairly regular disruptions and discipline incidents. I was frustrated. Like many beginning teachers, I pictured a classroom of well-behaved, motivated learners who all succeeded academically. What frustrated me the most was that I didn't know what else to do.

The next summer, a professional development opportunity changed my approach to teaching, and as a result it transformed my classroom and my life. It was a four-day training in William Glasser's Choice Theory and Quality Schools, an approach that emphasizes positive relationships and intrinsic motivation. Gaining an understanding of what motivates all human behavior enabled me to apply Glasser's ideas to my own classroom. What resulted was a classroom climate characterized by a sense of order (sometimes noisy, yet productive), positive relationships with and among my students, and significantly better learning and student performance. In addition, it was a lot more fun and professionally satisfying.

Because of my success, I was given the opportunity to share Glasser's ideas with my colleagues, which eventually led to a professional development position at our local Board of Cooperative Educational Services. Since then, I have had the opportunity to travel all over North America as well as to Australia, Europe, and South America teaching both the concepts and specific strategies that transformed my classroom, passing on to others the ability to create a classroom and school climate of success for all. One such experience, described as follows, was well-researched and documented.

For three years, I worked as director of training and curriculum for Smart Character Choices (SCC), a character education program in Michigan developed by CS Partners, a charter school management company funded by a grant provided under the federal Safe and Drug-Free Schools Act. During the three-year initiative, my colleague Diane Vance and I implemented the strategies explained in this book with four demographically diverse schools in Michigan:

The Dearborn Academy, a K–8 charter school just outside Detroit whose student population was made up of 85 percent Arabic children (many recent immigrants from Iraq and Lebanon), 10 percent African-American children, and 5 percent other ethnicities, with a high poverty rate (94 percent free and reduced lunch).

The Chatfield School, a predominantly Caucasian (92 percent), middle class K–8 school in the small city of Lapeer.

Randels Elementary, a K–6 public school in the economically challenged city of Flint with 53 percent of its students receiving free or reduced lunch. Its population was 50 percent African American, 42 percent Caucasian, and 8 percent other ethnicities.

Creative Technologies Academy, a predominantly Caucasian (97 percent) rural K–12 charter school in Cedar Springs, about 20 miles outside of Grand Rapids.

The SCC initiative was investigated by a team of researchers from the University of Minnesota. This research was focused on the impact of the program on student behavior, student attitudes toward school, and parent perceptions of the schools. It compared the differences in pro-social behavior and attitudes among eight randomly selected schools—the four schools implementing the SCC initiative and four schools that did not. The research showed that in the schools that went through the SCC program, "students reported better attitudes toward school, themselves, and others, and that parents reported being more satisfied with their children's schools."[14]

Besides these positive outcomes, two schools involved in the initiative received additional recognition. In the third year of the program, the Chatfield School won the Michigan State School of Character Award and a national Character Education Partnership "Promising Practices" designation. The same year, Randels Elementary School was featured on ABC News for a service learning initiative it began during our program, raising over $6,000 for Habitat for Humanity.

Additionally, the SCC initiative negated typical predictors of behavior problems: poverty and high class size. Whereas the control group showed significant correlations between those predictors and problem behaviors, there was no similar relationship between the two in the SCC schools.[15] Lastly, the University of Minnesota researchers stated that the approach we used in the SCC initiative—the approach contained in this book—has a proven record of effectiveness in urban, suburban, and rural schools and has shown to level the playing

[14] Szadokierski, I., et al, 2010.
[15] Parker, D.C., et al, 2010.

field for schools with high poverty rates and/or high class sizes.

An Overview of This Book

Chapter 1. Getting Started. Chapter 1 will help you make your own school climate plan. It contains guidelines for whole-school as well as smaller initiatives. After that chapter, the book is divided into three parts:

- Part 1. Setting the Foundation: Safety and Relationships

- Part 2. Essential Tools: Teaching Social-Emotional Skills

- Part 3. Optimal Conditions: Creating a Needs-Satisfying Environment

Each chapter introduces a new concept along with guidelines for introducing it to your students (and, at times, other staff) and provides community meetings and activities to help reinforce the material. Every activity begins with guidelines to help you adjust it to different audiences (including very young students) as well as the time, materials, and prep work required. Most of the activities can be done in less than a typical class period (usually about 20 minutes) without much, if any, prep and require no materials beyond what you are likely to have in your classroom. Some activities include handouts. These are noted in the materials list and thumbnails of the handouts can be found at the end of each chapter. The handouts are included in the digital content for this book and can be downloaded and printed out. See page 191 for download instructions. You will need to print out copies of the handouts before the sessions. Some of the handouts can be modified before printing to personalize them to your situation.

Part 1
Setting the Foundation: Safety and Relationships

This section provides important beginning steps to creating or improving a positive school environment by focusing on providing a sense of physical and emotional safety and a sense of community.

Chapter 2. The Community Meeting. This chapter explains the community meeting, a protocol designed to be used by principals, teachers, coaches, club advisors, parent-teacher organization officers—anyone who works with or supervises others. The community meeting creates a safe, structured approach to improving group communication and building a sense of community.

Chapter 3. The School Touchstone. One important way to engage the school community in clarifying a shared vision is by creating a school touchstone: a word, phrase, statement, or image that represents the school's core values. This chapter is intended for school leaders or leadership teams as a guide to facilitating the touchstone development process with their school community, although teachers and other leaders might consider creating a classroom, team, or club touchstone, as well.

Chapter 4. Bringing the Touchstone Values to Life. Once a school touchstone has been established, the strategies in this chapter help school leaders, school counselors, teachers, coaches, and club advisors bring it to life by integrating it into the school, classroom, or team culture.

Chapter 5. Integrating the Touchstone Values into the Academic Curriculum. Intended particularly for classroom teachers, this chapter provides ideas, model lessons, and resources for integrating the touchstone values into the academic curriculum in ways that satisfy the Common Core State Standards (CCSS).

Chapter 6. Inspiring Student Leadership. This chapter explains how to select, train, and provide opportunities for students to lead and serve the school community in ways that can have a profound positive impact on the school.

Part 2
Essential Tools: Teaching Social-Emotional Skills

This section provides school leaders, counselors, teachers, coaches, and others with specific games, activities, and discussions that teach adults and students the most essential social and emotional skills not only for creating a positive school climate, but also for improving academic, professional, and personal success. Each of the chapters works off the metaphor of the "behavioral car," which makes understanding social and emotional skills more accessible to students of all ages. Additionally, each chapter provides specific suggestions for student performance tasks that help integrate SEL into the core curriculum in ways that satisfy the CCSS, particularly in English language arts. Additional resources are also listed at the end of each chapter.

Chapter 7. Introducing Social-Emotional Learning to Your Students. This chapter offers a research-based rationale for integrating SEL into the curriculum and introduces the behavioral car. It explains specific ways of teaching important foundational concepts and connecting these concepts to the academic curriculum.

Chapter 8. The Five Basic Human Needs: The Fuel for the Car. This chapter explains the Five Basic Human Needs that drive all human behavior and provides activities that help people understand what motives them and others, so they can gain insight into their own behavior and develop acceptance of others.

Chapter 9. Understanding Emotions in Ourselves and Others: The Lights on the Dashboard. This chapter provides engaging ways of helping people accurately identify emotions in themselves, a first step in self-regulation. It also provides activities that help people learn to identify emotions in others, so that they can be more sensitive in their social interactions.

Chapter 10. Self-Regulation: The Four Wheels of the Car. This chapter, one of the most important in the book, provides resources to teach an essential skill for students and adults: self-regulation—the ability to control impulses, manage anger and stress, and regulate emotions in ourselves. It includes mini-lessons, activities, community meetings, and other resources.

Part 3
Optimal Conditions: Creating a Needs-Satisfying Environment

When people work and learn in an environment designed to meet the Five Basic Human Needs, they behave more responsibly and perform at higher levels. The chapters in Part 3 provide strategies that leaders of both adults and students can employ to create the conditions for such an environment.

Chapter 11. Addressing the Needs for Emotional Safety and Connectedness. This chapter provides specific strategies for creating a physically and emotionally safe environment and building trusting relationships.

Chapter 12. Addressing the Needs for Power, Freedom, and Fun. As people feel an increased sense of safety and connectedness, they can be provided with a greater voice in decisions that affect them (power); more choices and autonomy (freedom); and more opportunities to play and have fun. This chapter provides strategies and structures you can use to create a climate where people are empowered, liberated, and joyful.

Chapter 13. A Social-Emotional Approach to Behavior Management. No matter how positive a school climate is, adults and students will, at times, break rules, behave irresponsibly, and come into conflict. This chapter provides approaches to behavior management and discipline that keep relationships and the school and classroom environment intact.

While attaining the ideal learning and working climate in a school takes time and effort, the journey itself can be inspiring. I wish you the best as you begin the important work of developing and sustaining a school climate, one which brings out the best in everyone, students and adults alike. I would love to hear about your experiences with the school-wide climate solution—your success, challenges, and ideas. Please write to me in care of Free Spirit Publishing at help4kids@freespirit.com.

All the best to you,

Jonathan Erwin

Getting Started

You may be a principal or other administrator starting from scratch—perhaps you've been charged with reducing violence, increasing attendance, or improving achievement at your school. If so, *The SEL Solution* provides a thorough and effective program. Share this book with your staff and communicate with them regularly about progress. This chapter provides a roadmap for working with staff and students throughout the school year. Or maybe you're already using an anti-bullying or social-emotional program in your school; if so, the ideas and activities in this book can be a great complement, easily integrated into what you're already doing. Reading this chapter will help you figure out which aspects of the book to introduce at your school. Guidelines for a whole-school approach begin on this page.

If you're a teacher, coach, club advisor, counselor, or other leader looking for ways to build community in your smaller groups, feel free to pick and choose aspects from this book that make sense for your situation. Suggestions for where to begin and what to include are provided in this chapter. Go to page 15 for guidelines on individual use.

Whatever your situation, I recommend you make the climate solution your own. While my recommendations are based on my years of experience in improving school climate and culture, the way you implement in your situation may need to be modified because of your school's unique resources, opportunities, and challenges. Every successful school climate initiative eventually takes on its own unique personality, which is one of the best aspects of the climate improvement process. It shows that a school has taken ownership of the process and has a compelling shared vision.

As you read these recommendations for beginning and sustaining the climate improvement process, you will find that there are many opportunities to make it your own, while still maintaining the integrity of the general program.

The Whole-School Climate Initiative

As the leader of the climate improvement initiative, whether you are a school administrator, faculty member, or school counselor who has been delegated the responsibility of leading the process, it is critical to involve—right from the beginning—various stakeholders in the school community: staff, faculty, students, administrators, and parents. If students and other members of the community see the initiative as a program driven from the top down, it is unlikely to succeed. On the other hand, if you are able to garner grassroots support from the beginning, the initiative is likely to catch on like wildfire.

One of the most effective ways to establish support is by creating a Climate Improvement Team (CIT).

Create a Climate Improvement Team (CIT)

A CIT is made up of a diverse group of people who represent different stakeholder groups: faculty, administrators, counselors, staff, parents, and students. Members of this team will serve as representatives of their groups and communicate with them, both to advise and make decisions in the implementation of the initiative and to champion the effort. The CIT will meet early on—ideally in the summer before school begins—to help get your initiative off the ground as smoothly as possible and continue to meet throughout the year to keep everyone informed of what's working and what can work better.

Although it's important all these subgroups in the school community are represented, keep the size of the CIT manageable. Even in a large school, more than 25 team members is too many, making scheduling and decision-making cumbersome and slow. Three to four representatives from each stakeholder group is ideal, making the size of the team between 16 and 21 members. In smaller schools, it may not be practical or necessary to include as many representatives from each subgroup, so the CIT may be even smaller.

During the summer, as the school year approaches, send an email or letter to every member of the school community explaining your school climate initiative, describing the CIT, and inviting anyone who is interested to apply to be on the CIT. Writing to the entire school community helps ensure that faculty members, staff, and students see membership on the CIT as open to all, not as an elitist group or the principal's inner circle. This helps prevent complaining and blaming behavior later on in the process.

Your letter to adults and older students might look something like my sample (see the thumbnail on page 18). (Feel free to modify this reproducible handout for your letter.)

In addition to sending this general invitation to the school community, you may want to personally invite individuals who you know have an interest in school climate and who you believe would be a positive asset to the initiative.

To reach students, send an email or hand out a letter to secondary students and copy parents.

Because of the time commitment required to be on the CIT (and the shorter attention spans of younger kids), I recommend limiting elementary kids' participation to fifth graders and up. To contact them, consider having teachers make an announcement in class and send home notes to parents. See the thumbnail on page 18 for an example of a note that could go home to students' families. Here are a few other suggestions for establishing your CIT.

- Include union and parent-teacher organization leaders. They will add credibility and a sense of cohesion to the initiative.

- Personally invite leaders among the custodial, food service, and transportation staff.

- Include a variety of grade-level teachers and at least one school counselor, social worker, or school psychologist.

- In secondary schools, choose students from a variety of grade levels, based on recommendations from their counselors or teachers. Ideally these are students who are both liked and respected by their peers and who are on solid ground academically. It is also important to choose students who are comfortable voicing their opinions at team meetings and making presentations to their peers, faculty, and parents.

Hold Your First CIT Meeting

Hold your first CIT meeting just before school begins or within the first week or two. The purpose of the meeting is to build relationships among team members, clarify roles among the various stakeholder groups involved, and clarify what is involved in the process.

After welcoming and having team members introduce themselves, lead a group discussion around the following talking points and questions:

- We're here to improve our school climate. What, in your mind, is a positive school climate?

- What motivated you to be a member of this team?

- How would it benefit staff to achieve a more positive school climate? Students? Parents?

I recommend that you follow this discussion with the PDF presentation included in the digital content of this book. The presentation gives a brief overview of how positive climate results in better student and staff attitudes toward work and school, improved attendance, fewer behavior problems, and higher achievement. It also gives an overview of what makes a school climate positive and how the activities in *The SEL Solution* can help achieve that climate.

You may want to take extra time with the slides that discuss community meetings, which are an important foundation of the initiative that teachers in particular will need to know how to conduct.

After the presentation is finished and you have answered any questions raised, go through the following timeline for the year (this is also summarized as a chart on page 15 and provided in the PDF presentation), setting dates for meetings and giving jobs to team members.

Schedule Your School Year

The following steps are described with minor detail to provide a rough overview of the school year and help you make decisions about what steps to cut or modify. They will also help you set up dates for your school year and assign roles to members of the CIT. Information and guidelines for all the parts of the school climate solution are covered in detail in the other chapters of this book.

Scheduling times suggested are deliberately general; you'll want to establish a more precise schedule based on your own situation. On page 15, you'll find a timeline that provides a snapshot of the year.

Recruit and Begin Working with Student Leadership Team (SLT)

Since students make up the majority of the school community, it is only logical to involve them as early as possible.

Chapter 6 explains in detail how to recruit, train, and employ student leaders as powerful agents of positive change in the climate improvement initiative. Ideally, student leaders are recruited in the spring and begin their training in August or early to mid-September, shortly after the first CIT meeting.

Present School Climate Initiative to All Staff

Within the first month of school, the CIT hosts a meeting for all faculty and staff to present the school climate initiative you're undertaking. The CIT may use the PDF presentation if desired. The goal is to make sure everyone understands and is on board with the plan. **Important:** At this meeting, pass out the "Faculty and Staff School Climate Survey" (see the thumbnail on page 18) to everyone present and collect the completed surveys by the end of the meeting.

Present Climate Initiative to Students

Shortly after the all-staff meeting about the school climate plan, teachers will hold community meetings in their classrooms to discuss school climate with their students. See page 23 for guidelines for this meeting. Teachers ask students about the kind of climate they would like at school, discuss the benefits of a positive school environment, and provide a brief overview of the climate improvement process. **Important:** Pass out the "Student Climate Survey" (see the thumbnail on page 19) to students and collect completed surveys at the end of the meeting.

Analyze and Present Survey Results

After the surveys have been collected from both groups, compile the results. Assign a point value of 1 for every answer of "Strongly Disagree," 2 points for "Disagree," 3 points for "Neither," 4 points for "Agree," and 5 points for "Strongly Agree." (You may want to ask for a faculty volunteer to do this.) Keeping the adult and student surveys separate, calculate the average response for every question. Create a slide or handout that summarizes the findings, and present them at your next CIT meeting. You will also want to present the results to your entire faculty and staff.

In both meetings, explain that the purpose of this is not to assign blame or invite excuses. It is simply a reflection of the current perceptions of students and staff. It is always interesting to note any discrepancies between staff perceptions and those of students. Any item receiving an average under 3.5 is worth examining. Discussion might follow, listening to suggestions about addressing the most pressing items immediately.

At the CIT meeting, you may also want to use the survey results to help shape the topics for future community meetings and activities in classrooms. You may also use this information as the basis for creating goals for the year, one of them being the development of the school-wide touchstone. Review the importance of the touchstone (see Chapter 3).

Begin the Touchstone Process

Working together, your school community will determine which values it holds highest—the values you want to guide the behavior and interactions in your school. The beginning of this process involves each of the stakeholder groups meeting separately to brainstorm values and narrow their lists to a manageable size. See Chapter 3.

As you discuss this at your initial CIT meeting, you may want to set dates for these meetings and direct the CIT members from each stakeholder group to communicate with its group about the meeting. You will probably want to host the student meeting yourself, but you'll need to enlist plenty of help. See page 36.

Try to begin this process by late October or so.

CIT Meets to Finalize Touchstone

Shortly after touchstone stakeholder meetings are completed, the CIT takes the lists from those meetings and works to establish a final touchstone and determine how to present it.

Hold an Assembly to Unveil the Touchstone

This is a fun celebration for all members of the school community, so be sure to invite everyone. Consider making it an evening meeting so more parents can attend. It should be held before winter break.

Teachers Begin Teaching SEL in Class

It's a good idea to start SEL (social-emotional learning) lessons for students as early in the year

as possible, but with the touchstone process also competing for limited time, you may not be able to begin these until right before or after winter break. It all depends on how much of a priority you're able to make them. It's also up to you how stringent you want to be regarding which SEL topics and activities you require teachers to conduct. You may require emphasis on certain topics based on the survey results from earlier in the school year, or you may simply direct teachers to work their way through Part 2 (beginning on page 84) on their own.

If you're in a secondary school, you will have to determine which classes will do SEL activities. It's often best to do SEL in advisory, homeroom, ELA, social studies, or health classes.

SEL lessons continue through the end of the school year. See the chapters in Part 2. You may want to schedule the activities you want teachers to do so that they can plan ahead to make time for them—and so that you can make sure everything is covered that you want covered. It's up to you to decide how precisely you want to schedule things from the beginning, and how tightly you want to control teachers' lessons.

End-of-Year Climate Survey/Data Collection

Toward the end of the school year, conduct climate surveys for both adult and student populations, and aggregate the data. Members of the CIT and SLT compare these results with the results from the beginning of the year, looking for areas of success and ongoing challenges. Using this book as a reference, make plans for your second year.

Summer SEL Training for Teachers

Consider holding a two- or three-day summer training on SEL for teachers to personally experience the SEL activities that they will integrate into their curriculum. This will give them the rationale and skills they need to begin implementing SEL in the classrooms.

Timeline for the First Year of Whole-School Climate Improvement

Spring
- ↓ Recruit Climate Improvement Team (CIT)
- ↓ Recruit Student Leadership Team (SLT)

Late summer
- ↓ Hold first CIT meeting
- ↓ Collect data such as absentee rate and behavior referrals
- ↓ Hold first SLT meeting

Early fall
- ↓ Present climate initiative to all staff; administer climate survey to staff
- ↓ Present climate initiative to students; administer climate survey to students
- ↓ Analyze and present survey results

Fall
- ↓ Begin touchstone process (separate faculty, staff, and student meetings to determine shared values)

Early winter
- ↓ Teachers begin teaching SEL in classes

Winter
- ↓ CIT and SLT meet to finalize touchstone and determine how it will be presented
- ↓ Hold assembly/celebration to unveil the touchstone

Spring
- ↓ Administer end-of-year climate survey
- ↓ Begin planning for second year

Summer
- ↓ SEL training for teachers

Other Things to Keep in Mind

The chapters in Part 3, Creating a Needs-Satisfying Environment, provide extensive guidelines for classroom and behavior management. As the leader of the school climate solution, it's up to you whether you require teachers to read these chapters and/or adopt their lessons. Read these chapters well before school begins and make a plan for your approach. You may want to weave information and lessons from them into your monthly CIT meetings.

The Smaller-Scale Climate Solution

If you aren't part of a whole-school climate initiative, your goal in reading this book may be to create and sustain a positive climate within your classroom, sports team, extracurricular club, musical cast, or other small group. This section provides guidelines for getting started. (I use the term *teacher* throughout this section, but if you are a coach or other leader, that word refers to you, too.)

Communicate and Garner Support

For these smaller efforts, the community of stakeholders is smaller than it is for a whole-school initiative, but you'll still want to communicate your plans with your school leaders and parents. Your principal will most likely be interested in what you are doing and the results. Keep her informed along the way; she may want to share what you're doing as she coaches other teachers. Parents will most likely be happy to hear you care about providing their children with a safe, connected, engaged learning environment. Sending home a regular parent newsletter or dedicating part of the classroom website to "climate news" will help parents keep up on the process.

A letter to families at the beginning of the year is a good idea. I've provided a sample in the digital content for this book (see the thumbnail on page 18). Feel free to use or modify this reproducible handout for your letter.

These efforts will pay off by helping you gain the support of your administration and your students' families.

Prioritize and Schedule Your Initiative

Read this book and choose what elements you want to use. With fewer stakeholders and a smaller community compared to a school-wide effort, you are free to pick and choose the elements of this book that are most appropriate for your situation, and you have the flexibility to make changes quickly if something isn't working. It's not necessary to plan every meeting and activity for the whole year, though it's a good idea to have a general plan. The general outline provided on this page can be used as a model.

I strongly recommend that you implement the elements of Part 1, Setting the Foundation, in your classroom. Introduce community meetings as early as your first day together, and use them throughout the school year. If you're teaching younger students, you may want to hold one meeting every day or three times a week. For older students, especially if you only have them for 50 minutes a day, once every week or two is sufficient. Begin working on a class touchstone in those early community meetings.

If you're not planning to use all the chapters of Part 2, Teaching Social-Emotional Skills, it's best to focus on the material in the first chapter or two, leaving off later chapters which may not stand up well without the foundation of the earlier material. Use the timeline model on this page to plan your approach.

The chapters in Part 3 provide extensive guidelines for classroom and behavior management. Reading these chapters before the school year begins will give you plenty of good ideas for running a more positive classroom and allow you plenty of time to prepare to institute them. Any classroom norms, rules, and procedures should be in place on day one.

Timeline for Classroom Climate Development

First day of school	↓ Begin community meetings
Early fall	↓ Discuss climate initiative with class; communicate about it with your principal and with families
	↓ Begin working on the class touchstone
Early winter	↓ Finalize touchstone and determine how it will be presented
Winter	↓ Begin teaching SEL in class
	↓ Hold celebration to unveil touchstone
Spring	↓ Hold end-of-year community celebration

Final Thoughts About Getting Started

As you think about setting up your unique approach to school climate change and what your school year will look like, here are a few important things to keep in mind.

Commit to Ongoing Evaluation

Throughout the climate improvement initiative, it is essential to continuously evaluate the effectiveness of the process. Use concrete quantitative data (climate survey, grades, attendance, and so on), but also use any information you can gather from what educators might call *informal formative assessment*. At CIT meetings, part of the meeting should include time to share anecdotes and information that might help the initiative. For example, a teacher on the team might have overheard students talking excitedly about the social-emotional learning that's happening in ELA. Or someone on the team might have had a conversation with a staff member who criticized the initiative as coming from "them" (the administration).

With anecdotal as well as quantitative data at its disposal, the CIT can evaluate progress and, if necessary, make adjustments or change behavior in some way. This evaluation process is called the Process for Positive Change (PPC) (see pages 167–177). In brief, PPC involves the team discussing the following questions:

- What do we want? What is our goal?
- What are we currently doing to achieve that goal?
- Is what we are doing working? What's working and what's not?
- What is our plan moving forward?

Ongoing evaluation not only allows you to make adjustments and see better climate results, it also helps establish and sustain universal support for the initiative through the first year.

Keep Up Regular Communication

All members of the CIT and SLT have the responsibility to communicate accurate information to the groups they represent: Parent members to the parent-teacher organization; teacher members to the faculty; students to a designated number of classrooms, and so on. Use group email, social media, a dedicated website, or an old-fashioned newsletter to keep school community members informed.

This ongoing communication is a great way to obtain the anecdotal feedback about how people perceive the climate initiative. It also serves to keep the topic at top of mind so community members are thinking and talking about it. This can only help the effectiveness of the program.

Celebrate Success

By the end of the year, if you have followed the processes described in this book and conducted at least most of the activities, you will see positive results. In my experience, the most salient improvements the first year are related to climate survey results, behavior referrals, bullying, attendance, and student grades. These improvements, even if they don't achieve the goals you set at the beginning of the year, show that the school community is doing something right and is moving in the desired direction. (One of my favorite sayings is, "Better is better!") It's wise even before the end of the year to mark your successes. Communicate improvements with the entire school community. Share anecdotes and qualitative evidence with students.

Many schools and classrooms will have some kind of end-of-year field trip, field day, picnic, or other event to celebrate progress made during the year. Use this as a way to celebrate ways that people in your community developed friendships, respected differences, and achieved and grew as learners and as people. You might hold an end-of-year community meeting focusing on those topics and challenging students to continue to learn, read, and grow their bodies, minds, and hearts over the summer. I encourage you to give students a voice in creating a celebration that is both fun and meaningful to them.

By marking and celebrating improvements—and by establishing new goals and a plan to move forward—you will most likely sustain the initiative for the following year. You will have the opportunity to make even more progress.

Let's get started!

Printable Forms

Letter Inviting Participants to Climate Improvement Team

Dear [Parents, Students, Staff Members, Teachers, etc.]:

Research shows that a positive school climate leads to improvements in everything from attendance and graduation rates to student learning and achievement. That kind of climate is based on safety and order, positive relationships, and engaging teaching and learning. To achieve that at [School Name], we will begin a school climate improvement initiative this school year, and I would like to invite you to be involved in the process.

I am creating a Climate Improvement Team (CIP) made up of representatives from different parts of our school community: teachers, staff, parents, students, and administrators. Your involvement would require attendance at our first meeting, a full day on [date and time], as well as shorter monthly meetings throughout the year. You will also be asked to communicate regularly with other [parents, students, staff, etc.]. Monthly meetings will be held on [recurring day and time] starting [date]. All meetings will be held in [room number] at the school.

If you are interested in participating in this exciting opportunity, please email me at [email address] by [date]. Because interest in membership may be very high, and in order to end up with a team of optimum size, I am limiting the number of [parent, student, teacher, staff] representatives to [three or four]. I will select members from the pool of applicants to create a team that is as diverse and representative as possible.

Thank you for your interest in helping make [school name] the best school we can be for your child.

Sincerely,
[your name]
[your phone number]
[your email address]

Letter Informing Families of Student Involvement on CIT

Dear Parent or Guardian:

Research shows that a positive school climate leads to improvements in everything from attendance and graduation rates to student learning and achievement. That kind of climate is based on safety and order, positive relationships, and engaging teaching and learning. To achieve that at [School Name], we will begin a school climate improvement initiative this school year, and your student is invited to be involved in the process.

If selected, your child would be part of a team made up of representatives from different parts of our school community: teachers, staff, parents, students, and administrators. His or her involvement would require attendance at our first meeting, a full day on [date and time], as well as shorter monthly meetings throughout the year. He or she will also be asked to communicate regularly with other students to get input and feedback about the initiative. Monthly meetings will be held on [recurring day and time] starting [date]. All meetings will be held in [room number] at the school.

If your child is interested in participating in this exciting opportunity and you give permission, please email me at [email address] by [date]. Because interest in membership may be very high, and in order to end up with a team of optimum size, the number of student representatives will be limited to [three or four]. Members will be selected from the pool of applicants to create a team that is as diverse and representative as possible.

Thank you for your interest in helping make [school name] the best school we can be for your child.

Sincerely,
[your name]
[your phone number]
[your email address]

Faculty and Staff School Climate Survey

Before you begin, please read the following information:

- You are being asked to complete this survey as part of an effort to understand how students and other members of the school community (teachers, staff, and so on) feel about the current school climate.
- Read the statements carefully and base your answers on your thoughts and feelings about your personal experience at school.
- This survey is completely anonymous. No one will know how you responded, so please be honest.
- There are no right or wrong answers. We want to gather information about how people feel while they are here in school.

Directions: Mark an *X* in the column that corresponds with how strongly you agree or disagree with the following statements.

	Strongly Disagree	Disagree	Neither Agree or Disagree	Agree	Strongly Agree
1. I always feel physically safe at school.					
2. While at school or at school functions, I rarely see students insulting, teasing, harassing, or otherwise verbally abusing others.					
3. Adults at school treat students as if they care about them as individuals.					
4. School leaders encourage and support collaboration among teachers.					
5. Discipline referrals are handled fairly and effectively by administration.					
6. Most staff in this school are generous about helping others with instructional or management issues.					
7. This school encourages staff to get involved in extracurricular activities.					
8. In general, students at my school treat one another with kindness. No one seems to go out of their way to treat other students badly.					

➡

Faculty and Staff School Climate Survey continued

	Strongly Disagree	Disagree	Neither Agree or Disagree	Agree	Strongly Agree
9. Students at my school accept one another's differences (race, culture, gender, appearance).					
10. There is clear and effective two-way communication between administrators and staff.					
11. Adults in my school treat all students fairly.					
12. I feel as if I have a voice in matters that concern me in school.					
13. I do NOT see fights or physical altercations between students at school.					
14. In school, I teach more than academics. I teach students about things like perseverance, self-control, self-regulation, and collaboration.					
15. The administration at this school is fair in the way it allocates resources.					

Student School Climate Survey

Before you begin, please read the following information:

- You are being asked to complete this survey as part of an effort to understand how students and other members of the school community (teachers, staff, administrators) feel about the current school climate.
- Read the statements carefully and answer based on your thoughts and feelings about your personal experience at school.
- This survey is completely anonymous. No one will know how you responded, so please be honest.
- There are no right or wrong answers. We want to gather information about how people feel while they are here in school.

Directions: Mark an *X* in the column that corresponds with how strongly you agree or disagree with the following statements.

	Strongly Disagree	Disagree	Neither Agree or Disagree	Agree	Strongly Agree
1. I feel physically safe at school.					
2. While at school or at school functions, I am not insulted, teased, harassed, or otherwise verbally abused.					
3. Adults in my school treat students as if they care about them.					
4. My school has clear rules against physically hurting other people (hitting, pushing, kicking).					
5. I have at least one friend at school I can talk to if I have a problem.					
6. Adults seem to like one another and work well together in my school.					
7. There is at least one adult at school that I can trust and talk to if I have a problem.					
8. In general, students at my school treat one another with kindness. No one seems to go out of their way to treat other students badly.					

➡️

	Strongly Disagree	Disagree	Neither Agree or Disagree	Agree	Strongly Agree
9. Students at my school accept one another's differences (race, culture, gender, appearance).					
10. My teachers have high academic expectations.					
11. Adults in my school treat all students fairly.					
12. I am encouraged to take part in extracurricular school activities.					
13. I feel a sense of pride in my school (school spirit).					
14. In school, I am learning more than academics like math and ELA—I also am learning how to be a good person.					
15. In my school, we learn and discuss ways to control ourselves—our thoughts, actions, and emotions.					

Letter to Families About Classroom Climate Initiative

Dear Parent or Guardian:

I am looking forward to getting to know your child this year. In the interest of creating the best learning environment for my students, I am going to be conducting activities throughout the year that are intended to create a positive classroom climate, one in which there is a sense of physical and emotional safety, positive relationships, and engaging teaching and learning. Research has shown that a positive climate not only improves students' attitudes toward school, but also improves learning and achievement.

Some direct instructional time will be sacrificed to intentionally creating a positive climate. Students will work together to develop a classroom touchstone and class constitution, and they will participate in regular community meetings and social-emotional learning activities. The problem-solving, interpersonal, and self-control skills children will learn through these activities will serve them well not only in school, but later in life.

If you have any questions or concerns about my classroom climate initiative, please call or email me.

Sincerely,
[your name]
[your phone number]
[your email address]

Part 1

SETTING THE FOUNDATION

Safety and Relationships

2

The **Community Meeting**

The community meeting is the keystone of a positive school climate. Community meetings facilitate effective group communication, which is essential for building and maintaining positive relationships, as well as for team goal setting, creative problem-solving, information sharing, strategic planning, and learning.

The Community Meeting in Your Setting

Community meetings can be used with anyone, from the youngest students to staff. All groups can benefit from this simply structured, highly flexible, and effective communication process.

I recommend that principals or leaders of the climate improvement initiative take time during their first Climate Improvement Team (CIT) meeting to explain the process of community meetings and engage in one. You might also use community meetings to structure discussions in faculty or department meetings. Superintendents can include them in administrative team meetings, department chairs in department meetings, or team leaders (custodial, food service, transportation) in staff meetings.

For preK through fifth grade, it works great as a daily morning meeting or circle time. For middle and high school students, it provides a useful structure for academic, social-emotional, and character education discussions. Classes at any level can use them for problem-solving. Coaches and extracurricular advisors will find them useful

for group cohesion and team, club, or group problem-solving.

Whoever the participants, the benefits are compelling. Community meetings create a sense of connectedness and cooperation among participants. They also provide participants with a voice and a sense of ownership, and they empower everyone in the group. Because community meetings encourage effective communication, they help avoid common pitfalls that can occur in group meetings such as people dominating the discussion, people not participating, off-task behavior, boredom, and lack of focus.

In addition, community meetings provide students with:

- opportunities to learn essential communication and social skills

- opportunities to solve problems and take ownership of their solutions

- a safe place to practice speaking and active listening skills

- a safe, predictable way to start and/or end the school day or week

Community meetings provide teachers with:

- a highly effective procedure for beginning and/or ending the school day in a structured, needs-satisfying way

- a useful pedagogical and educational diagnostic strategy

- a great way to get to know and build relationships with students

Finally, community meetings provide school and district leaders with:

- increased staff or department engagement
- an increased sense of faculty/staff empowerment
- a more efficient problem-solving process, saving time
- liberation from the traditional faculty or department meeting

The Community Meeting Basic Structure

In whatever setting or purpose you are using community meetings, the general structure is the same.

Sit in a Circle

Participants sit in a large circle—if possible, with no desks or other furniture in the way. The reasons for the circle are:

- The circle, an ancient symbol of unity, creates the image of community and connection.
- Everyone in a circle can hear, see, and make eye contact with everyone else.
- No one can hide in a circle.
- The circle structure shares power. In the traditional classroom (or faculty-meeting-in-the-auditorium) structure, with the teacher (or principal) in front and the students or teachers in rows, it is clear where all the power resides. In a circle, however, the leader retains his or her power of authority and experience, but the circle levels the playing field, creating a sense of equity. The power differential is less apparent, providing participants with a greater sense of ownership and creating a greater sense of community and encouraging a feeling of "power with" rather than "power over."

It can take some time and effort to move the furniture for this structure, but don't let that discourage you. This is a great opportunity to involve the participants in creating a simple, clear procedure to accomplish this task. Once students know exactly what their responsibility is, practice the procedure until your group can get into the community meeting structure in less than a minute. Remember to set the criteria—quickly *and* quietly. (You might make a game out of it, trying to shorten the time in two or three successful practice runs.)

Consider using music as a signal to get into a circle. Some suggestions: the final *Jeopardy!* thinking music, "Rawhide" from the *Blues Brothers* soundtrack, "Happy" by Pharrell, a favorite of yours, or something popular with the students. The goal could be to get into the circle by the end of the first verse.

Introduce a Talking Device

Once you and the participants are in a circle, introduce a Koosh ball, Native American talking stick, small stuffed animal, or other device to designate the speaker. This is useful for groups of all ages, even adults, to help keep the discussion focused and discourage interruptions and side conversations. At first, you may want to choose the speaker, but with time, participants will learn to invite others into the discussion. Those who want to contribute to the discussion can signal through eye contact with the speaker or by raising their hands. When a participant has spoken, he or she chooses the next speaker and gently passes or tosses the talking device to the next speaker.

The high school and middle school students I work with enjoy adding "deep" meaning to the Koosh I use in community meetings, referring to it as the "Sacred Talking Koosh." One student even brought in a special box to keep the Koosh ball in.

Note: The facilitator of the meeting always retains the power to reclaim the talking device to redirect or refocus discussion.

Set Ground Rules

It's important to set ground rules at your first meeting and consistently follow them at every meeting. Make it clear that these rules are nonnegotiable. I recommend posting them somewhere where participants can see them during community meetings and briefly reviewing them at the beginning of every meeting. At first, it is your responsibility to do this, but once participants know the ground rules, consider inviting them to do it. Ask for volunteers or assign the task yourself. From my own experience, if facilitators skip this step, they will need to come back and revisit it later on anyway. It's best to be proactive and make sure everyone is reminded of the expectations.

You may want to add to or adjust the rules to fit your setting, but here are the minimum basic guidelines for a respectful and productive community meeting.

Ground Rules for the Community Meeting

The person with the talking device is the designated speaker.

Everyone else's role is to listen actively.

Stay focused on the topic.

No put-downs or criticism (verbal or nonverbal).

No interruptions or side conversations.

Anyone who wants to may participate.

Use I-statements when sharing opinions ("I think" or "I believe" instead of "We think" or "We believe").

The reason for emphasizing I-statements is to give ownership and responsibility to the speaker and to avoid the perception of a group "ganging up" on another participant or the facilitator. If someone voices a popular opinion, others have the opportunity to agree.

Start with a Greeting

By starting the meeting with a formatted greeting, you ensure that everyone in the circle has made at least one personal connection with someone else in the circle. The greeting can also be used to teach social skills, such as eye contact and how to appropriately greet others in a variety of social contexts.

With primary-age students, I recommend starting every meeting with a greeting. With older students, it's sufficient to limit greetings to once a week (if you're meeting more often than that). For adult groups, you can reserve the greeting for times when you are meeting for the first time or after a long break.

To begin, explain the kind of greeting to be used that day (or provide a choice). Here are a few examples of greetings you can use. Of course, you should feel free to create your own, too.

- traditional greeting: firm handshake, eye-contact, "Nice to meet you, _____."
- high five
- low five
- fist bump
- elbow bump
- combinations of the above
- Australian greeting: high five and "Good-day, mate!"
- Tanzanian greeting: fist bump and "Jambo!"
- cowboy greeting: two twirls of an invisible lasso, high five, and "Howdy, buckaroo!" or "Howdy, partner!"
- greetings in other languages

Stand up, approach one of the participants, and greet him or her in the manner of the day. In turn, that student approaches another student and follows suit. This goes on until the last person greets you. In order to help everyone see who has and has not been greeted, ask participants to keep their hands on their laps before they've been greeted and behind them after.

An alternative is to give each student an index card with a different set of variables (a person in a certain place or event) and, sitting in the circle, ask one participant to approach another and greet that person in the manner described on her card. After that greeting, the class guesses the person and situation. Next, the person who was greeted approaches another member of the circle and greets that person in the manner described on his card. The process continues until everyone has greeted and been greeted.

Here are some examples of variables for the greeting cards:

- the Queen of England at a royal function
- a prospective boss at an interview

- a friend from childhood you see for the first time in years
- a friend at a party
- a parent of a friend
- an adult you've never met before
- someone from your sports team in the hall at school
- historical or cultural figures
- the guest speaker greeting the audience at a big event
- an adult greeting a small, shy child
- a sports player greeting an opponent after losing the game

While the greeting is important, it can be overused. The rule of thumb is the younger the participants in the community meeting, the more frequently you might use the greeting.

Have the Discussion

This is the principle component of the community meeting. Your role in the discussion is to introduce the topic, ask questions, keep the discussion focused, and make sure the group is following the ground rules. You will need to decide on a topic before you begin so you will be prepared (see pages 27–31).

I strongly recommend that you structure your meetings using the define-personalize-challenge process, which works with virtually any topic. As your group gets more experience with community meetings, a less-structured process may work fine.

As the name suggests, the define-personalize-challenge process consists of three parts.

Define

Of primary importance in any discussion is that the participants agree on the definition of the concept, problem, or topic under discussion. You do this by asking defining questions—questions that help everyone explore the meaning behind the subject. Here are some examples of defining questions.

In a primary classroom. If the topic is active listening, defining questions might include:

- What does it mean to hear?

- What does it mean to listen?
- Are listening and hearing the same?
- What are the differences?

In a secondary classroom. If the topic is stereotypes, some defining questions might include:

- What is a stereotype?
- What does oversimplification mean?
- About whom or what do stereotypes exist?
- Why do stereotypes exist?

In an adult setting. If the topic is faculty relationships, some defining questions might include:

- What are the characteristics of a positive collegial relationship?
- What roles and responsibilities do you share?
- What differentiates your roles and/or responsibilities?
- What is necessary for positive, trusting, productive collegial relationships?

This part of the discussion generally goes quickly, but without the clarity and common understanding it creates at the beginning of discourse, the conversation may tend toward that of the proverbial five blind men describing an elephant (one describes it as a snake, one a tree, one a wall, and so on depending on where they stand). If your group can't agree on a definition, you can ask participants to accept a "working" definition of the terms for the sake of discussion.

Personalize

The personalizing questions get people engaged in the discussion because they get participants thinking about how the topic relates to them: "What does this have to do with me?" "How can I relate to this topic?" "How will learning about this topic or participating in this discussion add quality to my life?"

As all educators know, students need to be able to connect any new information to their experience, their schema, in order to integrate it. I believe that not only students, but adults, too, need to be able to personally relate to the topic or problem at hand before they will be engaged in the discussion or solution.

Here are some examples of personalizing questions using the same sample topics introduced in the "Define" section.

In a primary classroom. The topic is active listening.

- Do you know someone who is a good listener? How do you know?

- What do you think or how do you feel about people who are good listeners?

- Can you give an example of a time you "heard" but weren't listening?

In a secondary classroom. The topic is stereotypes.

- Have you ever felt like you were being stereotyped?

- How did you feel when you felt stereotyped?

- Do you know of someone who breaks a stereotype?

In an adult setting. The topic is collegial relationships.

- What are some of the best collegial experiences you've had as a teacher?

- Can you give an example of an outstanding team experience?

- Discuss a positive, trusting professional relationship you've experienced.

- How did this positive collegial relationship impact students?

Challenge

The purpose of the challenge component is to encourage group members to think more deeply about the topic: to solve problems, apply what they've discussed to real-world situations, synthesize what they've been discussing with other concepts, or make evaluations relating to the topic they've discussed.

Here are some examples of challenge questions using the same sample topics.

In a primary classroom. The topic is active listening.

- How does it benefit a person to be a good listener?

- When can you practice active listening?

- On a scale from 1 to 5 (5 being the best), rate your listening skills. What rating do you want? How can you make that happen?

In a secondary classroom. The topic is stereotypes.

- What are the problems with stereotyping?

- How can people rid themselves of stereotypical thinking?

- What can you do the next time you experience stereotyping?

- What can you do to prevent yourself from getting caught up in stereotypical thinking?

In an adult setting. The topic is collegial relationships.

- How can we as a faculty encourage better collegial relationships?

- What can you do as an individual to improve collegial relationships?

- What is an activity (or project or initiative) you might lead that would encourage positive collegial relationships?

The define-personalize-challenge format is designed to provide a basic structure, but often conversations take on their own life. An effective facilitator learns when to let the conversation continue and when to refocus or move on.

Close the Meeting

To bring the community meeting to a close, you can follow some or all of the following steps:

- summarize—or ask participants to summarize—any important points from the community meeting such as things learned, plans, next steps, and individual responsibilities

- set the agenda for the day (or week or month)

- make announcements

- schedule the next community meeting

- thank the participants

  In classrooms, you can also close by:

- having a student present the weather and calendar

- giving the answer to a daily brain teaser

- doing the "Kid of the Week" sharing time

- starting a transition procedure where students go back to their regular seats: This might be playing one minute of a song, directing students to be back in their seats by the time the music stops, or it might involve students filing past a table, picking up an assignment, and getting immediately reengaged in learning.

If you have students set up the circle at the beginning of the meeting, your closing can involve having them return the classroom to its original setup.

Three Kinds of Community Meetings

Generally speaking, community meetings can have one of three purposes.

Open-Ended. The primary purpose of open-ended meetings is to build a sense of community and to provide speaking and listening opportunities.

Problem-Solving. As the name suggests, the purpose of these meetings is to discuss class, faculty, or school issues and elicit solutions from the community.

Educational. The purpose of educational meetings is to prepare for a new learning experience or to instruct, informally assess, or extend student or adult learning.

The Open-Ended Community Meeting

The open-ended community meeting focuses on a topic of universal interest or one that relates to universal experience. It provides a nonthreatening environment for practicing effective speaking and listening skills and for members of the group to get to know one another better. Your priority is the process of communication, not the content.

I recommend starting with open-ended community meetings until the group demonstrates that everyone understands the process and ground rules. Once the participants are comfortable with the protocol, then the group is ready to engage in effective problem-solving or educational community meetings.

Running the Meeting

The define-personalize-challenge format is perfect for an open-ended community meeting. If the topic is something familiar to everyone, such as food or movies, you don't have to go through the define step. You can begin with personalize questions.

Topics for the Meeting

For initial community meetings, use topics of universal experience and interest so that everyone can be engaged and have something to share. Remember, the priority of open-ended meetings is working on communication skills rather than the subject matter. Eventually, you may include more difficult concepts or more controversial topics, depending on the age of the participants. In addition to topics that simply build relationships and help participants learn to communicate effectively in a group setting, some topics may involve social-emotional and character-related topics.

For example, if you're a classroom teacher with the goal of helping students gain empathy, a community meeting might focus on the topic of perspective taking or point of view. Example questions might include the following.

Define

- What does it mean to see something from another person's point of view?
- What does the phrase "walking in someone else's shoes" mean?

Personalize

- When is it important to you to have people see your point of view?
- When are some times you've looked at or felt something from someone else's perspective?

Challenge

- What are the benefits of being able to see things from different viewpoints?
- What are the challenges? When is it easy? When is it most difficult?
- When might you get a chance to practice perspective taking?

Chapters 6–8 have many ideas for community meetings based on social-emotional learning.

Open-Ended Community Meeting Topics

Here is a wide-ranging list of topics for open-ended community meetings:

- Food
- Music
- Books
- Pets
- Family
- Movies
- Television shows
- Video/Computer games
- Exercise
- Sports
- Poetry
- School events
- Holiday traditions
- Meaningful belongings
- Baby photos (bring one in to the meeting)
- Goals (short term, long term)
- Dreams
- Current world or national events
- Peer pressure
- Overcoming adversity
- Meanness and bullying
- Stereotypes
- Phobias
- Manners
- Movie manners
- Cell phone manners
- Character (in general or specific traits)
- Open-mindedness
- Acceptance
- Optimism
- Work ethic
- Responsibility (personal)
- Social responsibility
- Professionalism
- Personal strengths and/or challenges
- Community service
- Education (purpose, process)
- Emotions (in general or specific emotions)
- Social anxiety
- Regulating or controlling emotions
- Moral dilemmas

The Problem-Solving Community Meeting

Once participants understand the community meeting protocol and have demonstrated adequate group communication skills, the community meeting can be used to provide group members a voice in solving problems that affect the group and help students learn important problem-solving skills.

Running the Meeting

As with other types of meetings, the define-personalize-challenge format works well for problem-solving meetings. Your questions for the group will likely look something like these.

Define

- What is the problem we need to solve?
- How would (various stakeholders) view this problem?
- Is it a problem over which we have some control or influence?

Personalize

- How does this problem affect you?
- Have you ever solved a problem like this before?
- How will things be better for you (us) if we solve this problem?

Challenge

- What might we do to solve this problem?
- What are the best choices here?
- What is the first action required?

Another questioning format that works specifically for problem-solving meetings is based on reality therapy. To avoid the clinical sound of that term, I call it the "Process for Positive Change." Originally created as a form of psychotherapy, this process has been expanded into a highly effective approach for solving any problem. The process is as follows.

1. **Identify a shared goal.** You can use questions such as:
   - What do we want in this situation?
   - What is our goal?

- What will it look/sound/feel like if we achieve our goal? (Get specifics.)

- How will achieving this goal make things better for you (us)?

- Is this goal achievable?

2. **Examine current behavior in terms of the goal.** For example, ask:

- What are you (we) doing right now in terms of achieving your (our) goal?

- What have you (we) done in the past to achieve a similar goal?

3. **Evaluate current behavior.** You can ask:

- Is what you're (we're) doing going to get you (us) what you (we) want?

- How is what you're (we're) doing working?

- What's working? What isn't?

4. **Make a plan.** Start by asking:

- So what is your (our) plan?

- What do you (we) need to do to achieve your (our) goal?

- What is the first step?

- What are the next steps?

5. **Evaluate the Plan.** A good plan adheres to the SMART criteria. It is:

- **S**imple—the first step should not be 20 steps. Keep it simple. What is *one thing* that will get you closer to your goal?

- **M**easureable—set measurable goals to assess progress toward the goal.

- **A**ttainable—it's important that the plan meet with immediate success. Success in the first steps increases motivation to continue toward the goal.

- **R**epeatable—for example, if the problem you're trying to solve is poor scores on math quizzes, the plan might involve getting 100 percent homework completion. If everyone in the class does the homework one night, they can repeat that behavior again and again.

- **T**ry it out and evaluate again—you won't know if the plan works until you try it and evaluate your results against the goal using specific measurable criteria. If necessary, try again.

Topics for the Meeting

Problem-solving meetings can be used to solve any class, staff, or faculty problem, but they are not meant to solve individual problems (such as "Mr. Grant is late to work frequently" or "Miguel is calling kids names on the playground"). Individual problems require individual attention. The community meeting is not meant to be used as an intervention.

Here are some examples of appropriate problems to discuss in community meetings at the elementary, middle school, high school, and adult levels.

Elementary School Problems

- Students are not sharing the playground equipment during recess.

- During center time or independent work time, the classroom is too noisy.

- We want to go on a field trip and need to raise money.

- After recess, the floor is very muddy.

Middle School Problems

- The homework completion rate is low.

- We want to have community meetings, but we don't have space for a big circle of chairs in our room.

- Students have been spreading rumors.

- Students want more time to complete a project.

High School Problems

- Plagiarism is becoming widespread.

- Students want to address a local or national problem or issue (homelessness, hunger).

- Students want to create a more accepting classroom or school environment.

Adult/Staff Problems

- Enforcement of certain rules is inconsistent.
- Students are not complying with the school dress code.
- Teachers want time to collaborate with their teams.
- The school wants to increase parent involvement.

The Educational Community Meeting

The obvious purpose of this kind of meeting is to educate. Classroom teachers can use it to teach academic or social-emotional content, and school leaders can use it with faculty or staff as a professional development strategy.

Running the Meeting

For all topics that fit the educational meeting category, the define-personalize-challenge format works great.

Topics for the Meeting

Educational meetings can be used to introduce a new learning unit or concept, to integrate new content after an initial instruction phase, and to assess learning. Here are examples for all three categories.

Introducing New Learning in Elementary School: Habitats Example

Define

- What is a habitat? (If no one knows, tell them.)
- Who needs a habitat?
- What different kinds of habitats do you know about?

Personalize

- What kind of habitat do you need?
- What kind of habitat does a [specific animal or plant] need?
- How does your habitat have an effect on you?
- Do you have an effect on your habitat?

Challenge

- How might your habitat change? If your habitat changed, how might you have to adapt to the new environment?

Introducing New Learning in Secondary School: Interdependence (Symbiosis) Example

Define

- What does dependence mean?
- What does the prefix "inter-" mean (as in interactive, intergenerational)?
- How would we define interdependence?

Personalize

- Have you ever been in an interdependent relationship?
- In your future, what interdependent relationship might you experience?

Challenge

- Is interdependence a good thing? Can it be negative?
- What characteristics are needed for a positive interdependent relationship?
- What questions might we ask about the concept of interdependence?

Introducing New Learning to Adults: Student Motivation Example

Define

- What is motivation?
- What kinds of motivation are there (extrinsic, intrinsic)?
- Why is motivation important?

Personalize

- When, as a learner, have you been highly motivated?
- What were the characteristics of that experience that motivated you?
- When have you experienced a high degree of motivation from your students?

- What seemed to be the characteristics of that experience that motivated your students?
- How would your teaching experience be better if you knew more about human motivation?

Challenge

- What questions do you have about motivation?
- What do you want to learn about motivation?

Integrating Learning for All Grade Levels

Define

- How might we put [the concept or academic content] in our own words?
- What different kinds of [the concept or academic content] do we know about?
- Who can give an example of [the concept or academic content]?

Personalize

- How does [the concept or academic content] relate to your life?
- Have you ever experienced (or known someone who has experienced) [the concept or academic content]?
- How is [the concept or academic content] like or unlike other concepts or content we've learned about?

Challenge

- What real-world examples or applications can you think of, now or in the future?
- What questions can we still ask about [the concept or academic content]?

Assessment of Learning

Before a formal assessment, hold a community meeting and ask questions that students will be asked on the assessment. If students are struggling with the answers, you might determine that some content needs to be retaught to all or part of the class before assessing them.

Frequently Asked Questions About Community Meetings

What do I do if I cannot put chairs or desks in a circle?

If it is physically impossible to create a circle of chairs (for example if the desks are bolted to the floor or the desks and chairs are connected), it is still possible to hold a community meeting. You might hold meetings standing or sitting on the floor in a circle, sitting outside on the lawn, moving desks or tables into a large rectangle, etc. The key is to try to make sure everyone can hear and make eye-contact with everyone else.

How do I introduce the community meeting and help participants feel comfortable with sharing in a circle?

Explain that the community meeting is a way of giving participants a chance to talk and be listened to about topics that are important to them. Share with them that the circle is the most effective communication structure for groups of people and that you'd like to give it a try.

A particularly effective strategy to help participants feel safe sharing in the circle is the W.H.I.P. (Without Hesitation Immediate Participation) strategy. It requires a very low level of risk and encourages 100 percent participation right away. After the group is seated in a circle, the talking device has been introduced, and you have explained the ground rules, it is time to do the W.H.I.P. You provide a sentence starter and pass the talking device to your left, and the next participant fills in the blank in the sentence starter with a word or brief phrase without spending more than a second or two thinking about it. That person then passes the talking device to the next person, who does the same. This way, everyone gets to participate, and everyone has to say only a few words. Once participants understand that the community meeting is a safe place, they will be more likely to volunteer to share in the future.

Suggested W.H.I.P. Sentence Starters

These can work with students as well as adult participants.

My favorite dessert is . . .

A food I used to dislike, but now I like is . . .

A food I used to like that I don't like anymore is . . .

An unusual food that I've tried is . . .

A place I'd love to visit is . . .

One of the best places I've ever been is . . .

Somewhere I spend a lot of time is . . .

If I could meet anyone from history (or alive today), it would be . . .

A person I respect is . . .

One of my favorite sayings is . . .

My favorite musical band or artist is . . .

Something that I enjoy doing in my free time is . . .

A word (or two or three) that describes me is . . .

Someday I would like to . . .

One of my favorite movies is . . .

You can also have participants create sentence starters and submit them to you for screening.

How long should my community meetings be?

A simple rule of thumb is approximately the age of the student multiplied by two. For example, a community meeting for kindergartners (ages five and six) will be about 10–12 minutes, while seniors in high school can meet for about 35 minutes. Adults usually can remain attentive for approximately 45 minutes to an hour, depending on how engaged they are in the topic.

Community meetings do not have to last that long, however. For most students, a daily (for elementary) or weekly (for secondary) community meeting of 15–20 minutes (less for younger kids, obviously) suffices, unless there is a particularly important issue or topic at hand.

What if participants break the ground rules?

With adults, reminders are usually sufficient. With students, I have a different approach. In the first class meeting, intentionally break one of the rules early on in the discussion. (I usually have a side conversation with the person next to me.) Invariably, a student will call you on your behavior. Now, you have the opportunity to model for the group what you will ask of them when they violate one of the ground rules. Say, "Yes, you're right. I was having a side conversation. I'm sorry. It won't happen again." Then, teach them the simple process you just used:

- Admit the mistake
- Apologize to the group
- Change your behavior

Explain that you don't expect perfect adhesion to the rules. Perfection is not a human condition. What you do ask is that students comply with the rules the best they can. Everyone makes mistakes, like you just did. It is how we handle our mistakes that is important. Denying your mistake or blaming your behavior on someone else puts you in a bad light. Just admit it, apologize, and move on. To emphasize the point, you might post this simple process where everyone can see it.

If participants continue to break the rules after a reminder, ask them to sit outside the circle and find something to do: read, write in a journal—anything as long as it does not disrupt the community meeting. They should understand that after a short break (maybe three to five minutes) they are invited back to the community meeting as long as they are willing to comply with the ground rules. One brief invitation is sufficient; you don't want to encourage attention-seeking behavior.

If a student continues to disrupt the meeting, he or she should be removed from the room—to another teacher-buddy's room, the time-out room, or the school disciplinarian—wherever you typically send students who are insubordinate. Before holding another community meeting, hold a brief conference with the student about expectations and gain her or his compliance. If the student is still unwilling to comply, continue holding community meetings with this person sitting out. In my experience, community meetings are so needs-satisfying (safe, empowering, connecting, and fun) to students, eventually resistant participants willingly join in.

What if my discussion questions are met with stone silence?

When people are reluctant to share, they are not feeling safe. You might continue with short W.H.I.P. topics for a few more meetings before attempting the define-personalize-challenge format. It's also possible that the topic you've chosen is inappropriate for the current comfort level of the group. Focus early community meetings on topics that are noncontroversial or of general interest (food, hobbies, music, and so forth) and work up to more controversial or emotionally laden topics.

Two other proactive strategies you might use are:

Journal writing. Before moving into the community meeting, ask participants to formulate answers in their journals to some of the questions you will ask during the discussion. This gives participants time to think and formulate appropriate, coherent responses.

Heads together. This is another way of giving participants time to compose a response. Before opening up discussion to the whole community circle, have participants turn to a partner or two to discuss their responses. After approximately 30 seconds to one minute, repeat the question for the entire group.

How do I make time for community meetings with all the curriculum I have to cover during the school year?

This is one of the most common concerns I hear, and as a former teacher, I do understand. However, the regular use of community meetings has such a positive impact on the classroom climate, and subsequently student behavior, that it saves time in the long run by saving time that otherwise would be spent dealing with disruption, conflict, or off-task behavior. Fifteen minutes a day spent in a community meeting may save you more than twice that time managing behavior. Furthermore, it provides a great venue for announcements, taking roll, daily weather report and calendar (for primary students), and class discussions—things that need to occur anyway.

3

The **School Touchstone**
Discovering the Core Values of Your Community

A touchstone is a word, phrase, or slogan that expresses clearly and succinctly the shared values of an organization. It is a shared vision that you create based on mutually agreed-upon core values. This vision is like a destination for the climate improvement journey. If you set out on a journey but don't have an agreed-upon destination, the journey might be very long and unpleasant, and you might end up somewhere you don't want to be. The touchstone is like "true north" on a compass, providing clear direction for your efforts.

Furthermore, the *process* of creating a touchstone together—the focus of this chapter—is quite valuable. This process helps your community develop a sense of "we" as a class, team, or school; encourages pro-social behavior; and establishes a shared vision of what is possible. It builds and improves relationships among various stakeholders in the community. It also:

- Empowers members of the school community by providing them with a voice regarding the kind of school they want to become. This is particularly important for those who often feel powerless in their school, including students, staff, parents, and even teachers and administrators.

- Teaches students how to collaborate, cooperate, and achieve consensus.

- Sets a solid foundation on which a socially responsible school can be built and maintained.

When the process is complete, your touchstone provides a constant reminder of the community's shared values. Students, teachers, parents, and staff bring to life your school's touchstone values as they refer to them, model them in their daily interactions, and integrate them into their academic lessons. This creates the potential to revitalize a school's climate and culture.

This chapter explains why and how to create your school or classroom touchstone.

Examples of Touchstones

Just as every school community is unique, so is every touchstone. Here are some touchstones from schools I have worked with.

Creative Technologies Academy (CTA), a K–12 Charter School near Grand Rapids, Michigan, chose the motto "The CTA Way: character, respect, and acceptance" as their touchstone.[1] They display posters of the CTA Way in every classroom and throughout the school.

The Campus Community Elementary School in Dover, Delaware, developed a touchstone they titled "Campus Friends," with their values displayed as an acrostic:[2]

One noteworthy thing about the Campus Community touchstone is the number of values

---

[1] "The CTA Way" is used with permission from Creative Technologies Academy in Michigan.
[2] "Campus Friends" acrostic is used with permission from Campus Community Elementary School in Delaware.

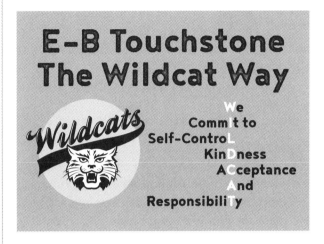

club also made a huge papier-mâché touchstone, and every student in the school puts his or her thumbprint on it. It is prominently displayed in the school foyer.

(10) they were able to incorporate: commitment, learning, community, caring, acceptance, mutual respect, performance, unity, social responsibility, and friendship. While I generally recommend limiting the number of values to seven or fewer so that everyone will be able to remember them, the acrostic format helped make the Campus Community touchstone easy to remember. And because it included everyone's most important values, the learning community enthusiastically endorsed it. One tradition the school has begun is having the entire school community recite the touchstone statement every morning at the end of announcements. One of the school's student leaders reads the announcements each morning and leads both the "Pledge of Allegiance" and touchstone.

The Emmet-Belknap Intermediate School in Lockport, New York, decided to include the school mascot, the Wildcat, into their touchstone: The Wildcat Way.[3]

During an inspiring student leadership training day at Emmet-Belknap, one of the boys excitedly shouted, "We should get a really big stone, write our touchstone on it, have everyone in the school put their thumbprint on it in colored paint, and put it next to the front door. Touch the stone, get it?" I loved that idea. They didn't do that exactly, but the school's art teacher engaged the art club in making papier-mâché stones for each classroom, on which students put their thumbprints to symbolize their commitment to the touchstone and so they could see it and refer to it every day. The art

Since Lockport High School's mascot is a lion and students wanted to be remembered for their shared values, their touchstone looks like this:[4]

The Lockport High School website included a link to a page devoted to their climate initiative. Their leadership team elicited input from as many of the school community members as possible, involving everyone from students to bus drivers. The website featured a blog titled "What's Your Print?" where students posted essays, videos, and songs they'd written and recorded about values embedded in the touchstone. Chapter 4 has more ways schools can make use of the touchstone for a variety of purposes.

---

[3] "The Wildcat Way" was created by the Emmet-Belknap Intermediate School in New York. Used with permission from Lockport City School District.

[4] The "Leave Your Print" touchstone was created by Lockport High School in New York. Used with permission from Lockport City School District.

Creating the School Touchstone

This process is the same for all the groups invited to be part of the touchstone development: teachers, students, paraprofessionals, administrators, other staff, and parents.

The process of establishing your school's touchstone can (and should!) be fun and affirming for everyone. To help achieve that goal, be sure to:

Engage everyone. Like the school climate initiative itself, the touchstone is not effective or engaging if members of the community feel like it was developed by a select group (such as school leaders, character education committees, or student council) and handed down to them. Invite as many stakeholders to be involved as possible.

Take your time. In order to arrive at universal buy-in, everyone must feel as if their point of view has been heard and that disagreements have been resolved satisfactorily. This takes an investment in time. It's important to remember that the process is at least as important as the final product.

Reach consensus. The touchstone is built on consensus, which does not mean that everyone gets exactly the wording that he or she wants. Nor does it mean simple majority rule. Arriving at consensus means everyone involved is thinking "we," not "I," and is willing to compromise at times so you can achieve unanimous agreement on the final product. Sometimes that agreement means trying the touchstone one way for a set amount of time and reevaluating its effectiveness at a later time, perhaps later in the school year. It is important that, once the group reaches consensus, members support the touchstone both in the room and out in the school. In other words, group members don't leave the session thinking or saying things like, "I wasn't for it, but they decided . . ." Instead, they're thinking, "We came to a consensus and our decision was . . ."

Here are the steps to follow to create your school touchstone. For a classroom or other setting, this process can be completed in one meeting with your small group.

Step 1: Introduce the Touchstone to All Stakeholders

Set up separate meetings for each of the stakeholder groups that will be involved in establishing the school touchstone (faculty, paraprofessionals, students, parents, and so on). Depending on your community, the group sizes can vary widely, but if a group has fewer than 10 members, consider combining it with a similar group (for example, support staff with food service staff). Make sure you will have enough co-facilitators to manage each group (about one co-facilitator for every 12 to 20 participants). For adult group meetings, you can use adult members of the CIT as co-facilitators (see page 12).

When you meet with the student population group, which will be your largest, use members of your SLT (see Chapter 6) as co-facilitators. In addition to providing extra hands and helping things run smoother, using student leaders sends the important message that this initiative is not a top-down, adult-centered process, but that students' voices are valued highly.

Hold your meetings in a location such as the cafeteria where participants can sit at tables to work in groups of four to eight. It's best to separate best friends or cliques and create groups as diverse as possible. One way to do this is to use playing cards. Pass out one card to each participant and group the participants by card value: all the aces at one table, all the kings at another, and so on.

Begin each of these meetings by explaining the purpose and rationale (or benefits) of creating a touchstone. Use the information at the beginning of this chapter.

Step 2: Reflect on Behaviors and Attitudes

Ask participants to think about the kinds of behaviors and attitudes they would like to experience at school and those they would *not* like to experience. Ask them to write their ideas on a T-chart or copies of "The School Touchstone" handout (see the thumbnail on page 41), being as specific as possible. Students tend to write "bullying" on their lists. Ask them, what are people doing or saying when they are bullying? Also, you may notice students writing down things they'd like changed in the school. "No homework!" for example, or "Better food in the cafeteria." Remind them that this is about how people interact; it's about behavior and attitudes, not changing school rules or lunch menus.

If you're using the handouts, ask students to leave the "Values" section at the bottom of the sheet empty for now.

With younger students, you may want to use the "The Schoolhouse Touchstone" handout instead (see the thumbnail on page 41). The directions on this graphic organizer are the same as they are on "The School Touchstone" handout, except students are to write the behaviors they do not want on the outside of the schoolhouse and those they do want inside of it. Again, they should leave the "Values" section (the foundation) of the sheet empty for now.

Here's a sample T-chart:

Behavior (Words and Actions)	
I would LIKE to see and hear	**I would NOT like to see and hear**
Recognition for what I'm doing right	Criticism
People waiting their turn	Gossip
Listening	Being ignored

Step 3: Compile T-Charts in Small Groups

Ask each group to identify someone to be a recorder and to compile all the items from their individual T-charts onto one large T-chart. You might have them do this on a fresh piece of paper or on large chart paper. Tell them to make sure everyone's ideas are recorded on the group chart.

Step 4: Create Values and Principles

This critical step requires the groups to shift from focusing on the specific to the general. Ask the table groups to develop a list of the values or principles that their list expresses. For example, if put-downs are something we do not want and being listened to is something we do want, they might identify the values *respect* or *caring*. Ask the groups to try to limit the values they list to five or six. This helps avoid redundancy and accelerates the next step in the process.

Before students get started on this step, talk about the difference between behaviors and attitudes on one hand, and values and general principles on the other. Behaviors are words and actions that we can directly observe. Values are the inner beliefs or guiding principles that underlie a person's words and actions.

Giving some guided practice on this difference is helpful, particularly for younger students. Say something like, "We might see Ali helping his classmates in math and sharing his cookies at lunch. Are we seeing a behavior or value?" Guide kids to the answer, behavior, then continue: "What *value* might Ali hold that is demonstrated by this behavior?" Answers could be kindness, generosity, or caring. You will get an idea of how many examples your students need as you informally assess the guided practice. Older students and adults will need fewer examples, if any. Some values or principles that are often listed are:

- Respect (almost always)
- Fairness
- Open-mindedness
- Compassion (or empathy or caring)
- Honesty
- Responsibility (personal, social, and civic)
- Learning
- Creativity
- Optimism
- Diversity
- Strong work ethic

When doing this step with students, it is particularly helpful to have members from your SLT helping out, since they already have been through the process when doing their training (see Chapter 13) and have their own touchstone. They can help students better understand the kind of big ideas we are looking for. It is also important that teachers and other adults circulate and guide the table groups away from behaviors and attitudes and toward values and principles.

Step 5: Combine and Condense Lists

Join two or three tables together and give them the task of coming to consensus on three to six words or phrases that express the most important values and principles from their group lists. Again, when working with groups of students, student leaders and adult group facilitators can advance this process by helping participants find common ground and looking for words or phrases that might be combined. For example, if the values of kindness and caring are listed, a facilitator might ask, "How are these the same and different? Do we need both or does one include the other? Can we agree on one or the other?" If so, cross one off the list. If no agreement can be reached, you might table that for the large group discussion that will come later in the meeting. For now, include both words with a slash between them (caring/kindness).

Once these groups have come to consensus on their lists, it is time to do so as a whole group. To do this, have each group present its final list to everyone in the room. As they do, write all of the values and principles on a flip chart or whiteboard. Once you have the complete list, your job is to facilitate the process of coming to consensus on the final three to six values and principles. These will be the values and principles that your community finds most compelling and important.

In a process similar to Step 4, look for common ground first, then for words or phrases that are redundant and/or that seem to incorporate the meaning of others. As you attempt to pare down the list, make sure to ask for any objections before eliminating words or phrases. Throughout the process, you might check for consensus using thumbs up (agree), thumbs down (disagree), or thumbs

sideways (need clarification). If there are objections, discuss the reasons for the objections as well as the rationale for eliminating the items from the list.

The reason to work toward a list of only three to six touchstone values is so that anyone in the school community can keep the values in mind and articulate them at any given time. With that in mind, remind the group of the importance of compromise and coming to consensus, which means everyone is able to live with and support the touchstone, even if it isn't exactly the way each person wants it.

Note: This is a crucial part of the process. It is important that all members of the group feel that their voices are heard and that their points of view have been understood. This takes patience on everyone's part. At some point, however, there needs to be a call for consensus: "Can we all agree to support the following values and principles as the basis of our touchstone?" If there is still a person or a few people who are resistant because of one value that was included (or not), ask if they would be willing to support it as is for one semester or year.

If this still doesn't achieve consensus, ask the resistant person what it would take for him or her to support the touchstone. Ask the rest of the group if it would support the touchstone with this person's suggested changes for a certain period of time. In my experience, at this point in the process, people are willing to concede and support the touchstone, at least for one school year.

Step 6: Bring the Groups Together to Establish the Touchstone

Once all of the groups in the community have met and come to consensus on their values, the CIT and SLT meet to finalize the list of touchstone values and principles. Using the final lists from each group, they create one final list of core values to be used for the touchstone.

Using that list, the two teams can brainstorm and discuss choices for how the touchstone will be depicted and published. Some possibilities include:

- an acronym, like at Buena Vista High School (RANCH)

- a catch phrase, like at The Creative Technologies Academy (The CTA Way)

- a statement, like the Campus Community School (We commit to being a caring learning community encouraged and supported by . . .)
- a phrase involving the school mascot like Emmet-Belknap School (The Wildcat Way)

Or you may come up with some other way to decide how to express the core values that is both memorable and unique. You could have the CIT and SLT discuss the options and determine the final phrasing by vote or other method. Or you could have a school-wide contest letting the school community vote on the various touchstone phrases.

Step 7: Present the Touchstone

Finally, when you've arrived at your touchstone, have an assembly or an evening presentation to officially unveil it. You might invite the school band to play, invite a guest speaker, or make it like a pep rally. Since self-control was the number one value listed under The Wildcat Way, the Emmet-Belknap Intermediate School unveiling involved a martial arts demonstration and a follow-up discussion on the importance of self-control in martial arts training and in life. This demonstration helped students understand self-control and added excitement to the event.

Another way to share the touchstone is to create a short video that depicts images of students demonstrating the values articulated in their touchstone. One of the schools I work with, North Park Junior High, decided to focus on acceptance. They created a video using Miranda Lambert's song "All Kinds of Kinds" as the background music, with images of their students, teachers, administrators, and staff holding whiteboards showing the "kind" they are, such as *Caring Kind, Sporty Kind, Child-of-Divorced-Parents Kind,* and *Funny Kind.* The principal published the video on YouTube and it received a lot of attention. Miranda Lambert herself even commented on the video, saying "North Park Junior High gets it."

Frequently Asked Questions About the School Touchstone

What if members of the community choose not to participate at all or refuse to take part in the small-group activities?

To encourage stakeholders to participate, communication is essential. As mentioned in Chapter 1, it's important to be invitational from the beginning, explaining the purpose and anticipated benefits of the climate improvement initiative and inviting various stakeholders to join the Climate Improvement Team. Representatives on the CIT have the responsibility to communicate and continuously invite feedback and input from their constituent groups. If people choose not to participate, trying to coerce them is likely to lead to further resistance. Continue to be invitational and communicative with them. At some point, they may choose to be involved.

For people who choose not to participate during meetings, quietly pull them aside and explain that this is their chance to have their voice heard and make a positive difference in the school climate. Emphasize that their individual voices are as important as anyone else's in the process, and explain that if they choose not to have their voice heard, they are letting others make choices for them—in essence taking away their power. If they remain withdrawn or antagonistic, thank them for their honesty and proceed without their input.

Some people are not comfortable working in small groups. For those people, invite them to create an individual T-chart. You can include their ideas along with those that are generated in the small groups.

What is the best way to display the touchstone?

Most schools create posters of their touchstones and display them in the entrance of the school and in every hallway and classroom. Some schools have acquired an actual stone (a boulder), painted the touchstone values on it, and set it outside the front door so that people entering the school could touch it. Many schools integrate the touchstone with other mascots or slogans that they've created over the years.

When groups of people become excited over a project, such as the touchstone, they become creative. Allow unique ways of displaying or publishing the touchstone to come from members of the school community.

Once we have a touchstone, how do we keep it from being one more document that gets filed away and forgotten?

While developing a touchstone goes a long way toward improving the school climate, unless teachers, school leaders, students, parents, and staff bring it to life in the classroom, the board room, faculty meetings, and in the school in general, it will soon be forgotten and may be perceived as a waste of time. However, through an ongoing, intentional effort to integrate the touchstone values into every aspect of school life, you develop and sustain a more positive school climate. Chapter 4 explains specific ways the touchstone and its values can be used to enhance instruction, discipline, supervision, and management.

How often should we revisit the touchstone or change it?

In a perfect world, every time a new class entered the school, they would be engaged in developing a touchstone. If you're working on a small scale to develop a classroom or team touchstone, this is easily accomplished. But because of the amount of time needed to develop a school-wide touchstone, it may not be feasible to develop a new one every year. I encourage revisiting and possibly revising the touchstone every three to four years, after the whole student body has turned over since the last touchstone was developed. This schedule gives students a sense of ownership over the touchstone and keeps it from becoming stale.

For the years in between, members of the CIT and SLT can hold an orientation program at the beginning of the school year for incoming students. At the program, they can explain the purpose of the touchstone and the process that was involved in developing it, emphasizing student voice. You might have classroom teachers lead their students through a T-chart activity like the one in this chapter and show students how the behaviors they listed on their T-charts align with the touchstone. This can help create buy-in with new students and begin the process of developing a social contract (see pages 46–51).

Printable Forms

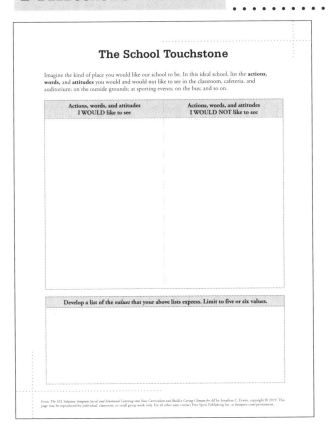

The School Touchstone

Imagine the kind of place you would like our school to be. In this ideal school, list the **actions, words,** and **attitudes** you would and would not like to see in the classroom, cafeteria, and auditorium; on the outside grounds; at sporting events; on the bus; and so on.

Actions, words, and attitudes I WOULD like to see	Actions, words, and attitudes I WOULD NOT like to see

Develop a list of the *values* that your above lists express. Limit to five or six values.

From *The SEL Solution: Integrate Social and Emotional Learning into Your Curriculum and Build a Caring Climate for All* by Jonathan C. Erwin, copyright © 2019. This page may be reproduced for individual, classroom, or small group work only. For all other uses, contact Free Spirit Publishing Inc. at freespirit.com/permissions.

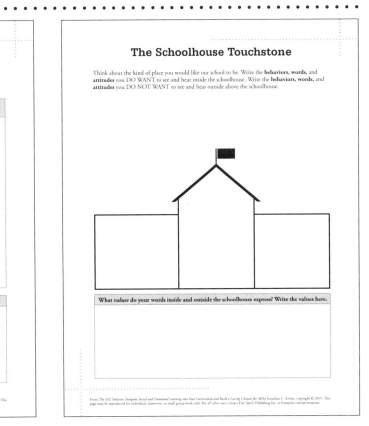

The Schoolhouse Touchstone

Think about the kind of place you would like our school to be. Write the **behaviors, words,** and **attitudes** you DO WANT to see and hear inside the schoolhouse. Write the **behaviors, words,** and **attitudes** you DO NOT WANT to see and hear outside above the schoolhouse.

What *values* do your words inside and outside the schoolhouse express? Write the values here.

From *The SEL Solution: Integrate Social and Emotional Learning into Your Curriculum and Build a Caring Climate for All* by Jonathan C. Erwin, copyright © 2019. This page may be reproduced for individual, classroom, or small group work only. For all other uses, contact Free Spirit Publishing Inc. at freespirit.com/permissions.

See digital content for full-size reproducible pages

4

Bringing the **Touchstone Values** to Life

It is critical that every member of the school community understands that he or she plays an important role in—and has responsibility for—attaining the shared vision articulated in the touchstone. It is every individual's social responsibility to act and speak in ways that are aligned with the touchstone's values and principles. This chapter provides several ways of reinforcing the touchstone values and principles and teaching everyone—adults and students—how to internalize those values and act in ways that express them.

Virtually all of the ideas and activities in this chapter are designed to be used with adult groups, such as staff and faculty, as well as with student groups such as classrooms, team practices, club meetings, and so on. However, the first two activities—The Touchstone Pledge (below) and The Touchstone Wall of Fame (page 43)—involve the whole school.

Note: The only activity designed to be used exclusively with students is the Behavior Matrix (page 51). Also, Triangles (page 44) is best suited for students ages nine and older. Other than those limitations, I recommend using all the activities and strategies for a school-wide approach.

The Touchstone Pledge

Many schools recite their touchstone every morning following the "Pledge of Allegiance" or at assemblies or other events. A touchstone pledge might be a simple recitation of the touchstone itself, if it is phrased as a statement, or a short new statement you write that contains a promise to uphold the touchstone values within it.

Emmet-Belknap Intermediate School in Western New York began each day with a student leading all students and staff through a recitation of the Wildcat Way Pledge:[1] "We commit to self-control, kindness, acceptance, and responsibility!"

Every morning at Randels Elementary School in Flint, Michigan, students recite their pledge:[2]

At Randels, I . . .

Respect others, myself,
and my school,

Always do my best and
am ready,

Make responsible choices,

Show self-control.

This is who I am, even
when no one is looking.

Having students recite a touchstone pledge doesn't make them behave in perfect alignment with the school values any more than saying the "Pledge of Allegiance" guarantees absolute loyalty to the United States, but it does have an important benefit: Everyone in the school will be able to list the school values without hesitation.

---

[1] Used with permission from Lockport City School District in New York.
[2] Used with permission from Randels Elementary School in Michigan.

The Touchstone Wall of Fame

A touchstone wall of fame is an excellent way to keep school community members aware of the touchstone values while providing a venue for celebrating them and giving thanks and recognition to people who demonstrate them.

People and organizations move toward what they focus on. If we're riding a bicycle through city traffic, we should not look at the cars on either side of us. We most likely would veer toward them and maybe crash. We should, instead, look at the space between the cars, where we want to maneuver safely. If we want a school based on kindness, looking for meanness would take us off course. Instead, looking for and celebrating simple acts of kindness will lead us to more acts of kindness. However, as human beings (and all other species), in order to survive, we naturally tend to look for what's wrong in a situation, anything that might threaten our safety and security. Therefore, at school, it is important to consciously look for and acknowledge what is right. The touchstone wall of fame helps that happen.

A touchstone wall of fame is simply a place in your school where students and other members of the school community can anonymously give recognition and affirmation to people who have demonstrated any of the touchstone values. It could be a bulletin board or just a hallway or lobby wall. It's important that it's placed where both students and adults can see it, such as in the school entrance or where students line up.

You will want to develop specific procedures for posting these affirmations on the wall of fame. For example, at one school I've worked with, teachers are provided with a stack of paper paw prints (their mascot is a lion) to keep in a designated spot in their classrooms. When the teacher or a student notices an act of kindness, social responsibility, self-control, or one of the other touchstone values, he or she writes a simple note of recognition and appreciation on a paw print and inserts it into a box near the teacher's desk. The note might include the values (like the examples that follow) or be a simple statement of thanks or appreciation. Some of the notes may say things like:

- Kindness: Mr. Lopez came in early to help me with my writing assignment.
- Social Responsibility: On the bus, Zeinab and Becky told an older kid to stop calling me names or they would report him. Thanks!
- Kindness: Thanks, Mr. Ngu, for helping me move my heavy desk! (From a teacher to a custodian.)
- Self-Control: Roberto, you demonstrated self-control today when Sarah called you a name. Thank you.
- Responsibility: Mr. Levi came in to let me into school early on Saturday morning to set up for the Young Authors' Fair. (From a teacher to principal.)

In this school, the teachers screen the paw prints for appropriateness and submit them to a parent volunteer (or sometimes the assistant principal), who each Monday replaces the previous week's paw prints with new ones. Changing the notes on a regular basis helps avoid too much clutter and provides everyone with an opportunity to have their notes included on the wall of fame.

You may find that students and adults will often stand, seemingly transfixed, in front of the wall of fame reading the various affirmations. People enjoy the recognition of seeing their own names but also love to read about the acts of kindness, responsibility, acceptance, and so on that others have noticed. This public celebration of the touchstone values encourages even more pro-social behavior, helping create a school climate that is safe, connected, and focused on positive values all the time.

Community Meetings: Touchstone Values

One way of engaging community members in the process of climate improvement is through community meetings focusing on the touchstone values. (See Chapter 2 for guidelines on running community meetings.) The define-personalize-challenge format will facilitate discussion and guide people toward a clear understanding of the touchstone values and their individual social responsibility in bringing the touchstone to life. Hold one community meeting to discuss each of your touchstone values.

Define

- What does [a particular value] mean?
- Are there different kinds of [the value]?
- How do you know [the value] when you see it? What does it look and sound like?

Personalize

- When are times you have acted (or seen others act) in ways that reflect [the value]?
- When are times you have acted in ways that do not reflect [the value]? What were the results of those actions?
- How might it benefit you to demonstrate [the value]?
- What might be the benefits to the school community?
- Can I make you act in ways that reflect [the value]? Who can?
- Who is responsible for achieving our touchstone goals?

Follow the responses to this final question with a statement such as: This is what our social responsibility is, to act and speak in ways that align (match up, conform, fit) with our touchstone.

Challenge

- What kinds of actions and words align with [the value] in the classroom? (Depending on the group you are facilitating, you might also ask about: in faculty meetings, in the teachers' lounge, in parent-teacher conferences, at school board meetings, at PTA meetings, on the bus, in the cafeteria, in the hallways, at sporting events, and so on.)
- What kinds of actions and words do not align?
- What are some things you can do (or not do) today to get us closer to achieving [the value]?

ACTIVITY

Triangles

Triangles is one of the most effective activities for helping everyone understand their responsibilities and individual roles in improving the school climate and having fun at the same time. Triangles can be used with many different-sized groups, including a class, team, or whole grade level, and any adult group, including school faculties, administrative teams, custodial crews, or parent groups—basically any group as small as 15 and as large as 150, as young as 9 and as old as 109, working toward a common goal.

Time Required: About 20 minutes

Materials Needed: A large empty space—a gymnasium or, even better, an outdoor space like an empty parking lot or playing field, and at least one facilitator, such as the school principal, a teacher, a school counselor, an officer with the PTO, or a coach

The Activity

Step 1: Gather your group into one big circle with everyone standing. (Holding hands is optional.)

Step 2: Tell everyone the name of the game and ask everyone to secretly and randomly choose two people from the group. Emphasize that they are not to indicate to anyone what two people they are choosing. You might also want to emphasize that the activity works best when the people they choose are not predictable (not a close friend, for example).

Step 3: Explain that everyone's task will be to form an equilateral triangle (defined as a triangle with three equal sides and angles) with themselves representing one point of the triangle and their secret partners as the other two points. They do not actually connect with their triangle partners physically; they simply must maintain the shape of a triangle with equal sides by moving around the space. But here's the catch: No communication of any kind (verbal or nonverbal) is allowed.

Demonstrate making a triangle using yourself and two randomly selected people from the group. You might say:

Suppose I chose Chase and Lauren as my two secret partners. My goal would be to form an

equilateral triangle like this. However, it is improbable in a group this size that Chase chose me as his secret partner, so he may need to move to form another triangle with his two chosen people. So I would need to shift my position like this.

Demonstrate what that would look like to shift so that you remain equally apart from and at equal angles from both your chosen partners.

Likewise, it is unlikely that Lauren chose me or Chase, so she may end up standing very close to Chase in order to form an equilateral triangle with her secret partners, so again, I will have to shift my position.

Again, demonstrate the shifting of positions. Have Lauren move close to Chase, forcing you to also move close to Chase and to her, keeping all three sides of your imaginary triangle equal.

The size of the equilateral triangles will vary, with some stretching across most or all of your open space and others quite small. The end result, with everyone in all these differently shaped triangles, will not look like a single neat geometrical pattern but a somewhat chaotic blob.

Step 4: Check to see if the participants are clear about the directions and ask if there are any questions. Emphasize that it is against the rules to change partners during the activity, and remind them that no communication of any kind is allowed. (Laughing and groaning are okay, however.)

Step 5: Tell them to begin, and observe the group's behavior as they attempt to get into their equilateral triangles.

Step 6: Usually within two or three minutes, the goal has been accomplished. At that point, call for applause, tell everyone to let their secret partners know who they were, and return to the training room (or their seats) to process the activity.

If students are unable to accomplish the goal, call time after about three minutes.

Step 7: Immediately after the activity, hold a discussion. Begin by directing participants to form groups of three or four and ask the question: How is participating in Triangles like being a member of a school community?

Explain that dozens of connections can be made and no answers are wrong. Give the groups three or four minutes to discuss the question, with someone at the table acting as a recorder to jot down answers. Reconvene as a larger group and ask each of the smaller groups to share one idea. After each group has shared, invite people to share any other significant points that came up. Some of the connections that might be brought up are:

- We have to work together to accomplish our goals.
- Sometimes it seems impossible to achieve our goals, but if we persist we can succeed.
- Sometimes it's frustrating.
- We have to be flexible and adjust to the needs of others to achieve our shared goal.
- Each of us has a role to play.
- Some people may feel left out.
- It's chaotic at times.
- It can be fun.
- Having a clear goal from the beginning helps us be successful.
- At times we wanted to control other people (the other points of our triangle), but the only person we could control was ourself.
- Every individual's actions affect the whole group.

That last one is the key point. Make sure it is emphasized. If it isn't brought up in the discussion, make sure to point it out yourself. To help lead the discussion toward some of the points, you may ask some of the following questions in order to elicit them:

- Did you think it would be impossible to achieve the goal?
- What enabled us to be successful? (Or, why weren't we successful?)
- How did you feel during the activity?
- Who did you want to control or influence during the game? Who could you control?
- What would have happened if one person, who one or two people chose as their triangle partners, didn't follow the guidelines and just kept moving around?

Step 8: After this discussion, summarize the ideas and connect your discussion to the touchstone. Make the following points:

- Without a clear goal at the beginning of Triangles, we would still be milling around the parking lot, trying to achieve our own individual goals. Having a touchstone gives us all a target to shoot for.

- ⋇ Many people might think becoming a school based on [your touchstone values] is impossible. But working together and being persistent, like we were in Triangles, it can happen.

- ⋇ Instead of focusing on trying to control other people, if we simply focus on our own behavior, aligning it with the touchstone, we can all be successful. This is being socially responsible.

- ⋇ Like in the Triangle activity, each of us influences (sometimes without knowing it) the entire school community, positively or negatively.

- ⋇ Sometimes it's frustrating, but again, with patience and persistence (and any other pertinent character traits) we can experience the fun, or joy, of making our touchstone come to life.

Note: Even if your group was unsuccessful in completing Triangles, the activity is still valuable since the discussion is the important part. Analyzing why the goal wasn't accomplished can bring out points that relate to school climate as well. For example, one person may not have understood the goal. In that case, we might learn that it's important to provide clear expectations. Or, if one person chooses not to follow the rules, the result could be chaos. Triangles helps people understand the significance one person's behavior can have on the whole school.

Social Contract

Behavioral norms—recurrent patterns of interpersonal behavior—emerge in any group of people who interact with each other regularly. Think of the different groups you interact with: your family, a circle of friends, coworkers, a civic or religious organization. "Normal" behavior in each of those groups probably differs significantly. For example, the accepted behaviors in a group of old college friends of the same gender would be very different from those in a faculty meeting. (At least, let's hope so!)

In some groups, the norms of behavior that emerge are based on cooperation, mutual respect, and courtesy. In others, the patterns of behavior are more indicative of competition, mutual distrust, and contempt. When a group comes together, if we allow these norms to develop naturally over time, then we give up all control over the kinds of patterns of behavior that may emerge and that can be risky.

On the other hand, if we are intentional about creating positive norms as a team, we can come to an agreement on what behaviors are acceptable and what behaviors we want to avoid. Creating a social contract for a group of students or adults is one way of ensuring that the behavioral norms are clearly understood by all and align with the core values of the school community.

School leaders may want to create a social contract for the school as a whole, but it's equally as effective, and more personal for participants, if social contracts are made for each of the smaller group contexts (classrooms, teams, staff, and so on).

Steps for Developing a Social Contract

The process of developing a social contract is like the touchstone process in reverse. In creating the touchstone, we begin with specifics and arrive at general principles or values. Now, after the values have been established through the touchstone process, the social contract clarifies how the values inform behavior in a specific context: during class, in rehearsals for the school musical, during faculty meetings, in team practices, at board meetings, in department meetings—any situation in which people will be working together for a significant period of time.

Step 1: Do the Math

Divide your group or team into groups of four to six and explain that the purpose of the social contract is to be proactive about the kinds of norms, or patterns of behavior, that we want to see and hear. For students, that means everyone feels safe (emotionally and physically) and gets along in the place where we work and learn every day. For adults, that means creating an optimal working/learning environment that aligns with our core values.

With students, start with a quick arithmetic exercise. Ask if anyone knows how many days are in a school year. The answer in New York state is about 180. Then ask how many hours or minutes we are together each day. (About six hours, or 360 minutes a day for elementary students; for secondary students, about 45 minutes a day.) Multiply the number of days by the number of minutes or hours and write the number on the board. That's 64,800 minutes or 1,080 hours for elementary students; 8,100 minutes or 135 hours for secondary students.

Your students may groan. Those are big numbers. Next, ask if they'd like those hours to be pleasant or unpleasant. (Most students agree on pleasant.) Explain that the process you're about to begin is a way of ensuring that those minutes or hours are as pleasant as possible for all of you.

Step 2: Brainstorm Behaviors

Pass out one copy of "The Social Contract" handout (see the thumbnail on page 52) to each group, or have them make a T-chart on blank paper. At the top of the page, have them write the values from your touchstone. On the left side of the T-chart, have groups list the specific behaviors and statements they would see and/or hear in your group context that align with those values. On the right side, list behaviors and statements that do *not* align and would be considered unacceptable. See the sample chart in the next column.

Younger students may need more hands-on help. They might say things like "Be nice" or "Be good." Asking, "What do you see or hear when someone is being nice?" will elicit more specific responses. Students can use invented spelling or even pictures to express their ideas.

Step 3: Combine Lists

Once the groups have created their lists, create a shared list on a large sheet of chart paper or whiteboard. Write down every behavior from every list, eliminating redundancies as you go. With all the behaviors collated onto a single list, discuss with the group whether anything should be added, changed, or removed. It's important to come to consensus on every item on the group list. If certain behaviors become too controversial to be agreed upon, you can temporarily table them to be discussed at a later date. (And make sure this happens.)

Step 4: Write the Contract

Use the results of the combined T-chart to create the social contract. On a new sheet of paper, write an introductory statement at the top that says that everyone who signs the contract promises to uphold the values of your touchstone and engage in the positive behaviors on the chart while avoiding the negative ones. You might add a flourish to the language to make it more fun, perhaps by mimicking language from a historical document like the Declaration of Independence: "We, the students of room 203, in order to form a more perfect classroom, promise to take responsibility for all that we do, respect others and ourselves, maintain positive and helpful attitudes, be inclusive, practice teamwork, and adhere to the behavior guidelines below—even when no one is looking."

Ask for a commitment from each individual to do his or her best to follow the social contract, and symbolically seal that commitment by signing the bottom of the final draft of the document. Alternatively, students might enjoy showing their commitment by placing their thumbprint in colored paint on the document. This document can be posted in the room, or copied for every student to use as the first page of their notebooks.

Your social contract can be as elaborate or simple as you see fit for your group. With younger kids, it may not make sense to have a long document that is likely to be overwhelming to them. On the other hand, it may be effective to create a more complex document for adult groups.

On the following page is an example of a social contract developed by the facilities team of a small city school district in Western New York. The team leaders referred to the social contract daily during regular team meetings. Soon, the team members were referring to it with each other (sometimes jokingly). What's significant is that the social contract, for this team, became part of their daily routine and interactions. The members of the facilities team said that their jobs and their interactions with other team members became more pleasant because of the social contract.

Custodial and Maintenance Team Agreement[3]

As members of the Custodial & Maintenance Team, in order to create a positive working environment for ourselves and our team members, we agree to be guided by the following values and principles in our interactions with one another.

Safety: Being mindful of our own and others' safety and well-being at all times.

Respect: Treating ourselves and others with the dignity we deserve as people and as contributing team members.

Honesty: Being truthful with ourselves and others.

Strong Work Ethic: Being there and being on time. Performing high quality work in a timely manner. Pitching in to help others when needed. Doing our best work.

Leadership: Understanding that we all have the capacity to be leaders.

Fairness: Being equitable with all those on the team. Not showing favoritism.

Pride: Being aware that our work truly matters in the lives and education of the children and adolescents of our school community.

We will see these values exhibited among members of the team when we

See or hear:	Do not see or hear:
Common courtesy and manners	Bad mouthing
Positive attitude and willingness to work	Complaining
Listening	Pushing off work
Cooperation among members of the team	Back-stabbing
Follow-through	Nosiness
A task-oriented focus	Whining
Consequences dispensed when required	Bad attitudes
Taking initiative	Empty promises
Everyone helping keep clean and secure	Shoddy or poor quality work
Recognition (private)	Criticism
Thanks	Being looked down upon
"How can I help?"	Selfishness
Sufficient supplies	Poor hygiene
Clear direction	Disrespectful emails
Effective communication among team members	Unreasonable demands
	Rumors

[3] This social contract is from the Lockport City School District in New York. Used with permission.

Variation for Developing the Social Contract

The following variation of the social contract is interactive, requires creative and abstract thinking, and is lots of fun for both adults and students. It is particularly useful for younger students because it involves drawing, but teenagers and adults will enjoy it just as much. However, if you are not in a setting where you can display your social contract on a wall, the previous approach is probably more practical. That version easily lends itself to being copied and put in every student's notebook.

This variation begins in the same way as the previous approach, but after small groups have completed their T-charts differentiating behaviors that align with and violate the touchstone values, try the following activity.

Groups Draw a Living Space

On a big piece of paper (flip chart paper or a piece of paper tablecloth), each group creates a "living space"—that is, any place where living creatures can be together. It might be an island, a baseball diamond, a school house, a hot air balloon, a tree house, a ship, a castle, an aquarium, a petri dish, and so on.

Then have the groups create symbols for the behaviors listed on their T-charts. Ideally, the symbols align with the theme of the living space. Students can choose to have one symbol represent all positive behaviors and one symbol represent all negative behaviors. For example, a group with an island as their living space might have palm trees as their positive symbol and sharks as their negative symbol. Or they could have a distinct symbol for every behavior—a monkey with big ears for active listening, a sun for positive attitude, a palm tree for helping others, and so on.

Place Symbols on Drawing

The groups place the symbols of positive behaviors inside the living space (on the island, on board the ship, inside the castle walls) and place the negative behaviors outside the living space (in the ocean or outside the castle walls). Give people the opportunity to be creative, and they will align their symbols to fit the living space. The participants may also want to label their symbols to help make them clear.

Present Drawings to the Large Group

Give each group an opportunity to present its living spaces and symbols to the large group and explain what their symbols mean.

As groups present, have two volunteers compile all the behaviors listed—one keeping a list of all the positive or acceptable behaviors and the other recording all the negative or unacceptable behaviors. Here are two examples of small-group living spaces from groups I've worked with.[4]

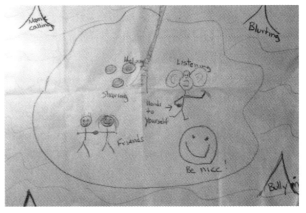

The island above was created by a small group of second graders. They chose to depict positive behaviors (helping, listening, hands to yourself,

[4] These social contracts are from the Lockport City School District in New York. Used with permission.

etc.) with various symbols on the island and negative ones (name-calling, mean words, etc.) as sharks in the ocean.

Teachers at an alternative high school created the other example as part of creating a faculty social contract. Their creative variation shows the positive behaviors (good listening, encouragement, etc.) as bones that the dog apparently likes and negative behaviors (nagging, one-upmanship, sarcasm, etc.) as bones that the dog prefers to bury. (I choose to be flattered by the fact the group named the dog Erwin.)

Make and Post a Group Drawing

As the volunteers compile the list of behaviors, delete any redundancies. When everyone has presented, discuss the behaviors listed and, as with the previous version of the social contract activity, work to reach consensus on all behaviors you will include in the final contract.

Next, create a new whole-group living space, different from all those already created, complete with symbols for positive and negative behaviors. Depending on your setting, you may want to choose the final living space and symbols, or you might put up a couple options for a vote. This final poster becomes the social contract. Post the final version as well as all the small-group living spaces for a week or so in your room or meeting area to value the creativity and effort each group put in. But it is the whole-group living space that becomes the official social contract.

Keep the Social Contract Alive

Whichever version of the social contract you go with, keep your group engaged with the contract by referring to it regularly and, at first, often. While it's easy to refer to the social contract when someone is violating it, it is vital to intentionally refer to it when things in the group are going well. After a successful meeting or class, discuss what positive aspects of the social contract members of the group observed. Recognize the positive behaviors with a simple acknowledgment (for example, "Devante demonstrated active listening by being able to summarize Natalia's argument"). Teach members of the group to offer feedback in this way—not with

a value judgment or an evaluation (such as "Good job!"), but with an observation of a specific behavior that aligned with the social contract.

This kind of specific, positive, nonjudgmental feedback encourages more positive behavior.

If the social contract is referred to only when there is a violation—which is usually followed by an uncomfortable conversation for everyone in the group—then it is associated with negativity and discomfort. Instead, if it is revisited frequently to remind people of the values or to give recognition for pro-social behavior, it becomes part of the team culture. Once that occurs, the social contract is then also useful when members of the group are behaving in ways that violate the social contract.

Frequently Asked Questions About the Social Contract

If we have a school touchstone, isn't that enough? Why is the social contract necessary?
The touchstone process identifies the core values of the community, but we can't expect every member of the community to understand what those values look like in the various contexts of a school. For example, everyone has a personal perception of what the value respect means. During the process of creating the social contract, everyone in the group comes to a clear understanding of what respect looks and sounds like in a specific context. In this way, the social contract fleshes out the bones of the core values, clarifying behavioral expectations for all.

Is the "Living Space" variation only for elementary students?
I enjoy using that variation for all the groups I work with. It generates a lot of positive energy and laughter, putting the social contract in a positive light from the start.

What if an individual chooses not to participate in the process?
Privately discuss with the person the purpose and benefits of the social contract and explain how nonparticipation is giving away power and control to others. Be clear that nonparticipation in the process does not mean exemption from the final document, just as choosing not to vote does not exempt one from the laws enacted by Congress. If

the person continues to choose nonparticipation, at least he or she made an informed decision.

Behavior Matrix

If you create social contracts for individual class-rooms and other small groups and spaces in the school and do not have one for the whole school, you may want to create a behavior matrix for certain locations, situations, and activities at the school—for example, hallways, restrooms, school events, buses, lunchtime—that aren't covered by a social contract.

To do this, assemble a representative team of teachers, students, parents, and administrators. Using the touchstone values that the school chose to inform behaviors and interactions, you can establish and communicate behavioral expectations for all school contexts. The final result will be a grid, or matrix, with the touchstone values listed horizontally and the various school contexts vertically. In the boxes of the grid, list the behaviors expected. While this approach is less democratic than the social contract, it is based on the values that the members of the school community chose and is created not just by the school disciplinarian, but by a team that includes a variety of stakeholders.

Below is an example of a behavior matrix.

Your behavior matrix can be made into posters and placed in strategic locations around the school and grounds, ensuring that behavioral expecta-tions are clear in every context and align with your touchstone's core values.

Model the Values

The activities and measures discussed in this chapter will help your students keep your school's touch-stone values in mind. But the loudest and most influential message about values that adults can send is to demonstrate those values through their actions and words on a daily basis. It's important that educators are mindful that students are watch-ing and learning all the time. The way teachers and administrators interact with their peers, the way they discipline students, their "off-the-record" com-ments, even the way they dress—all these things speak volumes about the kind of values they hold.

Students, particularly adolescents, are keen to pick up on inconsistencies, contradictions, and hypocrisy. It sends a powerful message if a teacher can ask a student, "Have I ever treated you disre-spectfully?" and be confident that the student will say no. The message will be just as potent, but it will have powerfully adverse results if a teacher gives lip service to the touchstone then belittles, publicly humiliates, laughs at, ignores, threatens, unfairly punishes, or yells at students. They may say they support the touchstone, but what they are teaching instead is bullying behavior.

As we already know, being an educator is a huge responsibility. And we also know that perfection is not a human condition. So, what should an adult do when he or she makes a mistake and behaves in a way that does not align with the touchstone? What would we want students to do? Generally, we want them to 1) admit their mistakes, 2) apologize, and 3) change their behavior. We can do the same.

Behavior Matrix Example			
	Responsibility	Kindness	Acceptance
Hallways	Walking quietly	Saying "excuse me" if you walk in front of someone	Smiling at people you pass
Lunchroom	Cleaning up after yourself	Greeting the lunch monitors and cafeteria workers	Keeping your opinions of other people's lunches to yourself
Bus	Keeping hands and feet to self	Sharing a seat	Sharing a seat with anyone who needs it
Auditorium	Listening quietly	Polite applause	Listening with an open mind

Instead of making excuses or blaming our mistakes on someone or something else, we can admit that we messed up. We can apologize, if appropriate, and fix the problem or make sure that we don't make the same mistake again.

For example, if I promise a student I'll stay after school to help him with his essay, but I forget and go home early, I could call that student to my room first thing the next morning, admit my mistake, tell him I'm sorry, and reschedule the session. I may also need to give this student a short extension on the essay's deadline. By behaving in this way, I am teaching a much more important lesson than anything he learned in English that day. I am showing him how to be honest, humble, sincere, and responsible.

Just as every school's touchstone is meant to represent the unique learning community that created it, every school will have its own unique rituals, celebrations, and ways of integrating the touchstone into its culture. The ideas in this chapter are just a few classroom strategies that were effective in other schools. I invite you to consider other ways your school touchstone might be celebrated. When students, teachers, and other community members become inspired by what the touchstone represents, creative ideas will flow like white water rapids.

Printable Form

The Social Contract

Value(s): _____

When the value(s) listed above is (are) being supported, we will see and hear the following:	When the value(s) listed above is (are) being violated, we will see and hear the following:

See digital content for full-size reproducible pages

Integrating the Touchstone into the Academic Curriculum

One of the most effective ways to keep the touchstone values alive and simultaneously engage students is to integrate the concepts into the core curriculum. This not only helps keep students and educators focused on their shared values, it helps students see how these values are relevant to life outside of school and how they can inform their choices in meaningful ways throughout their lives.

This chapter explains how to create thematic integrated units that revolve around touchstone values, suggesting specific performance tasks that students might be assigned in a wide range of curricular areas. Because English language arts (ELA) and social studies so easily lend themselves to values-based learning units, this chapter provides specific ideas and guidelines for integrating touchstone values into those content areas in ways that satisfy the Common Core State Standards (CCSS). Sample lesson plans in those subject areas for various grade levels are included in this book's digital content. You can use the plans as they are or modify them for your own situation.

Building Integrated Learning Units Based on Touchstone Values

Thematic interdisciplinary units have several benefits over teaching any subject in isolation: They help students see the connections between various disciplines; they allow teachers to plan and work together, so their shared experiences and ideas create a better learning experience than any one of them might have developed alone; they encourage higher-level thinking skills (application, synthesis, evaluation, abstract thought); and they provide a novel and highly motivating learning experience.

Touchstone values—and themes related to touchstone values—provide excellent concepts around which to build learning units in any academic subject. For example, the concept of cooperation (and sharing) might make a wonderful literature unit for students in grades kindergarten through sixth. Even better, cooperation might provide a unifying concept for cross-curricular units, examining the same ideas in different academic areas. For older students, the theme of perseverance can be a way of learning about important figures who have overcome obstacles and achieved great things in any subject including art, music, history, culture, science, technology, and mathematics: Vincent van Gogh, Ludwig van Beethoven, Abraham Lincoln, Ray Charles, Stephen Hawking, John Forbes Nash Jr., and so on. As students learn about people overcoming adversity through perseverance and grit, they will also learn about the contributions those people made to their respective fields.

Steps for Setting Up

Here are the general steps for implementing a thematic integrated theme.

Step 1. Choose Your Value or Theme

In choosing the first theme, select one that will connect easily to content. The most frequently identified values—respect, caring, fairness, kindness, responsibility, community, friendship, self-control, and acceptance—have been themes in history and literature for centuries. So they are easy to connect to language arts and social studies.

For example, community is a topic that is easy to explore in all subject areas. Coincidentally, understanding community (what a community is, the importance of community, community resources, individual or group contributions to the community) is part of the CCSS for social studies for second grade and can easily be modified to work in any grade level.

If you are a primary teacher, you are free to make connections across subjects as you see fit. If you are a secondary teacher, you will most likely be teaming with other teachers. In that case, it's important to choose a theme that works well for every teacher. Review the standards for your subject and grade level, then meet with a team to decide on a theme everyone agrees on.

Step 2. Establish Learning Goals

Identify the specific information and skills in the various subject areas you want your students to learn during this unit, aligning them with state standards. For example, imagine you are teaching fourth grade in the state of New York and want to integrate a unit on cooperation across English language arts, social studies, and science. Using the CCSS for ELA and New York State (NYS) Standards for social studies and science, your learning objectives might look like this:

English Language Arts

- Students will read and demonstrate understanding of two nonfiction accounts of an event from the 16th or 17th century in North America in which cooperation played an important role. CCSS standards addressed: English Language Arts Standards » Reading: Informational Text » Grade 4 (ELA-LITERACY.RI 4.1–4.3 and 4.7–4.10).[1]

- Students will work in cooperative groups to make a presentation to the class on their chosen historical event. CCSS standards addressed: English Language Arts Standards » Speaking & Listening » Grade 4 (ELA-LITERACY.SL 4.1–4.6).[2]

Social Studies

Students will read nonfictional accounts of life and culture among the indigenous people of New York or accounts of the first settlers of New York, focusing on the need for cooperation. NYS Standards addressed: Connect local, New York State, and United States history, focusing on the following themes: Native American Indians of New York State; Colonial and Revolutionary periods; The new nation.[3]

Science

Students will research advances in science or technology during the 16th and 17th centuries (the time period relating to the social studies and English language arts content) that were developed cooperatively. They will choose one advance and make a computer presentation explaining what it was, who was involved, and how cooperation played a factor. NYS Science Standards addressed: Standard 2—Information Systems, Key Idea 1: Information technology is used to retrieve, process, and communicate information and as a tool to enhance learning.[4]

Step 3. Plan Lessons

Once you have clarified your outcomes, plan lessons in the three subject areas as you normally would. In a primary school setting, you may be able to teach English language arts and social studies simultaneously. For example, if you were teaching the unit on cooperation previously described, you would be using the same historical content for the reading and presentation assignments in both subjects. Emphasizing the theme of cooperation will help students see the connection to science.

---

[1] Copyright © 2010 National Governors Association Center for Best Practices and Council of Chief State School Officers. All rights reserved.

[2] Ibid.
[3] Learning Standards for Social Studies, Copyright 1996, New York State Education Department, used with permission. www.p12.nysed.gov/ciai/socst/pub/sscore1.pdf.
[4] Learning Standards for Science, Copyright 1996, New York State Education Department, used with permission. www.p12.nysed.gov/ciai/mst/pub/elecoresci.pdf.

Step 4. Community Meeting on Your Value

Begin your unit with a community meeting focusing on the value you are using as your theme. Use the define-personalize-challenge format. For our sample fourth-grade unit on cooperation, your questions might include:

Define

- How can we define cooperation in our own words?

Personalize

- Have you ever cooperated with a group or a team? What was it like?
- When have you achieved success in a cooperative situation?
- Do you know any people who are extremely cooperative? How do you feel about working with them? (Don't name any names.)
- What situations do you know of in which cooperation is important?

Challenge

- Which is more important, cooperation or competition? (There's no right answer, but this question gets students thinking.)
- What might the world be like if there were less cooperation? (Give hypothetical examples.)
- What might it be like if there were more? (Give examples.)
- What are some examples of times in the past or present when cooperation was (or is) in short supply?
- What are some examples when cooperation was (or is) in abundance?
- What are the results of each?

Step 5. Introduce the Unit

Explain that you'll be learning about your value or theme across several subject areas and discuss how the value can be seen though literature, history, and science. Then share the specific expectations for this unit and the timeline. (A good timeline for a unit is around two weeks.)

Step 6. Teach and Assess the Unit

At the end of the unit, hold another community meeting to reflect on your value, asking students to talk about what they have learned about the value during the unit. Ask: Why is the value so important?

Sample Integrated Learning Unit: Community

Here is an integrated learning unit based on the common touchstone value community, presented for primary and secondary classrooms. You will likely want to adjust these examples to fit your particular setting. Literature and social studies provide the foundational connections, with other subjects being brought in whenever possible.

Primary School (Grades K–5)

Language Arts. Research a specific aspect of your community (government, religious organizations, civic organizations, businesses, resources, and so on) and create a presentation for the class. Kindergartners might choose a "community helper" (police officer, librarian, baker, teacher), find out what he or she does, and make a short report to their class. Older students might research and write a report about a person in the community who has (or has not) demonstrated one or more of the touchstone values.

Social Studies. Compare and contrast your community with a different kind of community. *Community* could be defined broadly. Students might compare their town or city to another one of similar size, or one that is very different. They could compare their family to a friend's family, their school to another, or a club, team, or group they are a part of to another club, team, or group.

Math. Use numeric data about the community in mathematical problems: population, number of students, number of households, number of police, size of parks, cost of licenses, and any other information you can think of. Many pertinent statistics can be found on your town or city website. Using information about the students' own community makes the math problems more meaningful.

Music. Sing and listen to songs about community and friendship.

Art. Have students paint or draw local landmarks or a cartoon map of the community or neighborhood; or bring in "found art" from the community at large.

Science. Study the different habitats found in your community and the variety of plant and animal life found there.

Secondary School (Grades 6–12)

Language Arts. Students might address the theme of community through a variety of writing or reporting assignments. Here are some examples.

- Students research and write a report about a person in the community who has (or has not) demonstrated one or more of the touchstone values.

- Students identify and research a problem in their community and write or present a report on the current state of the problem, what has been done to address it, and make suggestions for solving it.

- Students write a letter to a community leader explaining a problem in the community and persuading him or her to address the problem in a specific way.

- Students write nonfiction narratives about times when they or someone they know in the community exhibited (or did not exhibit) one of the values articulated in the touchstone.

Social Studies. Students research and report on an aspect of their community's social, political, economic, or cultural history, such as people, historic events, or natural events.

Math. Have students use numeric data about the community such as population, number of students, number of households, number of police officers, size of parks, cost of licenses, and so on, in mathematical problems. All of this information can be found on your town or city website. Using information about the students' own community makes the math problems more meaningful.

Music. Students research music that is indigenous to their community (such as jazz in Louisiana, blues in the Mississippi Delta or Chicago, rock and roll in Cleveland or Memphis, country in Nashville, bluegrass in the Appalachians). Or have them research music that is about their part of the country. Or they may locate, interview, record, and create a presentation about a local musician.

Art. Invite local artists as guest speakers or guest teachers. Or have students write a biography of an artist: They might research and report on community artists who have exhibited social responsibility or other touchstone values.

Science. Students could research and report on issues affecting their community, such as changing habitats, toxic waste issues, changing animal populations, climate change, and air and water pollution.

Foreign Language. Students might discuss how language affects a community. Discussion might center on questions such as:

- How does language bring people together?

- Can language create barriers to community?

- Should our country adopt an official language? Why or why not?

Sample Integrated Learning Unit: Friendship

Another value that almost always appears on school touchstones is friendship, a theme that students of all ages can relate to. Here is an integrated learning unit based on that value, presented for primary and secondary classrooms. You will likely want to adjust these examples to fit your particular setting. Literature and social studies provide the foundational connections, with other subjects being brought in whenever possible.

Primary School (Grades K–5)

Language Arts. Students create collages of what friendship means and present them to the class. Or have students read stories or novels involving friendship, discuss them, and write essays or make presentations analyzing the friendship between the two characters, using concrete support from the text. Friendship is a main theme in the following titles, and many of these titles are already part of the curriculum in schools:

- *Frog and Toad Together* by Arnold Lobel
- *Owen & Mzee: The True Story of a Remarkable Friendship* by Isabella Hatkoff, Craig Hatkoff, and Paula Kahumbu
- *Farfallina & Marcel* by Holly Keller

Social Studies. Students study relationships between groups or individuals from history, looking at how and why they developed and whether they can be considered friendships. One example could be the relationship between European fur traders and Native American groups in the Great Lakes region that began during the 1500s. Students create a visual representation (drawing, diorama, collage) of the relationship.

Music. Students listen to and sing songs about friendship. Discuss their meaning.

Math. Create math friends—collaborative pairs who work together on math assignments, checking each other's work as they go. This is a great process to help students move from guided practice to independent practice. You can give the class a problem to solve, let the pairs briefly discuss how to solve it, have them each individually solve it, and have them check each other's work. Afterward you can go over the problem with the class and discuss solving methods.

Another way to use math friends is to pass out a math worksheet, assign one partner odd numbers and the other even; after students complete their half of the assignment, they check each other's work and agree to turn in a final completed worksheet.

Secondary School (Grades 6–12)

Language Arts. As with elementary students, a great way to integrate friendship into the ELA curriculum is to have students read stories or novels involving friendship. You can assign groups to discuss the friendships featured in the text and make presentations analyzing them. Of course students can be assigned essays or other ways of showing their analysis of the book and the friendship in it.

Friendship is a main theme in the following titles, many of which are likely to be part of the curriculum at your school:

- *Bridge to Terabithia* by Katherine Paterson
- *Tuck Everlasting* by Natalie Babbitt
- *The Outsiders* by S.E. Hinton
- *Adventures of Huckleberry Finn* by Mark Twain
- *A Separate Peace* by John Knowles
- *One Flew Over the Cuckoo's Nest* by Ken Kesey

Social Studies. Students read and research about interesting friendships from history or the current time and write an informative essay or create a presentation explaining the historical/cultural significance of each person and detailing their friendship. Here are a few examples of historical friendships:

- Octavian and Agrippa (Roman Era)
- Helen Keller and Mark Twain
- Henry Ford and Thomas Edison
- Mark Twain and Nikola Tesla
- Groucho Marx and T.S. Eliot
- Marilyn Monroe and Ella Fitzgerald
- Emily Dickinson and Thomas Wentworth Higginson
- Ulysses S. Grant and James Longstreet
- J.R.R. Tolkien and C.S. Lewis

Music. Students research famous songwriting pairs and present their findings about their relationship as well as their body of work. Some famous songwriting partnerships include:

- W. S. Gilbert and Arthur Sullivan
- John Lennon and Paul McCartney
- Carole King and Gerry Goffin
- Richard Rodgers and Oscar Hammerstein II
- Cynthia Weil and Barry Mann
- Naomi and Wynonna Judd
- Jimmy Jam and Terry Lewis

Technology. Students participate in discussions about social media and friendship. Here are some discussion questions around which you might build assignments:

- How do you and your friends use social media?
- What is the impact of social media on friendships?
- Are all your Facebook or Instagram (or other social media platforms) friends real friends?

- What do you need to consider before accepting a friend request?
- Is social media and technology making it harder for you to have a face-to-face conversation?

Making Touchstone Connections in English Language Arts and Social Studies

English language arts (ELA) and social studies are the easiest content areas to make connections between the touchstone values and academic curriculum. That is because the study of literature, both fiction and nonfiction—as well as history, culture, and current events—is really the study of human behavior.

Teachers of ELA and social studies will find that they already make connections between values and literature, history, culture, and current events. It is hard to read literature or study history or current events and *not* make observations about the values of the characters and people involved. Touchstone units simply are more intentional about making touchstone values part of the ongoing discussion.

There are generally two ways to begin. One way is to start with the value or values you want to focus on and find thematically appropriate materials to use as the academic content. For example, if the value you want to study is responsibility, you could use a version of the folktale *The Little Red Hen* for kindergarten; *The Story of Ruby Bridges* by Robert Coles for fourth grade; *The Outsiders* by S.E. Hinton for eighth grade; and *The Grapes of Wrath* by John Steinbeck for eleventh grade. Each of these books examines an aspect of personal responsibility that relates to students' lives and experiences. *The Little Red Hen* is about one's responsibility to the common good. *The Story of Ruby Bridges,* about the first black girl to attend an all-white school in Louisiana in the 1960s, focuses on her courage in taking responsibility and breaking the color barrier so others might follow. *The Outsiders* focuses on three orphaned teenage brothers and their responsibility to one another. And

two of the main themes of *The Grapes of Wrath* are family and social responsibility during the Dust Bowl years of the 1930s.

Another way to begin is by connecting one of the school's touchstone values to the fiction or nonfiction that you already have on your syllabus. This is probably the most economical approach because you already have the materials. This isn't as difficult as it might seem at first. Literature often explores values that pertain to how humans treat one another—such as with (or without) respect, honesty, or kindness. Many books' themes pertain to how a person should treat herself—by persevering, by having self-respect, or by having empathy. Interpersonal conflicts in literature will certainly touch on issues of respect, kindness, honesty, empathy, and other common touchstone values. Internal conflicts will often touch on issues of self-control, perseverance, self-respect, self-esteem, being true to yourself, personal responsibility, and so on. By looking carefully at how characters in literature and humans in history/social studies act, we can start to see where our touchstone values have played a role. Start with considering works of literature you are already comfortable with teaching and look for connections to the touchstone values. Choose the literature that makes the most obvious connections.

The following sections provide ideas for student performance tasks you might consider as either formative or summative assessments that connect to touchstone values. Many of these performance tasks are general enough to be assigned to students at a variety of developmental levels. You can modify and adjust the time, reading level, and performance expectations according to your students' needs and abilities.

Literary Analysis

Analyzing literature is a straightforward way to bring touchstone values into the curriculum. Students can consider the value you're studying through characters or literary themes.

Character Analysis

Have students read a work of literature and carefully track a major character's thoughts and actions (collecting quotations and specific references from the text), assessing the character's behavior in terms of the touchstone value being studied. This will help students understand how authors use character development and character change to develop their themes.

It also helps students learn to infer the value that a character holds dear (or ignores). In *The Little Red Hen*, every animal refuses the little red hen's request for help in baking a loaf of community bread. The little red hen does everything from growing the wheat to baking the bread. At the end of the story, all the animals want to help eat the bread. The story is clearly a lesson in social responsibility and cooperation. In the novel *Adventures of Huckleberry Finn*, Huck decides not to turn in his companion Jim, a runaway slave, despite the fact that Huck believes he will go to hell for this "sin." The values that might be discussed are loyalty, empathy, and friendship.

In terms of performance tasks, students might be asked to:

- Write a traditional literary expositive essay (or paragraph for younger students) explaining how their character exhibits (or acts contrary to) the touchstone value under study.

- Collaborate with another student who focused on a different character to write an essay comparing and contrasting their characters in terms of the touchstone value.

- Write a personal nonfiction narrative comparing an event in the student's life with an event from the literature in which the character demonstrates the touchstone value.

- Create a multimedia presentation about their character and the touchstone value using video clips, music, and images.

- Create and present a poster about their character.

- Draw a picture of their character and a list of important actions that demonstrate the touchstone value.

- Create a comic book or short graphic novel depicting relevant actions and words of their character.

- Write and perform a song or rap about the character and the touchstone value (or put new words to a well-known song).

- Create and unveil a monument for their character out of clay or Legos with a plaque explaining the character's actions in terms of the touchstone value.

- Act out an important scene from the literature and explain how that scene demonstrates the touchstone value.

- Write an obituary or deliver a eulogy about their character that focuses on the touchstone value.

For all performance assessments, students must support their claims with concrete supporting details from the text.

Thematic Analysis

In a thematic analysis, instead of focusing on one character throughout a story or novel, students look for examples of behavior that demonstrate the touchstone value under study (or demonstrate an important lack of the value). If kindness is the value, for example, students would track all characters as they read, writing down events, actions, and quotations that show examples of kindness and contrasting acts of meanness or cruelty.

Performance tasks for thematic analysis would be similar to those for character analysis, but with the focus on the bigger picture of theme. For example, students might be asked to:

- Write a traditional literary expositive essay explaining how various characters' actions demonstrated the touchstone value and help develop it as a theme.

- Write an essay comparing and/or contrasting two major characters in the story in terms of the touchstone value, noting how their differences help develop the theme.

- Create and present a poster dedicated to the touchstone value depicting the characters and their significant actions or words.

- Create a multimedia presentation dedicated to the touchstone value and including various characters' important words and actions demonstrating it.

- Act out two or more important scenes from the literature involving at least two different characters, and explain how those scenes and characters demonstrate the touchstone value.

- Write and perform a poem, song, or rap about the touchstone value, including specific references to characters and events in the story that demonstrate the value.

- Create a drawing or a model out of clay or Legos of an important scene from the story including two or more characters and explain how that scene helps demonstrate the touchstone value.

For all performance assessments, students must support their claims with concrete supporting details from the text.

Historical and Current Event Analysis

By studying the actions of people in history and current events, your students have many opportunities to see touchstone values upheld, embraced, or—just as important in terms of learning opportunities—ignored. Consider approaching this through biographical analysis, perspective taking, or political analysis.

Biographical Analysis

In a biographical analysis, students learn—through class discussion or their own research—about a particular historical or contemporary figure, focusing on his or her actions and written words, and assess that person in terms of one or all of the touchstone values. Students can learn how these values have informed important decisions in history for better or worse.

In terms of performance tasks, students might be assigned to do any of the tasks described on pages 58–59 for "character analysis," replacing the literary character with the real person.

Perspective Taking

Older students, grades five and up, might be encouraged to look at events and behavior from differing perspectives and consider how the values underlying the behavior may shift with our perspective. While the values that various figures demonstrate may or may not align with your school's touchstone, perspective taking is a way of having empathy, which is often a part of school touchstones in one form or another. Looking at how values can change with different perspectives

is a great way to exercise that empathy muscle in a safe environment.

For example, the American colonies revolting against the British throne is seen as a struggle for freedom from an American patriot's perspective. Besides freedom, a colonist's values might have been persistence and loyalty to the other colonists. From the point of view of a member of the British Parliament, however, the early acts of revolution would be considered immoral acts of terrorism. The Englishman's values might have been security and loyalty to England. To take it a step further, what perspective might people from different Native American nations have had? What about people from other European nations? What about Canadians?

For another example, the American Civil War offers a wide variety of perspectives. The opening battle at Fort Sumter might be considered from the point of view of a Confederate or Union soldier, an abolitionist, a slave, a plantation owner, an army nurse, and a member of the British Parliament. Each point of view has some value or values at its core: The soldier might act out of a sense of loyalty to his country while the abolitionist's perspective would likely be based on compassion. The slave holds a desire for freedom while the plantation owner values financial security.

One final example is the Vietnam War. From the official U.S. perspective, the purpose of this conflict was to save the world from the tyranny of communism. The value: freedom. From the Vietcong perspective, it was a war for independence from decades of colonial rule. Same value: freedom. The meaning of what freedom means, however, shifts with perspective.

Performance tasks can be modified versions of the "thematic analysis" assignments on pages 59–60.

Political Analysis

Through political analysis, instead of looking at the behavior and belief systems of individuals, we study the behavior and belief systems of political entities—nations, states, political parties, and other groups. Touchstone values provide a useful lens through which to analyze the behavior of different groups, particularly when they are in conflict.

After learning about a particular country's policies and actions, a particular political organization's beliefs, or a conflict between two nations or organizations, students might be assigned to:

- Write a paragraph or short essay about how that country's or organization's behavior aligns with (or conflicts with) a touchstone value. For example, discuss how the United States or Canada coming to the aid of its Allies during World War II demonstrated the value of loyalty. Or discuss how the U.S. government's relocation of the Cherokee through the forced migration known as the Trail of Tears conflicts with the stated American values of life, liberty, and the pursuit of happiness.

- Create a poster depicting a nation's or an organization's policies or actions and the touchstone value that they seem to demonstrate (or contradict). Students might write the value in the center of the poster surrounded by quotations, facts, events, and images that demonstrate it. Alternatively, students could create a multimedia presentation explaining the same.

- In pairs, students look at a particular war or conflict from two different perspectives and write an essay or prepare a report comparing and contrasting the values that seem to be behind each country's actions.

ELA and Social Studies Unit Examples

Three different examples of values-based units—one designed for third grade, one for sixth grade, and one for eleventh grade—are available in this book's digital content. While the third-grade unit is primarily social studies and the other two are primarily ELA, all three units have elements of both subjects. The point of these examples is to provide models for you to build your own units appropriate to your students' grade and situation (see the thumbnails on pages 65–68).

The unit plans begin by stating the objectives, which include academic as well as social-emotional objectives. Next, each unit lists the Common Core State Standards that it fulfills. Prerequisites are listed next, followed by resources that help provide background knowledge or give additional information and materials required. The units are then divided into an introduction, the instruction phase, and the assessment phase.

Suggested Literature for Touchstone Units

The charts on the following pages list some books that make connections to a variety of common touchstone values. They are organized into four different levels: Early Elementary (grades K–2), Upper Elementary (grades 3–5), Middle School (grades 6–8), and High School (grades 9–12). Along with the title and author are some of the values the title explores. Some titles are well-known classics that are already found on many classroom shelves; others may be new to you but are just as relevant and in some cases are more engaging. Explore this list and your own classroom bookshelf to start making touchstone connections.

When touchstone values become part of the core curriculum, they become an integral part of the school and classroom culture. When schools deliberately and continuously move in the direction of those touchstone values, a positive school climate becomes ever more likely.

Suggested Books for Touchstone Connections

Early Elementary (grades K-2)

Title	Author	Touchstone Value(s)
FICTION		
The Giving Tree	Shel Silverstein	responsibility, kindness, caring
The Lorax	Dr. Seuss	responsibility, caring
The Little Red Hen	Margot Zemach	responsibility, work ethic, perseverance
The Little Engine That Could	Watty Piper	optimism, perseverance
Cat Up a Tree	John and Ann Hassett	caring, kindness, helping
How Humans Make Friends	Loreen Leedy	friendship, cooperation
The Great Kapok Tree	Lynne Cherry	responsibility, caring, interdependence
Saily's Journey	Ralph da Costa Nunez	caring, empathy
The Rainbow Fish	Marcus Pfister	selflessness, generosity
Love Monster and the Last Chocolate	Rachel Bright	empathy, sharing
NONFICTION		
If You Sailed on the Mayflower in 1620	Ann McGovern	cooperation responsibility, courage,
A Voice of Her Own: The Story of Phillis Wheatley, Slave Poet	Kathryn Lasky	optimism, perseverance
Quakers in Early America	Melinda Lilly	friendship, cooperation
If You Were at the First Thanksgiving	Anne Kamma	kindness, generosity
Thank You, Sarah: The Woman Who Saved Thanksgiving	Laurie Halse Anderson	optimism, perseverance
A Picture Book of Paul Revere	David A. Adler	responsibility
The Bald Eagle (Symbols ofFreedom)	Tristan Boyer Binns	respect
The Life of Benjamin Franklin: An American Original	Yona Zeldis McDonough	responsibility
Finding Winnie: The True Story of the World's Most Famous Bear	Lindsay Mattick	caring, perseverance

Upper Elementary (grades 3-5)

Title	Author	Touchstone Value(s)
FICTION		
The Harry Potter Series	J.K. Rowling	courage, responsibility
Judy Moody Saves the World!	Megan McDonald	responsibility, caring, cooperation
King of the Kooties!	Debbie Dadey	acceptance, kindness
The Hundred Dresses	Eleanor Estes	caring, empathy
Just Juice	Karen Hesse	perseverance, learning
The Library Card	Jerry Spinelli	empathy, learning
Walk Two Moons	Sharon Creech	empathy, compassion, acceptance

Suggested Books for Touchstone Connections continued

Hey, Little Ant	Phillip and Hannah Hoose	kindness, empathy
A Long Walk to Water	Linda Sue Park	perseverance, courage, kindness

NONFICTION

Island of the Blue Dolphins	Scott O'Dell	responsibility, friendship, loyalty
Through My Eyes	Ruby Bridges	courage, responsibility, empathy
Lewis and Clark	Andrew Santella	cooperation, courage
Sacajawea: The Journey West	Elaine Raphael	kindness, perseverance
The Amazing Impossible Erie Canal	Cheryl Harness	optimism, perseverance
You Want Women to Vote, Lizzie Stanton?	Jean Fritz	perseverance, equality
They Called Her Molly Pitcher	Anne Rockwell	responsibility, kindness
I Am Malala	Malala Yousafzai	social responsibility, courage, perseverance

Middle School (grades 6-8)

Title	Author	Touchstone Value(s)
FICTION		
The Outsiders	S.E. Hinton	kindness, acceptance, loyalty
Buddha Boy	Kathe Koja	acceptance, nonviolence, empathy
Flush	Carl Hiaasen	responsibility, social responsibility
Where the Red Fern Grows	Wilson Rawls	work ethic, kindness, optimism
Bud, Not Buddy	Christopher Paul Curtis	optimism, perseverance, kindness, friendship
Of Mice and Men	John Steinbeck	empathy, responsibility, kindness, friendship
A Christmas Carol	Charles Dickens	kindness, generosity, social responsibility
A Tree Grows in Brooklyn	Betty Smith	optimism, perseverance
The Call of the Wild	Jack London	courage, kindness, perseverance
My Side of the Mountain	Jean Craighead George	perseverance, courage, friendship
Wonder	R.J. Palacio	empathy, compassion, acceptance
NONFICTION		
Harriet and the Promised Land	Jacob Lawrence	responsibility, kindness
Hannah's Journal: The Story of an Immigrant Girl	Marissa Moss	courage, optimism, perseverance
Beating the Odds: A Teen Guide to 75 Superstars Who Overcame Adversity	Mary Ellen Snodgrass	optimism, perseverance, responsibility
The Flight of Red Bird: The Life of Zitkala-Sa	Doreen Rappaport	respect, perseverance
Harvesting Hope: The Story of Cesar Chavez	Kathleen Krull	kindness, responsibility
I Have a Dream	Dr. Martin Luther King Jr.	optimism, equality
Boys in the Boat (Young Readers Adaptation)	Daniel James Brown	grit, courage, teamwork

Suggested Books for Touchstone Connections continued

High School (grades 9-12)		
Title	Author	Touchstone Value(s)
FICTION		
Touching Spirit Bear	Ben Mikaelsen	responsibility, self-control, friendship, forgiveness
A Separate Peace	John Knowles	friendship, responsibility, acceptance
The Merchant of Venice	William Shakespeare	fairness, kindness, acceptance
King Lear	William Shakespeare	responsibility, kindness, loyalty
One Flew Over the Cuckoo's Nest	Ken Kesey	social responsibility, acceptance, kindness
The Great Gatsby	F. Scott Fitzgerald	honesty, optimism, friendship
The Grapes of Wrath	John Steinbeck	responsibility, fairness, kindness
To Kill a Mockingbird	Harper Lee	acceptance, integrity, fairness, equality, courage
The Adventures of Huckleberry Finn	Mark Twain	social responsibility, friendship, kindness, loyalty
The Hunger Games Trilogy	Suzanne Collins	courage, responsibility, friendship, optimism, perseverance
The Fault in Our Stars	John Green	courage
NONFICTION		
Beating the Odds: A Teen Guide to 75 Super-stars Who Overcame Adversity	Mary Ellen Snodgrass	optimism, responsibility, perseverance
Malcolm X: A Fire Burning Brightly	Walter Dean Myers	equality, responsibility, perseverance
Working: People Talk About What They Do All Day and How They Feel About What They Do	Studs Terkel	optimism, work ethic
A People's History of the United States	Howard Zinn	optimism, perseverance, kindness, cooperation, equality
The Untold Civil War: Exploring the Human Side of War	James Robertson	loyalty, kindness, friendship, perseverance, equality
The Greatest Generation	Tom Brokaw	responsibility, courage, cooperation, kindness
Dispatches	Michael Herr	courage, responsibility
Boys in the Boat	Daniel James Brown	grit, perseverance, teamwork

Printable Forms

Grade 3 Sample Unit: The Theme of Kindness

The Theme of Kindness in *Sacajawea: The Journey West* by Elaine Raphael

Touchstone Connection: Kindness

Academic Objectives
Students will:
- Demonstrate their understanding of the historical context and purpose of Lewis and Clark's expedition.
- Demonstrate their understanding of the literal level of *Sacajawea: The Journey West*.
- Be able to identify specific acts of Sacajawea's kindness.

Social-Emotional Objectives
Students will:
- Demonstrate their understanding of the meaning of kindness.
- Gain an understanding of the importance of kindness.

Third-Grade CCSS Addressed*
Reading: CCSS.ELA-LITERACY.RI 3.1–3.3, 3.7 and CCSS.ELA-LITERACY.RF 3.3–3.4.
Speaking and Listening: CCSS.ELA-LITERACY.SL 3.1–3.2, 3.4

Resources
Sacajawea: The Journey West by Elaine Raphael
A Picture Book of Lewis and Clark by David A. Adler
Kids' Discover Magazine: Sacajawea (www.kidsdiscover.com/shop/issues/sacagawea-for-kids)
The Story of Sacajawea: Guide to Lewis and Clark by Della Rowland

Other Materials Needed
Chart paper or large sheets of white construction paper (one per group)
Graph paper with 1 cm grids (optional for drawing strategy)
Construction paper, clay, play dough, or other art supplies (for monuments or posters)

Introduction
Journal Entry
Give students a few minutes to write about the following prompt: What does kindness mean? Tell about a time someone has been kind to you. How did that feel?

Community Meeting: Kindness
Define
- How can we define the word *kindness*?

Personalize
- Has someone been kind to you? Give an example of kindness.
- Tell about a time you've been kind to someone. How did it feel?
- How did the other person respond?

Challenge
- When is it important to be kind to people? (If students answer "always," ask them when is it *particularly* important to be kind to people.)
- We are going to read a true story about a brave Native American woman who helped a team of white explorers survive a very hard journey out West in the early 1800s. What do you know about the West in the early 1800s?
- What acts of kindness might we expect to read about?

After the community meeting, you may want to talk briefly about Lewis and Clark and the Corps of Discovery to provide background to the reading.

Instruction
- Read aloud the first several pages of *Sacajawea: The Journey West*, noting the hardships Sacajawea endured.
- Divide students into productive pairs, and assign them to finish reading the story, each taking turns reading one page aloud and then switching.
- After they have completed the reading, put students into groups of four to discuss and list (on chart paper or large sheets of construction paper) acts of kindness Sacajawea performed to help the Corps of Discovery.
- Have students present their lists to the class.

Assessment
Students create a statue or a mural of Sacajawea including a plaque dedicated to her honor. The plaque will list the acts of kindness she performed for the Corps of Discovery.
Consider having students try the grid drawing system at the end of *Sacajawea: The Journey West* to help them with their drawings. This will help them extend and apply fine motor skills and their skills of observation as well.

Closing
Wrap up the unit by discussing in a community meeting what was learned. Ask:
- What hardships did Sacajawea endure?
- What kind of person did she turn out to be?
- Might you someday experience hardships? Or are you right now?
- How might the kindness of others help you?
- How might you be kind to others?
- How can we, in this classroom, make sure kindness is something we practice, not just talk about?

Grade 6 Sample Unit: The Theme of Work Ethic

The Theme of Work Ethic in *Where the Red Fern Grows* by Wilson Rawls

Primary Touchstone Connection: Work ethic

Secondary Touchstone Connections: Responsibility, kindness

Academic Objectives
Students will:
- Demonstrate their understanding of *Where the Red Fern Grows* on the literal and thematic level.
- Demonstrate an understanding of the literary concepts of setting, flashback, and foreshadowing.
- Explain how the characters and events in the novel demonstrate the importance of a strong work ethic and responsibility, using concrete supporting details from the text.
- Make connections between events and characters in *Where the Red Fern Grows* and their own lives, and articulate those connections through speaking and writing.
- Write a first-person, nonfiction narrative relating to one of the topics or events in *Where the Red Fern Grows* OR a research paper relating to one of the topics in the novel.
- Use effective communication and social skills in a community meeting format.

Social-Emotional Objectives
Students will:
- Understand that in life, as in literature, our choices determine our character and our destiny.
- Understand that one person's choices can profoundly affect many others.
- Understand the connection between positive character (specifically a strong work ethic, kindness, and responsibility) and personal happiness.

Sixth-Grade CCSS Addressed*
Reading: CCSS.ELA-LITERACY.RI 6.1–6.3, 6.5
Writing: CCSS.ELA-LITERACY.W 6.1–6.3, 6.5, 6.7
Speaking and Listening: CCSS.ELA-LITERACY.SL 6.1, 6.4

Resources
Where the Red Fern Grows by Wilson Rawls
Where the Red Fern Grows movie
Watersheds.org: "An Old-Timer Remembers Bryant Creek's Cashless Economy: Farm Life" (www.watersheds.org/history/oldtimer.htm#farmlife)

Prerequisites
- Students have a working understanding of the touchstone values of work ethic, kindness, and responsibility.

- Background knowledge includes general information about life in the Ozarks during the early 20th century, particularly rural life. Much of this can be learned online such as through the Watersheds.org resource. One option is to talk to a social studies teacher in your school about the possibility of doing an interdisciplinary unit.

Introduction Lesson 1
Journal Entry
Give students about five minutes to write about the following prompt: What makes a good friend? Who are some people you would consider good friends? What personality or character traits do they have? Why do you consider them good friends? Are you a good friend? Why might you be considered a good friend?

Community Meeting: Friends
Define
- We use the word *friend* a lot, sometimes when we just mean someone we spend time with or with whom we share a common interest (sports, music, video games, and so forth). What is the difference between someone we might enjoy spending time with and a true friend?

Personalize
- Do you know someone who has been a real friend to you or someone you know? Tell about it. (Teacher Note: Consider giving an example from your own life.)
- Have you ever been a real friend to someone? Tell about it.

Challenge
- How could you be a better friend to someone whose friendship you value?

Close the meeting by having students freewrite about a true friend of theirs. What did the friend do that proved he or she was not just a buddy or fair-weather friend? Or, write about a time you were a real friend to someone else. What did you do that proved your friendship?

Introduction Lesson 2
Continue introducing the unit on the second day with the following activities.

Journal Entry
Do you have or have you ever had a dog? If not, do you know someone who has a dog? What is the dog's name? What personality or character traits describe the dog? For example, is it friendly, active, nervous, lazy, affectionate, or smart? Do you have any interesting memories or stories about this dog? (If you can't think of a dog, discuss another pet you have had or know.)

Concentric Circles
Have your students count off by twos (one, two, one, two) and direct the "ones" to stand in a circle (almost shoulder to shoulder) and turn around so that they are facing out. Now direct the "twos" to create an outer circle in which each of them is facing one of the "ones."
1. Give the students a simple direction to greet the partner they're facing, such as "Shake hands with the person you are facing and say 'Good morning!'"
2. Next, have them share their dog (or pet) information and any stories they have.

See digital content for full-size reproducible pages

3. After a minute or two, have one of the circles move one to three spaces to their right, and repeat the two steps above.

4. Repeat the whole process three or four times.

Journal Entry
Give students about five minutes to respond to the following prompt: What did you learn about other people's pets? Did any other stories about your pet come to mind? Jot down a few notes to remind you of those stories for another time.

Community Meeting: The Friendship of Dogs
Define

- Yesterday, we had a community meeting about friends. An old saying is that dog is "man's best friend." What do people mean when they say that?

Personalize

- Does your dog (or pet) fit that description? Why or why not?
- What are some of the interesting stories you heard about someone else's pet during the Concentric Circles activity?

As students identify some of the interesting stories they heard from their classmates about pets, invite the classmates themselves to share more about their stories.

Challenge

- Have you ever read or heard other true stories about dogs (or other pets) that explain why they are called our best friends?
- What can we learn about friendship from our pets?

Finish the meeting by explaining that tomorrow you will begin reading a novel set during the first decade of the 1900s about a boy in the Ozark Mountains and his two hunting dogs who turn out to be his best friends.

Instruction Lesson 1
Journal Entry
Give students a few minutes to try to define the following literary terms in their journals: *flashback, setting, foreshadowing.*

Introduction to Where the Red Fern Grows
Engage the class in a review of the following literary terms, finding out what they already know about them. Then give them the following definitions.

- **Flashback.** A literary or cinematic device in which an earlier event is inserted into the normal chronological order of a narrative. (In this case, the flashback is the main part of the story.)
- **Setting.** The time and place a story occurs. In *Where the Red Fern Grows,* the Ozark Mountains during the Great Depression in the early 20th century.
- **Foreshadowing.** To give clues or hints about an action that will happen later on.

Read the first chapter aloud, stopping to check for understanding when necessary. You might tell students to be looking for examples of foreshadowing as you are reading the chapter. You will be

asking them to predict events that happen later on. You also might want to point out, or have them point out, some examples of foreshadowing.

Journal Entry
Give students a few minutes to journal in response to the following prompt: What do you predict the story is going to be about and what might you expect to happen based on the foreshadowing the narrator provides in chapter one?

Instruction Lesson 2
Journal Entry
Have students spend a few minutes responding to the following prompt: Have you ever wanted something so much that it hurt, but your parents would not or could not provide it? What was it? Did you ever get it? How?

Community Meeting: Predictions
Ask for predictions about what will happen in the story. Be sure to ask for support for the predictions from the chapter you read.

Community Meeting: Hunting and Trapping
Without some background knowledge on hunting and trapping, many students will be unable to understand much of what happens in the novel. I suggest holding a community meeting about hunting, using the following questions.

Define

- What kinds of animals do people hunt where you live?
- Why do people hunt?
- What do you know about trapping? Why might people trap instead of hunt? (It may be easier to trap some nocturnal species than hunt them, among other reasons.)

Personalize

- Have you ever been hunting with older family members? What were you hunting? What did (or would) you do with the animals?
- Have you ever gone trapping? What was it like?

Challenge

- Do you think hunting is right or wrong? Why?
- Do you think there is a difference in morality between hunting today as opposed to a hundred years ago? If so, why?

Explain that in *Where the Red Fern Grows,* hunting and trapping were an important part of life. Among the Ozark Mountain people like Billy's family, who had little money, hunting was an important way of putting food on the table, and any money they could make from selling fur was a big help. Some of the animals they hunted and trapped were deer, squirrel, fox, opossum, rabbit, and raccoon (or "coon" in Appalachian/Ozark dialect). Raccoons were particularly valuable because of their thick, water-resistant fur. They are also very smart and elusive prey. Only a skilled hunter with particularly skilled hunting dogs could be a successful coon hunter.

After this meeting, read the second chapter aloud to the class.

Instruction Lesson 3
Journal Entry
Give students five to ten minutes to write about the following prompt: Have you ever saved up for something you wanted? How did you get the money? How long did it take? How did it feel when you finally got the money you needed?

Community Meeting: Work Ethic
Define

- What does it mean to have a strong work ethic?
- What are some other words we use to describe people with a strong work ethic? (Look for answers such as *hard-working, conscientious, responsible, dependable, dedicated,* and so on.)

Personalize

- Who do you know who has a strong work ethic? How do you know?
- When have *you* demonstrated a strong work ethic?

Challenge

- What is good about having a strong work ethic? What's in it for you?
- Why would it be good for you to work hard when you are young, as opposed to enjoying yourself now and working hard later?
- Is there any downside to having a strong work ethic? Could someone have too strong of a work ethic?

Explain that while you are reading, the class will keep a double-entry journal, listing times in the book when they notice someone:

- having a strong work ethic
- being responsible
- demonstrating kindness

Read Chapter 3 aloud, encouraging students to raise a hand when they notice one of these values being demonstrated. Keep a record as you go on a document projector or whiteboard. Your journal might look like this:

Character Trait	Actions and/or Quotations that Demonstrate the Trait
Responsibility	Billy starts saving money in an "old K.C. Baking Powder can."
Work ethic	Billy "worked like a beaver" catching crayfish and trapping minnows and selling them (along with fresh vegetables) to fishermen. He also picked blueberries and sold them to his grandfather for 10 cents a bucket.
	Billy trapped "harder than ever" and his grandpa sold the hides to fur buyers.
	It takes him two years to save up enough money for the dogs.
Kindness	Grandpa gives Billy a sack full of candy.
Responsibility and kindness	Billy shares candy with his sisters.

Introduction Lesson 4
From here to the end of the reading, start each class with a journal entry and vary other activities to suit the needs of your group. Here is a sample format:

Journal Entry
Have students write for a few minutes on a topic related to incidents in the chapter. Try to elicit personal stories that relate to events in the novel. For example, a prompt for Chapter 4 could be: Tell about your first time in a new place (big city, different country, new school).

Reading Quiz
Ask four or five questions about the content of the previous reading to check for understanding and that everyone is keeping up.

Reading
You may want to continue reading aloud to the class through to the end of the book. Another option is to have students read in or outside of class. Or, if you have a small group where the noise won't get too loud, or you have spaces where your students can spread out, you might also pair up students and have them take turns reading aloud. While one reads, the other completes the double-entry journals.

Community Meetings
Close lessons with a community meeting focusing on helping students develop an understanding of the literal level of the novel and discussing the character traits of work ethic, responsibility, and kindness.

Assessment
Choose one of the following two assessments. These assessments will need to be written in student-friendly language and accompanied by rubrics or checklists that make expectations clear.

- Students write a first-person, nonfiction narrative that addresses one of the themes (work ethic, responsibility, or kindness) in *Where the Red Fern Grows.* The narrative should explain, in context, one important event in the novel and go on to tell a personal story that relates to it, explaining how both reflect the themes. The personal anecdote should use literary conventions appropriate to the genre, including foreshadowing, flashback, setting, and dialogue.
- Students research one of the main topics in the novel and write a report using a variety of sources (not only electronic). Possible topics include Ozark culture (music, food, folk art, storytelling), trapping history, and hunting with dogs. Note that this option does not address the touchstone values, but it is a good alternative for students who don't want to write about their own lives.

As an option, you may require students to prepare an oral multimedia presentation of their narrative or report.

Closing
Provide a day to a few days at the end of the unit during which students who need more time to achieve quality can receive correctives. Those who do not need more time can participate in extension activities for additional credit.

Grade 6 Sample Unit continued

Correctives
- One-on-one teacher-student tutoring.
- Peer tutoring (student does this as an extension activity).

Extensions
- Students act out an important scene from the novel and submit an accompanying paper that includes the script and two paragraphs: one explaining how this scene is important to the overall plot, and one discussing how this scene connects to one of the major themes of *Where the Red Fern Grows*.
- Students draw, paint, or sculpt a work of art that relates to the plot or theme of the novel and write an accompanying paper explaining its importance to the overall plot or major theme.
- Students write a poem or rap that summarizes the plot and theme of the novel.
- Students tutor a classmate during gap time.

Grade 11 Sample Unit: The Theme of Responsibility

The Theme of Responsibility in *The Grapes of Wrath* by John Steinbeck

Primary Touchstone Connection: Responsibility

Secondary Touchstone Connections: Kindness, optimism, perseverance

Academic Objectives
Students will:
- Understand *The Grapes of Wrath* on the literal and thematic level.
- Be able to describe how the characters and events in the novel develop the themes of personal and social responsibility, kindness, optimism, and perseverance, using concrete supporting details from the text.
- Make connections between events and characters in *The Grapes of Wrath* to their own lives, and articulate those connections through speaking and writing.
- Make a poster presentation explaining how literary characters help develop a novel's theme, using concrete support from the text.
- Write a literary expositive essay on one of the themes in *The Grapes of Wrath*.
- Use effective communication and social skills in a class meeting format.

Social-Emotional Objectives
Students will:
- Understand the importance of personal and social responsibility, optimism, kindness, and perseverance to the individual and society.
- Understand that, in life as in literature, our choices determine our character and our destiny.
- Understand that one person's choices can profoundly affect many others.

11th- and 12th-Grade CCSS Addressed*
Reading: CCSS.ELA-LITERACY.RL 11–12.1, 11–12.2, 11–12.3, 11–12.4, 11–12.6
Writing: CCSS.ELA-LITERACY.W 11–12.1, 11–12.4, 11–12.5, 11–12.6
Speaking and Listening: CCSS.ELA-LITERACY.SL 11–12.1, 11–12.4, 11–12.5

Resources
The Grapes of Wrath by John Steinbeck
The Grapes of Wrath movie
Wessels Living History Farm: Farming in the 1930s
 (www.livinghistoryfarm.org/farminginthe1930s/farminginthe1930s.html)
Wessels Living History Farm: The Dust Bowl
 (www.livinghistoryfarm.org/farminginthe1930s/water_02.html)
United States History: The Dust Bowl (www.u-s-history.com/pages/h1583.html)

*Copyright © 2010 National Governors Association Center for Best Practices and Council of Chief State School Officers. All rights reserved.

Grade 11 Sample Unit continued

Prerequisites
- Students have a basic understanding of the touchstone values of responsibility, kindness, optimism, and perseverance.
- Background knowledge includes general information about life during the Dust Bowl years of the Great Depression. Much of this can be learned through the suggested Web resources. One option is to talk to a social studies teacher in your school about the possibility of doing an interdisciplinary unit.

Introduction Lesson 1
Journal Entry
Give students the following prompt: What does the term *responsibility* mean to you? What kinds of responsibilities are there? What are some of your responsibilities? What are the benefits of being responsible?

Community Meeting: Responsibility
Define
- How would you define *responsibility*?
- What different kinds of responsibilities are there?

Discuss the three main types of responsibility: personal (responsibility to self), social (responsibility to others), and civic (responsibility to the community at large).

Personalize
- What are some of your personal responsibilities now? How about your social responsibilities? Civic?
- How does taking responsibility affect you? What's good about it? What's not so good?

Challenge
- What will be some of your responsibilities in the future? Consider all three types.
- How important is it to be responsible to self, others, and the community? Why?

End the meeting by going around the circle and doing a W.H.I.P. (Without Hesitation Immediate Participation) activity (see page 31 of *The SEL Solution* to review). Provide the sentence starter in the following first bullet and pass the talking device to a student to your left to a student who fills in the blank in the sentence starter with a word or brief phrase without spending more than a second or two thinking about it. He or she then passes the talking device to the next person, who does the same, until everyone has answered the sentence. Be sure to answer the prompt yourself. Then provide the second sentence starter and repeat the process.
- On a scale of 1 to 10, how would you score yourself on your personal, social, and civic responsibility (1 being totally irresponsible, 10 being almost perfect)?
- What's one thing you can do today or this week to be more responsible?

Introduction Lesson 2
Journal Entry
Have students write on this topic: What are a parent's responsibilities to his or her children?

Grade 11 Sample Unit continued

Class Discussion
Lead a group discussion in which you talk about the following questions:
- What are a parent's responsibilities to his or her children?
- What might responsible parents do if they lost their job, and there weren't any welfare money, social services, or jobs available where they lived?
- Where might they go? Why there?

Introduce the Novel
Share photos or videos of the Dust Bowl as you read a summary of the history of those years to students (you can use one of the Dust Bowl websites listed in the Resources of this unit). Explain that thousands of families faced this dilemma in the 1930s: They lost their farms, jobs weren't available, there was a terrible drought, and there was no welfare system to save these people. Introduce *The Grapes of Wrath* by telling students that it's about one family living through this situation.
 Begin reading Chapter 1 to the class. Assign the rest of the chapter for homework, if necessary.

Instruction Lesson 1
Journal Entry
Give the students a couple minutes to journal about the different reactions to the turtle crossing the road. Have them stop writing and review the concept of foreshadowing. Then have them write on the following prompt: What might be John Steinbeck's purpose in starting out his novel with this chapter?

Class Discussion: Chapter 1
Lead a group discussion covering the following questions:
- What are the different responses to the turtle crossing the road?
- What would you do?
- What might the turtle represent?
- Have you ever been in a situation where you felt helpless, like the turtle? What did you want from others when you felt that way? How were you treated?
- What does the way people treat those who are helpless say about them?
- What do you think Steinbeck's purpose is in starting the novel with this chapter?

Introduce the Touchstone Values
Explain that during this unit students will be assigned specific touchstone values to identify throughout the novel: responsibility (personal, family, and social), kindness, perseverance, and optimism. Before students can find examples of these traits, it is important that they clearly understand the character traits they are looking for. Students probably have a strong grasp of kindness, so you can simply hold a short discussion on that value, and you had a community meeting on the different kinds of responsibility on the first day of the unit. You may need to prepare a short lesson or class discussion on perseverance and optimism.

Instruction Lesson 2

Journal Entry

Give students five minutes to write on the following topic: What are the responsibilities of people in a society regarding the health and well-being of the dispossessed, the homeless, or the helpless?

Consider also holding a community meeting on this topic. It is sure to be a lively one, especially if you bring up welfare, the ongoing health insurance debate, and similar subjects.

Reading and Tracking Values

Divide students into five groups and assign each group to track one of the following character traits throughout the novel:

1. Personal and family responsibility
2. Social responsibility
3. Optimism
4. Kindness
5. Perseverance

Read aloud Chapter 2 and model citing examples of the values as you go. You can use a whiteboard or document projector to make a T-chart with the values on the left and the examples (with page numbers) on the right. Students will read the rest of the book independently, tracking the one value they are responsible for. Be sure to include non-examples as well (times when the values are violated).

Instruction Lesson 3

From here to the end of the unit, students are reading independently outside of class (you may allow for some in-class reading time, too, including you reading aloud). At each class meeting, build a lesson based on the following model (making adjustments to fit your classroom situation).

- Journal entries in which students write about events, characters, and themes in the novel, connecting them to their own lives when appropriate.
- Reading quizzes.
- Class discussions on the journal topic.

At the end of the unit, students will turn in their list of touchstone value examples. You can have them turn them in independently or give time to compile their lists, which can be a great springboard for group discussions about examples individuals may have missed, disagreements about certain inclusions, and so on.

Assessment

Formative Assessment

Give each value group a set of index cards with the name of each important character on a separate card. Ask them to place the cards on a continuum with the character who most exhibits their value at the top to the person who least exhibits it at the bottom. For example, most kind to least kind, or most responsible to least responsible. Once they have ranked them, students write on the cards the reason(s) they are where they are in the continuum. Reasoning should include support from the text.

As a class, try to come to a consensus on the continuum for each value.

➡

Summative Assessment

Have students do both of these assessments—one as a group and one as an individual.

1. Working in their cooperative groups, students develop and present a 10-minute poster presentation on their touchstone value, including a visual depiction of one character they believe most exemplifies their group's value and lyrics to a theme song for that character. (You can allow them to make up a song or use an existing one.) The presentation should focus on demonstrating how the character's actions and beliefs in *The Grapes of Wrath* help develop the themes of responsibility, kindness, optimism, or perseverance.

2. Each student writes a literary expository essay on the touchstone value they focused on during the novel, demonstrating how that value is developed as a theme in *The Grapes of Wrath*.

Closing

Provide a day to a few days at the end of the unit during which students who need more time to achieve quality can receive correctives. Those who do not need more time can participate in extension activities for additional credit.

Correctives

- One-on-one teacher-student tutoring.
- Peer tutoring (student does this as an extension activity).

Extensions

- Students write a first-person, nonfiction narrative about a time when one of the character traits played an important role in their lives.
- Students draw, paint, or sculpt a work of art that relates to the plot or theme of *The Grapes of Wrath* and an accompanying paper explaining its significance.
- Students write a poem or rap that summarizes the plot and theme of the novel.
- Students research a current event or situation in which people are experiencing suffering like the migrant workers in Steinbeck's novel and write a persuasive essay calling for action.
- Students tutor a classmate during gap time.

Inspiring Student Leadership

This chapter is intended for administrators, school counselors, and any other adults (including teachers, school psychologists, social workers, and parent volunteers) who have an interest in advising a student leadership team.

One of the most powerful catalysts in the process of developing and sustaining a positive school culture and climate is a Student Leadership Team (SLT). These student leaders provide often missing but essential elements of an effective school improvement initiative: student voice, empowerment, and ownership of the climate improvement process. When these students see themselves as active agents of positive change, they will take personal and collective ownership of the vision and work hard to make it a reality.

Once a group of student leaders becomes engaged in the process of creating a better school, their positive energy is contagious. Other students are more likely to buy into the process once they are aware of their peers' enthusiasm and determination to have a positive impact on the school climate and culture—to make it "our school." Student leaders also provide excellent models of social responsibility and the values of the school touchstone, helping the general population see and hear what those values look and sound like from kids their own age in a variety of school contexts.

This chapter explains how to select, train, and employ student leaders in way that will inspire not only the students on the leadership team but also the entire school community. Starting student leadership training at the beginning of the school year (or even better, during the summer break) has important benefits. Student leaders can be actively involved in the school climate improvement process from the beginning, helping in the development and promotion of the touchstone values and acting as peer SEL educators, counselors, and mentors.

Before assembling a team of student leaders, identify two or three adults willing to act as student leadership advisors. They may be members of the Climate Improvement Team (CIT), but that is not required. What is important is that they are passionate about educating the whole child, character education, and social-emotional learning. Usually advisors are teachers, counselors, or social workers. You may approach people who you think might be interested and invite their leadership, or you may open up the opportunity to staff at a faculty meeting. The best student leadership advisors are adults who students and faculty like and respect and who are sincerely invested in the climate improvement initiative.

What to Look for in Student Leaders

The efficacy of a group of student leaders is in large part related to the size of the group, which students are chosen, how they are chosen, and how they are trained and developed into a team. Here are some things to consider when looking for inspiring student leaders.

Optimum Size of the Team

A team of student leaders needs to be small enough to develop close, supportive relationships but large enough to reflect the diversity of your school. The most effective groups of students I've worked with have been between 16 and 20 students. It's a good idea to start out with a few more than you expect to end up working with because some students will discover that the responsibilities and/or time commitments are too much for them, and they'll drop out.

It is best if the student leaders come from the upper-two grades of your school, because students generally do not give younger students the same respect as their peers or students from a higher grade.

Diversity of the Team

The members of the SLT should reflect the diversity of the school population. Some kinds of diversity to consider:

- socioeconomic status
- living environment: rural, urban, or suburban
- gender
- gender identity
- interests (for example, art, music, drama, sports, technology)
- ethnicity
- cultural

The SLT should, as closely as possible, mirror the diversity within the school, but it doesn't need to become a quota system. Simply do your best to make the group as diverse as possible.

It might seem like a highly diverse group of students could have trouble relating to one another to form a cohesive unit, but in my experience, these groups come together beautifully after the first day of training. As one student leader remarked in a concluding activity, "We have more in common with each other than we have differences."

Leadership Characteristics

It is important that the students selected for the team be liked and respected by their peers and adults, and emulated by other students. Many of these student leaders will be "typical" leaders—

student council members, sports team captains, club officers, and so on. But leadership team membership should not simply be a popularity contest. Students who may not be leaders in any official capacity, but are liked and respected by their peers, can make excellent student leaders. Other students to consider are those who may not be highly social, but who model a positive attitude, responsible behavior, and academic excellence.

It is also important to recruit some students who may at times lead their peers slightly astray. This doesn't mean students who are involved in serious trouble, such as with drugs or gang activity, but those who at times have modeled less-than-responsible behavior among their friends and peers. These students often respond positively to being placed in a position of responsibility and turn themselves (and subsequently, their followers) around. If they choose to disrupt or push boundaries during the training, explain to them, as you would with any other student, that membership on the team is a privilege and if they continue disrupting, they will lose their place on the team. Even with that in mind, it is best to find the more "positive" leaders for at least 80 percent of the group.

Student leaders should also be made up of students who do not struggle academically. Training and other SLT activities may require them to occasionally miss class, and academic success is an important leadership quality.

The majority of the group should be outgoing students, since they will be asked to present and work with other students. However, introverted student leaders can often offer creative ideas and backstage support.

Inviting Leaders and Creating Your Student Leadership Team

As the initiator of the SLT, you will need to communicate to staff, students, and parents the purpose of the initiative, the responsibilities of members, and the process of team selection.

Get Recommendations

In the spring semester prior to launching the SLT (but after presenting the climate improvement initiative), send out an email to instructional, counseling, and coaching staff members inviting suggestions of students who might make good candidates to be student leaders.

Before selecting potential student leadership members, it's important to select the group's co-advisors and invite them to attend the next CIT meeting. See a sample letter to the right.

After collecting recommendations from the staff, take the list to the next CIT meeting and explain that you will be making the final selections, but would like their input before deciding. Go through the list with the CIT and co-advisors asking, 1) If you know this student, what strengths would she bring to the team? and 2) Does anyone have an objection to this student being invited?

Next, based on staff recommendations, co-advisor input, and CIT advisement, use the criteria regarding size, diversity, and leadership qualities previously explained to create a list of possible candidates.

Reach Out to Candidates

Once you have developed your list of potential candidates, invite them to a meeting—or simply send them a memo through their homeroom teacher or the teacher who nominated them. Print out copies of the "Student Leadership Team: Interview Questions" and the "Student Leadership Team: Parent Permission" handouts (see the thumbnails on page 82) and have them available at the meeting or distribute them with the memo. Tell candidates something like the following:

I am in the process of assembling a Student Leadership Team that will begin working together this summer and throughout the next school year. The purpose of this team is to help make our school a place where everyone can be safe, feel connected, be respected, and learn.

The responsibilities of team members will include attending all training sessions and meetings, working with your peers and younger students, making presentations, and leading discussion groups and small group activities. You also may be called on to mentor individual students and/or mediate conflicts between

Dear Staff Member,

In our efforts to improve our school climate, student involvement and support will be critical to our success. Therefore, we will be creating a Student Leadership Team (SLT) to provide students with a voice in the process and engage the entire student body. Students will be selected based partially on staff recommendations but also on student interviews, input from the Climate Improvement Team, and parent permission. Please consider the following criteria for membership on the SLT. We are looking for students who:

- are academically sound
- treat others with kindness and respect
- are liked and respected by other students
- model responsible behavior
- would be comfortable presenting to their peers and others

If any students you work with will be upper classmen next year and fit the above criteria, please respond to this email with their names and grade level by Friday.

In addition, I am looking for two faculty members who would be interested in being co-advisors for this team. Responsibilities will include:

- being involved in conducting one full day of student training this August (or on a Saturday in early September)
- taking time out of the classroom or office to conduct training and be involved in SLT initiatives (substitutes will be provided)
- holding monthly after- or before-school meetings
- communicating with me and the Climate Initiative Team

If this is something that interests you, please email me or stop by my office. I'd be happy to answer any questions.

Looking forward,

Mr. Erwin

students. The time required of you would be a full day of training in August (or a Saturday in early September), monthly meetings after (or before) school, and an average of one day out of the classroom per month. That means that you must make up missed work and keep your grades above a B average.

This is a great opportunity to develop your leadership skills, make new friends, learn about yourself, and make a positive difference in your school.

Everyone who is interested will have an opportunity to interview for a spot on the team. If you are interested in membership, please sign up on the sheet at the front of the room (or let your homeroom teacher know) and take a permission slip and the list of interview questions. Please return your permission slip by Friday and carefully go over the interview questions to help you prepare for the interview (feel free to bring your interview questions and any notes you take on them into the interview with you). Next week you will be notified about your interview time and place. Thank you for your interest. I hope to see you in an interview.

For secondary students, you may want to gather email addresses or phone numbers for texting.

Make the parent letter and permission form available on your school website in case students don't take a copy home with them. You may need to email it home to some families as well. Use this letter as is, or use it as a model to create your own.

Interview Process

Conducting interviews not only helps ensure you are recruiting the most promising student leaders, it also sends a message that being a member of the SLT carries a certain amount of responsibility and prestige. Again, I recommend passing out the interview questions at the initial meeting or making them available ahead of time some other way (see page 82), so students will feel less intimidated by the questions during the face-to-face interviews.

After conducting the interviews and selecting the team, send each team member a congratulatory note and invite them to the full-day summer training session.

Student Leadership Training Meeting

In order for your group of student leaders—that's just what they are, a *group* of individuals—to have a positive impact on the school culture, it is important to devote time and effort into transforming the group into a cohesive *team* with a clear purpose and a common vision. To achieve these goals, students need to feel emotionally (and physically) safe, get to know and like one another as well as the adult team advisors, be given a voice and choice in what they are being asked to do, and—maybe most importantly for students of any age—have fun. The community meeting and the following strategies have helped me develop strong, effective student leadership teams.

The first thing is to schedule your SLT training meeting for just before school begins in the fall or early in the school year—within the first two or three weeks. Select this date ahead of time and let students interested in applying know that this meeting is required. That way you assure yourself full participation. If you hold this meeting during the school year, schedule it on a Saturday so students won't miss class. Attendance on a Saturday will also demonstrate students' commitment. If possible, provide snacks and lunch at this meeting.

Here's a recommended agenda for the first training session.

Introduction to Student Leadership

When students, like many adults, enter into a new situation with a group of strangers (or mere acquaintances), they often feel uneasy and self-conscious. Your first task is to help break the ice and create a comfortable atmosphere. Start by placing chairs in a circle before the students enter the room. Greet and welcome students at the door, introduce yourself, ask their names, and direct them to sit anywhere in the circle.

After all the students are present, welcome them as a group, explain the purpose of the student leadership initiative, and share the day's agenda. You may want to have it posted on a flip chart or projected on the whiteboard (see the agenda

I created below). It's also a good idea to answer students' burning, as-yet unasked questions right away—when breaks will occur, when you will have lunch, and when you will conclude.

With the "nuts and bolts" out of the way, here's a script for getting things going:

The purpose of this group is to make our school, which is already a good school, into a place all students love coming to every day! For that to happen, you need the power to help it come about and a voice to help make it real.

Your responsibilities on this team will be to work directly with your peers as group leaders, make presentations, and be involved in a variety of ongoing initiatives and activities designed to improve the school climate. Some of these will be required, like helping out at school-wide touchstone meetings, which we'll talk about today. Others will be voluntary, for example, being a peer mentor or conflict resolution facilitator. Others we will choose and agree on as a group.

My hope is that you come to think of this school not as the teachers' school or the principal's school, but as YOUR school. Today, we're going to focus on getting to know one another, developing this group into a team, and beginning the process of transforming our school into a joyful learning community.

Here's the agenda I recommend:

1. Interviews and Introductions
2. The Name Game
3. Do You Know Your Neighbors?
4. Community Meeting: Bullying, Meanness, and Relational Aggression
5. The Five Basic Human Needs
6. Closing Team-Building Activity (for example, Group Juggle)
7. Community Meeting: The Closing

ACTIVITY

Interviews and Introductions

Students will most likely be sitting with their friends. Explain to them that the purpose of the first activity is to get to know and feel more comfortable with other members of the group.

Time Required: About 25 minutes

Materials Needed: A deck of regular playing cards

The Activity

Create pairs of students by taking a deck of regular playing cards and selecting two cards of each value: two aces, two kings, two queens, and so on, making sure that you have the same number of cards as students in the group. Shuffle the cards and pass them out, making sure that students don't get a card with the same value as their buddies. Keep one card for yourself so that you can participate, too. (If the group, including you, has an odd number of people, keep a joker as a wild card and join a pair as the third member.)

Next, tell students to find the person who has the value card that matches their own and sit together with their partner. Once everyone is partnered up, explain that partners are to interview each other and prepare to introduce each other to the group. Here is what they have to find out:

- their partner's name
- what he or she likes to be called
- what grade their partner is in
- something their partner likes to do in his or her free time
- one other interesting thing about their partner

Some students may have trouble with the "interesting thing," so you might make suggestions: pets they have, places they have traveled or lived, hobbies they enjoy, personal achievements, or anything that makes them unique.

Once the students understand the instructions, give them five minutes to interview each other. You interview your partner, too. When time is up, model what you expect by introducing your partner, then invite your partner to introduce you.

Next, introduce the talking device (explained on page 23), explaining that the person with the device has the floor. Ask who would like to introduce their partner next, and toss that person the talking device. Encourage the pair to start by having both partners stand and one beginning, *I'd like to introduce my (new) friend . . .*

When that pair has completed their introductions, direct them to pass the talking device to another pair and sit down. Continue until everyone has been introduced.

ACTIVITIES

The Name Game and Do You Know Your Neighbors?

These two games are fun ways to help students learn one another's names, learn more about one another, and get energized for the day's training. For complete directions on how to facilitate these games, go to page 162 for the Name Game and page 148 for Do You Know Your Neighbors?

Time Required: About 30 minutes for both

Note: It is important that all adults involved with the training participate enthusiastically in all the activities. The student-adult relationship improves and your enthusiasm will be contagious.

COMMUNITY MEETING

Bullying, Meanness, and Relational Aggression

The purpose of this meeting is to help leaders gain an understanding of the need for climate improvement.

Time Required: About 20 minutes

Invite everyone to sit in the circle next to someone they didn't know well before today. Remind them of the purpose of the Student Leadership Team: to help make the school a place where everyone can feel part of a safe, caring, joyful learning community.

Next, explain the community meeting ground rules (page 23), emphasizing that only the person with the talking device speaks and that everyone else should listen actively. The following questions are suggested for the first community meeting. To encourage participation, consider having students discuss their answers with a partner next to them before opening the floor to the whole group discussion. This can help students feel more prepared and less nervous about speaking in front of the group.

Define

- What are some attitudes and behaviors that prevent students from feeling safe and connected in school?
- What are some ways students are mean or aggressive in school?

- What are other ways students are mean to each other?
- What are some places where you witness meanness or aggressive behavior?

Personalize

- *Without mentioning anyone's name,* have you ever witnessed any of these kinds of behavior?
- Have you ever personally experienced them?
- How did you feel?
- How did they affect you?
- What did you do?

Challenge

- What are the effects of meanness and aggression on students in the short term?
- What might be the long-term effects of meanness?
- Who feels the effects of this kind of behavior?
- What would be the benefits of eliminating meanness and bullying from this school?

This meeting will help students see that bullying is more than the stereotypical physical bullying many people think of when they hear the word. Instead, it involves a continuum of mean and aggressive actions and words ranging from subtle put-downs (eye rolling, for example) through physical assault, including all of the behaviors described in the community meeting. Most, if not all students, will report having been a victim (or perpetrator) of meanness at some point in their educational lives.

Also, student leaders will come to understand that we all feel the effects of meanness and aggression. Anxiety and fear about being mistreated holds people back from achieving their potential, not only in school but in life. Envisioning a school environment where meanness is absent will help motivate students to continue their student leadership involvement.

LESSON

The Five Basic Human Needs

Through this series of lessons, discussions, and activities, student leaders will gain an understanding of the universal basic human needs that drive all behavior and how those needs relate to creating a positive school climate.

Time Required: About 3 hours

The lessons for teaching the Five Basic Human Needs are clearly explained in Chapter 8. Lead student leaders through all the activities, from Introducing the Five Basic Human Needs through the Personal GPS Collage, pages 95–100. It is unlikely that students will have time to complete their Personal GPS collages. Save them and explain they will have time to complete them at the next meeting.

ACTIVITY

Closing Team-Building Activity

Having another energizing activity close to the end of the first training session, one filled with fun and laughter (and learning), helps keep a positive attitude toward membership on the SLT and continues to bond the group. Choose any one of the team-building activities explained elsewhere, such as the Group Juggle (page 163), Musical Circles (page 98), the Group Knot (page 165), or another activity you like.

COMMUNITY MEETING

The Closing

A class meeting using the W.H.I.P. structure is an effective way to bring the first training session to a close. W.H.I.P. stands for "Without Hesitation Immediate Participation."

Give students a sentence starter from the list that follows (or another one you see fit), and give them 30 to 60 seconds to discuss with a partner how they will complete the sentence.

- Today, I liked . . .
- Today, I learned . . .
- A question I have after today is . . .

Next, start the W.H.I.P. by filling in the sentence starter for yourself and passing the talking device to the person to your right or left. That person shares her answer with the whole group and passes the device again in the same direction. The next person, in turn, gives his answer and sends

the device along. Continue until everyone has responded in sequence around the circle.

After every student has responded, summarize the day's learning, emphasizing any points you feel necessary, and answer any questions students have. If you're working with secondary students, get everyone's phone number or email address (if you haven't already) so you can communicate with them directly. You might also consider setting up a private Facebook group or making a simple group website to facilitate communication.

Touchstone Table Facilitators

Soon after the first training, it is important to give the student leaders a project. One way to immediately begin engaging them is through their involvement in developing the school touchstone (see Chapter 3: The School Touchstone). Schedule about three hours during school or on a Saturday morning to prepare students for their responsibilities as table facilitators during the touchstone process.

As students enter the meeting, greet them and allow them to informally work on their Personal GPS collages that they began in the initial training. This will serve as a reminder of their learning from the last session and keep them engaged while other student leaders arrive. Once all the students are there, call the meeting to order and have students sit in a circle.

Set the Purpose and Clarify Expectations

Explain to the student leaders what a touchstone is and why it is important. For example, tell them:

A touchstone is a word, phrase, or slogan that we develop as a school to represent the kind of school we want to become, based on values like fairness and respect. A touchstone provides the school community with an agreed upon goal or target to aim for. Without a target, chances are we will not hit the bull's-eye. The process of developing the touchstone is just as important as the final product. It helps people be aware of the kind of attitudes and behaviors we want and those we do not want in our school culture. It also encourages all of us to think about our own attitudes and behavior, focus on things we have in common rather than on differences, and understand the core values of the school.

Explain to students that one of their first responsibilities will be to lead their peers through the touchstone process:

Today, you're going to develop your own Student Leadership Team touchstone. The process you go through today is the same one you will facilitate for your peers, so you will want to pay close attention and take an active roll in this. The SLT touchstone will provide you all with a shared picture of the kind of team you want to be. We will use it during SLT meetings to guide our interactions with one another and help us come up with ideas for planning future projects. Our touchstone values eventually will be combined with those identified by other groups in the school and absorbed into a school-wide touchstone. Once the school-wide touchstone is completed, it will replace the SLT's touchstone.

Lead Students Through the Process

Chapter 3 is dedicated to touchstone development. Please refer to that chapter as a guide in developing the student leaders' touchstone.

Assign Facilitator Duties

After student leaders have experienced the touchstone process themselves, explain that they will be working in pairs as table facilitators to help other peer groups develop touchstone values. Their responsibilities will include:

- Helping ensure that students understand the task, which is not to rewrite the school rules, but to create a shared picture of the kind of behaviors and attitudes that help us feel safe and respected

- Helping keep students on task

- Making suggestions regarding the parts of the process, including behaviors and attitudes, living space choices, symbols, and so on

- Helping students understand how to make the shift from behaviors and attitudes to values and principles

- Distributing and collecting materials

- Being ambassadors of the process, spreading enthusiasm and confidence in the final product

Their responsibilities do *not* include:

- **Being a disciplinarian.** If students in the group are uncooperative, gently remind them that this is their opportunity to make a difference in the school; then leave them alone. If they are disruptive, ask an adult to intervene.

- **Imposing your ideas on the group.** Let the ideas come from the group as much as possible. If the group is struggling, provide some suggestions, but let them choose.

- **Taking abuse.** Again, ask an adult to intervene.

After the first session with the general population, hold a brief meeting with the SLT to process and evaluate how it went and adjust if necessary. Ask questions, such as:

- What went well?

- What challenges did you encounter?

- How did you respond to the challenges? Did that work?

- If not, what might you (or we) do or say differently?

- On a scale of 1–10, how well did you and your partner work together?

- What did you learn from this?

Ongoing Student Leadership Opportunities

Once you have established a team of student leaders, you can continuously engage them in numerous activities that benefit both the school community and the student leaders themselves.

After experiencing a successful and engaging first training and building momentum from the touchstone process, the student leaders will enter the next session with energy and enthusiasm. To keep that momentum going, it is important to continue providing opportunities for them to build positive relationships, learn, feel empowered, and have fun.

Begin training them in the SEL skills in Chapters 7–10 as well as in the Process for Positive Change (pages 167–177). You will have to approach this training in a more intense timeframe than you would in a classroom so student leaders are prepared for various roles in the climate improvement process. Those student leader roles include the following.

Research Assistants

As research assistants, student leaders will be observing their peers and noting the frequency and type of certain behaviors. This activity is invaluable in helping student leaders see the need for improving the school climate and culture and increasing responsible social behavior in various contexts in the school. It also helps them gain a clear picture of the kinds of bullying and meanness present in the school environment. Furthermore, it provides useful baseline data against which to assess the effectiveness of their leadership efforts on improving the school climate and increasing pro-social behavior.

To help student leaders understand what they will be doing and observing, hold a community meeting discussion about what behaviors they might see and hear or not see and hear in terms of each of the relevant touchstone values (respect, kindness, etc.). After the community meeting on the touchstone, student leaders will have clear expectations of what to look for in terms of behaviors that align with (and those that don't align with) their chosen values.

Next, your student leaders will conduct their primary research in the school by collecting examples of behaviors (words or actions) that embody or contradict a certain touchstone value. Put students in pairs and assign each pair a value to focus on, either positive or negative examples of that value, and a specific place to look for behaviors that fit their category. For example, one pair of students might be assigned to look for examples of kindness in the lunchroom. Another pair would then be assigned to look for examples of *unkindness* in the same location. Locations can include specific classrooms, the lunchroom, the playground, specific hallways, and so on.

One partner in each pair will simply make tick marks each time he sees an example. The other partner will write down the specific behavior observed. If the same behavior is observed twice, there would be two tick marks, but only one specific behavior described.

Be sure to assign two pairs of student leaders to each location for each value, one pair to note positive examples and one to note negative ones. Be creative in order to effectively cover your particular school in the most appropriate way. For example, if the lunchroom is too big for two pairs to effectively observe, divide it into parts and assign the necessary additional pairs. Fifteen to 20 minutes should be a sufficient amount of time for the students to observe.

Explain to the students that they are not to intervene in any way while observing; they are simply to be "flies on the wall." Tell them that good researchers do not want to have any effect or influence on the subjects of their study. When other students see them carrying clipboards and taking notes, they will invariably ask the student leaders what they are doing. You might tell the student leaders to simply tell their subjects, "We're collecting information for a school improvement project we're doing" or some other nonthreatening statement.

After their observation time, the student leaders will report back to the training room and share what they observed (without mentioning names). Ask them how many positive examples of each value they noted and how many negative. Then ask them to describe the specific behaviors they observed. In my experience, for whatever reason, the number of negative examples typically is far greater than the number of positive behaviors. That may be because negative examples are usually more obvious. (It's clear someone is being unkind, for example, when you hear name-calling. Kindness may not be as easy to observe when it is manifested in a quiet conversation between friends.) Usually, student leaders are surprised (often shocked) by the sheer number and variety of negative examples they share. Remind them, though, that they also observed positive behaviors.

End this discussion by telling them that the mission of the Student Leadership Team is to increase the number of positive examples and reduce, and ultimately eliminate, the negative.

After this data-collection activity, compile the findings and share the compilation in an assembly with the student body and staff—perhaps as part of the touchstone process. You might also share it with district leaders as a way of helping them see the need for a school-wide touchstone and for the entire school climate initiative. Students will need to conduct similar research several months later to look for any improvements.

ACTIVITY

Touchstone Champions

Students generally get excited over the touchstone and, if given the opportunity, will think of dozens of ways of championing it. Rather than dictating initiatives and activities, you can trust that students will have lots of ideas for supporting and celebrating the touchstone and its values. Here is a process that helps generate student ideas. Try it at one of your SLT meetings after the school has established its touchstone.

Time Required: 20 minutes

Materials Needed: Flip chart paper, markers, and masking tape

Getting Started

Before the meeting, write the school touchstone on a sheet of chart paper. Then write each touchstone value at the top of a separate sheet. Post the sheets at different spots around the room where students can access them, and leave a marker at each station.

The Activity

To begin, put students into groups of three or four and assign each group to a different poster (including the full touchstone poster). Explain that they have two minutes to come up with as many ideas as possible for bringing that value (or the touchstone itself) to life in the school—in other words, to encourage the behavior signified by that value or touchstone.

After two minutes, give a signal for groups to rotate to the next station to their left. Give them two minutes to read what has been written there and add as many new ideas as they can think of. After two minutes, rotate to the next station,

continuing the process until every group has visited every station.

When they have completed the circuit, hold a group meeting discussing what they thought their best ideas were. Go poster by poster to discuss ideas. Some of the ideas may seem wild at first, but if the group is willing to consider them and discuss modification, sometimes these "wild ideas" can turn into the most powerful suggestions.

Finish by having students choose one or two ideas to begin with. You can determine these by simple vote, or by using a priority voting procedure: Give each student 12 gold stars or something similar to designate their votes and tell them to put their stars on the chart paper next to the ideas they are voting for. They can distribute their votes any way they want: They can put one star on 12 different ideas, put all stars on one idea, or any combination in between. The idea(s) with the most votes become the next initiatives, which you can start developing and implementing at this SLT meeting or at a subsequent meeting.

Here are some ideas that student leaders I've worked with have come up with:

- Get an actual stone and inscribe the touchstone values on it.
- Make a large papier-mâché stone, inscribe the values on it in school colors, and have every student put a different color paint thumbprint on it to signify their commitment.
- Have "Random Act of Kindness Day" (or Week).
- Have students read the announcements and end with an inspiring quotation that relates to the touchstone.
- Sell silicon bracelets with the touchstone printed on them.
- Do an acts-of-kindness flash mob.
- Host a guest speaker on perseverance.
- Have a touchstone balloon release.
- Hold a student leader–led assembly unveiling the touchstone.
- Hold a multicultural day to celebrate diversity.
- Create a peer tutoring program.
- Make murals of the touchstone.
- Create multimedia presentations or videos that celebrate the touchstone or its values.

■ Sell touchstone T-shirts. For example:[1]

A video that one junior high school completed about acceptance went semi-viral. To watch the video and see how easy it is to do, go to: www.youtube.com/watch?v=TRfQ-L_HOXs.

The students and staff thoroughly enjoyed making the video, and the subsequent recognition the school received helped transform the negative public perception the school had been trying to shed.

Peer SEL Educators

While teachers will be teaching the majority of SEL information and skills to their students, involving the SLT as peer SEL educators has important benefits. One of the benefits is that it sends a message to the student body that this is not just an adult-driven initiative, students are an important part of the process. It also helps student leaders learn the information and skills at a deeper level. And finally, it can relieve classroom teachers of some of the responsibility for teaching basic concepts to students.

After student leaders have learned the SEL content, they can work in pairs or small teams to lead their peers through the same activities they experienced themselves. This can be done by student leaders "pushing in" to classrooms and leading an SEL activity. The SLT advisor or principal sends an email to faculty explaining that the SLT will be coming into their classrooms to teach a basic skill at a particular date and time.

Another approach is to arrange a workshop in which students (possibly a whole grade level) meet in the lunchroom or gym for an hour to 90 minutes. Divide student leaders into teams and have each team lead a different SEL activity in a different area of the room. Students attending the workshop would then rotate through the different activities so that all students receive all the information during the workshop. Student leaders would repeat their activity four or five times to accommodate all of the groups.

I recommend student leaders facilitate all or some of the following SEL content:

Motivation
- Stranded activity (page 95)
- The Needs and Social Responsibility activity (page 101)

Emotional Awareness
- Times When I've Felt… activity (page 112)
- Voice lesson (page 115)
- I Have a Feeling activity (page 116)

Self-Regulation
- Think Red activity (page 127)
- The Traffic Circle of Life activity (page 135)

Peer Mentors

Assign a volunteer student leader to a new student or a student who is struggling emotionally or academically (or, as is so often the case, both) to act as a mentor or buddy. Explain that the student leader's primary goal is to personally connect with the assigned student. At first, the mentors' responsibility is just to get to know their "mentees" by doing things like having lunch, listening to music together, taking walks, shooting hoops, playing cards, and just hanging out. As they get to know each other, the two will develop trust, and mentees will feel like they have at least one friend at school. Student leaders will need to be reminded to make sure they avoid being condescending or patronizing, their role is to be a friend (not a parent or savior). Once the trusting relationship is established, mentors might tutor their mentee in academics or teach them some social-emotional skills when situations call for it.

---

[1] The T-shirt examples are used with permission from Lockport City School District in New York.

Peer Counselors/Mediators

Teach students to use the Process for Positive Change (PPC) (pages 167–177) or the Solving Circle (pages 179–180). Pair up student leaders and have them use the counseling structures with peers experiencing difficulties or making irresponsible choices. Of course, these students will not be prepared to deal with extremely difficult or dangerous situations. Younger students would be equipped to resolve things like playground disputes, rumors, or lunchroom meanness. Older students (grades 9 and up) could help resolve conflicts between friends or classmates and help counsel students in academic trouble. Older students also will be able to resolve simple behavior issues working with students who come to class unprepared, are insubordinate, or say something inappropriate in class.

Some students might be given the *option* of working out their behavioral or academic challenges or conflicts with a pair of student leaders instead of having to meet with a building administrator. This would provide the school disciplinarian(s) a little more time and energy for more difficult situations.

Leaders of Service

Engaging students in service learning projects may be one of the most powerful ways of creating a climate based on caring and social responsibility. Service learning is not the same as community service. Instead of simply providing a service—a canned food drive, for example (which is a great thing to do, of course)—service learning integrates the service students are providing with the core academic curriculum. During a service learning project, students are both learning new curriculum and using their academic knowledge and skills in service to the community. They are also practicing the social-emotional skills they've been learning. Service learning inspires people because it can directly satisfy four of the Five Basic Human Needs (see Chapter 8):

- **Love & Belonging:** Working as a team and connecting with members of the community
- **Power:** Having a voice in the kind of projects chosen; making a significant difference in or contribution to the community
- **Freedom:** Experiencing a novel approach to learning and having many choices throughout the project
- **Fun:** Working with others to make a positive difference feels great

Engage student leaders in choosing a service learning project. At the end of one of your monthly SLT meetings, tell your student leaders to spend some time before the next meeting thinking about your community's needs. They can talk to parents, peers, and teachers and watch the local news to come up with ideas. Maybe a neighborhood park needs cleaning up, or a nearby elder facility needs volunteers, or a family just experienced a tragedy and needs assistance. At the next meeting, brainstorm a list of possible service learning projects. As a group, choose one service learning project to implement.

Service learning is too big a topic to cover in detail here, but Cathryn Berger Kaye's *The Complete Guide to Service Learning* (2010) truly lives up to its title. It provides all the information and resources necessary to launch a service learning program in a school.

The energy and excitement generated by a group of enthusiastic young people working toward a shared goal is palpable, contagious, and inspiring to adults and other students. Student leaders have the potential to transform a school.

Resources

These resources align with this book's approach to student leadership and provide activities and lessons that will extend and enhance those in this chapter. They can be used by teachers, counselors, coaches, or anyone who works with students.

Building Everyday Leadership in All Kids by Mariam G. MacGregor (Free Spirit Publishing, 2013). The activities in this book help promote an understanding of leadership, effective communication, and problem-solving. The book is primarily designed to be used with grades K–6 but can be adapted to other age groups.

Building Everyday Leadership in All Teens by Mariam G. MacGregor (Free Spirit Publishing, 2015). Designed to be used with middle and high school students, these activities help teens explore ethical decision-making, team-building, what it means to be a leader, how to work with others, risk-taking, communication, creative thinking, and more.

The Complete Guide to Service Learning by Cathryn Berger Kaye (Free Spirit Publishing, 2010). This outstanding resource provides everything you need to create and implement a high-quality service learning project, allowing all students to gain leadership skills, practice social-emotional skills, and bring their touchstone values to life. The author includes service learning themes, specific examples, and ways of linking community service to the ELA curriculum.

Emotionally Intelligent Leadership for Students: Facilitation and Activity Guide by Marcy Levy Shankman, Scott J. Allen, and Paige Haber-Curran (Wiley, 2015). This book provides a curriculum to help students in K–12 foster 19 emotionally intelligent leadership skills.

Inspiring the Best in Students by Jonathan Erwin (ASCD, 2010). Designed to be used with students K–12, it extends the social-emotional curriculum explained in this book, helping students gain a better understanding of themselves and others, and, through an extended social-skills section, how to get along better in a variety of social contexts.

The Leader in Me: How Schools Around the World Are Inspiring Greatness, One Child at a Time by Stephen R. Covey, Sean Covey, Muriel Summers, and David. K. Hatch (Simon & Schuster, 2014). Filled with success stories of student leadership, this book shows teachers how to use Stephen R. Covey's proven 7 Habits to help kids of all ages be more effective, more goal oriented, and more successful.

National Youth Leadership Council (www.nylc.org). The NYLC is a national nonprofit organization providing a support network, resources, and conferences intended to encourage youth leadership initiatives.

Teambuilding with Teens: Activities for Leadership, Decision Making, and Group Success by Mariam G. MacGregor (Free Spirit Publishing, 2008). The excellent selection of activities in this book can enhance team-building and group communication with groups in grades 6–12.

TEENERSHIP: Leadership for Teens by Randall Mitchell (Xlibris Corporation, 2013). This book, to be used with middle and high school students, provides approaches and metaphors that teach personal responsibility and help students perceive themselves as leaders.

Printable Forms

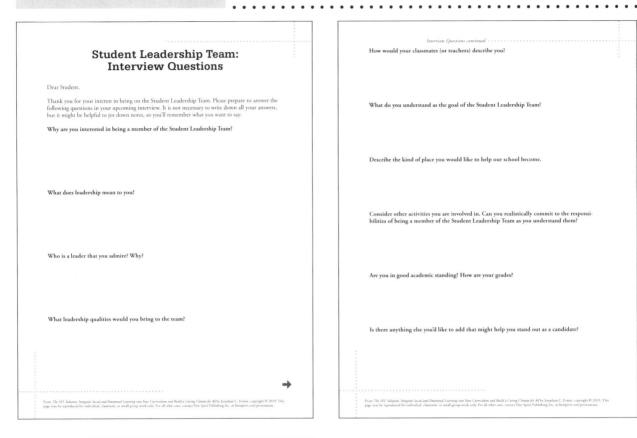

Student Leadership Team: Interview Questions

Dear Student,

Thank you for your interest in being on the Student Leadership Team. Please prepare to answer the following questions in your upcoming interview. It is not necessary to write down all your answers, but it might be helpful to jot down notes, so you'll remember what you want to say.

Why are you interested in being a member of the Student Leadership Team?

What does leadership mean to you?

Who is a leader that you admire? Why?

What leadership qualities would you bring to the team?

Interview Questions continued

How would your classmates (or teachers) describe you?

What do you understand as the goal of the Student Leadership Team?

Describe the kind of place you would like to help our school become.

Consider other activities you are involved in. Can you realistically commit to the responsibilities of being a member of the Student Leadership Team as you understand them?

Are you in good academic standing? How are your grades?

Is there anything else you'd like to add that might help you stand out as a candidate?

Student Leadership Team: Parent Permission

Dear Parent or Guardian,

Your child has been recommended by faculty—and is interested in applying—for a position on a new Student Leadership Team at our school. The purpose of this team is to empower students to make a positive difference in the school climate, helping create a safe, connected culture of excellence. They will learn leadership skills, make presentations to their peers, learn important social-emotional skills, and have the opportunity to mentor younger students and/or mediate conflicts.

Your child would be required to attend all training days, including a full day in August (or a Saturday in early September) and monthly after- (or before-) school meetings. She or he would miss classes about one day a month on average. It will be your child's responsibility to make up missed assignments and remain academically sound. Maintaining a B average is required for continued membership on the team.

I will be holding interviews next week. If your child is not selected this year, he or she will have other opportunities in the future.

Please sign and return to me the permission slip below if you would like your child to be considered for the Student Leadership Team.

Sincerely,
[your name]
[your phone number]
[your email address]

✂ -

I, _____ (parent or guardian's name), hereby give permission for

my child _____ (child's name) to be considered for membership

on the _____ (your school's name) Student Leadership Team.

_____   _____
Signature   Date

See digital content for full-size reproducible pages

Part 2

Teaching Social-Emotional Skills

7

Introducing **Social-Emotional Learning** to Your Students

While creating a set of shared values through your school's touchstone and introducing those values into the classroom in various ways is an important foundation to improving your school's climate, teaching social-emotional skills gives students the capacity to align their behavior with those values. These skills include self-awareness, the ability to focus, self-control, self-regulation, and social skills like the ability to empathize, actively listen, and cooperate. They are key to helping students behave in a way that aligns with their school touchstone's values.

Teaching SEL

If we compare teaching students to be responsible, respectful, and caring to coaching them to becoming skilled athletes or teaching them to be excellent readers, we can see the importance of teaching skills. Athletes need to develop hand-eye coordination, learn how to condition themselves, and analyze their performance based on specific criteria. Readers first need to understand letters, then phonemes; they learn vocabulary, gain word attack skills, and so on. We don't just tell them, "Be athletic" or "Be literate." We teach them step by step the skills they need to be those things, and we support them until they learn them.

Similarly, as educators, we can't just tell students to "Be respectful" or "Be responsible" until they understand what it means to be those things, how to be them, and—just as important—why to be them.

Social-emotional learning is the process through which students acquire the knowledge, attitudes, and skills to:

- identify and manage their emotions
- set and achieve positive goals
- demonstrate caring and concern for others
- make responsible decisions
- handle interpersonal situations effectively

Who Does What

This chapter provides specific strategies for teaching students important social-emotional information and skills. It is primarily designed for classroom teachers and educators who work directly with groups of young people.

Classroom Teachers

If you teach third grade or higher, follow the activities, lessons, and community meetings in the order they're presented. For teachers of kindergarten through second grade, I recommend teaching the behavioral car (pages 86–91) in terms your students will understand, perhaps through a short lesson using the "Behavioral Car" handout (see the thumbnail on page 93) as a visual (print out or display on the whiteboard). You can then skip the rest of the activities and discussions in this chapter and go directly to Chapter 8. In secondary settings, ELA or social studies are usually the most logical class in which to conduct SEL lessons because SEL concepts are so easily integrated into the core curriculum of those subjects.

Most of the activities, lessons, and community meetings in this chapter will last about 20 minutes, with a few going as long as 30 minutes. For elementary students, 20 to 30 minutes is about as long as you'll want to spend on SEL lessons in a given day. Students in grades 7–12 can stay focused and interested for up to an hour. Therefore—in this chapter as well as the other chapters in Part 2—elementary teachers will likely teach one lesson a day every day while secondary teachers can combine two and sometimes three activities into one class-length meeting.

The chapters in Part 2 proceed as if you are doing a whole-school climate initiative and have created a school touchstone. It works just as well if you are doing a smaller initiative, such as in a single classroom; prepare ahead of time to substitute pertinent vocabulary (such as changing "school" to "classroom") and make any other adjustments you find necessary.

School Leaders

The role of principals and other administrators (whoever is leading the school climate initiative) is to provide teachers with the resources and time to plan SEL lessons and to make teachers accountable for teaching SEL. Give this subject as much emphasis as academic subjects by requiring SEL lesson plans, observing whenever possible, and including SEL in the yearly professional review process.

Many adults can also benefit from learning and practicing social-emotional skills. Therefore, it is highly beneficial for school leaders to lead their staff through many of the activities and lessons of the chapters in Part 2 of this book during faculty meetings, department meetings, and conference days. The staff members will not only gain awareness of the SEL skills themselves, but they will have experienced the activities firsthand and will, therefore, be better equipped to teach them to students.

Parent workshops involving SEL can also be quite valuable. They increase parent involvement and help support what you are teaching their children at school about self-control and getting along. Finally, the entire school community using a shared language and set of social-emotional skills will increase a sense of connectedness, contributing significantly to the positive school climate and culture.

Why SEL Matters

Think of a student you have taught or are currently teaching who has the cognitive ability to succeed or even excel in school, but because of an inability to manage emotions, control impulses, persevere, self-motivate, focus, or get along with others, underperforms or simply shuts down and gives up when faced with academic challenges. These students' struggles in school frequently lead to frustration and anger, and subsequently result in insubordination, disruption of the classroom, aggression toward other students and/or teachers, or even dropping out. The impact of these problem behaviors on the classroom and school climate can be highly destructive, affecting all students' (and teachers') sense of safety, school connectedness, and learning (or ability to teach). Implementing academic interventions alone may only serve to increase the frustration these students and their teachers experience.

What these students need are the intrapersonal and interpersonal knowledge and skills to enable them to get out of their own way and succeed, not only in school but later in life. They need social-emotional learning (SEL).

A hard (and growing) body of evidence shows the positive impact of SEL on students. One compelling large-scale study was conducted by the Collaborative for Academic, Social, and Emotional Learning (CASEL), the nation's leading nonprofit organization researching and advancing the teaching of academic, social, and emotional skills. This meta-analysis of 213 school-based, universal SEL programs involved 270,034 kindergarten through high school students in urban, suburban, and rural settings. It found that in schools that implement SEL, statistically significant improvement occurred in the following areas:

- social and emotional skills (sometimes termed SQ and EQ)
- attitudes toward self, others, and school
- pro-social behaviors
- conduct problems
- emotional distress (anger, anxiety, and depression)
- academic achievement

Notably, SEL integration yielded an average gain on achievement test scores of 11 percentile points, and some schools in the study achieved gains up to 17 percentile points.[1] The academic impact alone may be reason enough to implement SEL.

But the implications of an effective SEL program go beyond the academic results. What SEL can do to promote a school climate with fewer behavioral problems, reduced stress, better relationships, and more positive attitudes makes SEL an essential component of overall school improvement.

The Elements of an Effective SEL Program

According to CASEL, an effective SEL program has the following four characteristics encapsulated in the acronym SAFE. SAFE stands for sequenced, active, focused, and explicit.[2]

Sequenced. Having a step-by-step teaching approach, breaking general learning outcomes into smaller segments, which provide students with opportunities to make connections between the smaller parts.

Active. Using student-centered activities and discussions to teach the concepts and skills.

Focused. Sufficient time and attention is devoted to learning the concepts and skills.

Explicit. Clear and specific learning objectives are preferred, rather than general goals.

The concepts and strategies included in this chapter are intentionally aligned with the SAFE elements. They are:

Sequenced. The activities and community meetings explained are meant to be administered in the order presented here, with some developmental exceptions as noted.

Active. The strategies involve both active learning and engaging community discussions. While an occasional lecture is necessary, all the concepts in this chapter and the next involve active learning.

Focused. Dedicate specific time to teaching the SEL concepts and skills. They should not be taught only when it's convenient (such as the day after a test or before a long weekend), but planned into the daily or weekly agenda on a consistent basis. For elementary students, the beginning of each day would be an ideal time to integrate SEL. At the secondary level, teachers should integrate SEL lessons into content, focusing on SEL at least once every week or two.

Explicit. The specific behavioral learning objectives are listed before each strategy. It's important to share those expectations with students.

In general, the strategies explained in this book provide some of the most important concepts and skills students need to:

- understand and identify their emotions
- self-regulate (manage stress, anger, frustration)
- control impulses
- increase self-efficacy
- identify emotions in others
- take others' perspective
- empathize
- understand what people have in common
- appreciate differences

All of these skills will increase students' self-control and ability to get along with others, skills that are essential to increasing a school climate based on physical and emotional safety, order, and sense of community.

The Behavioral Car Metaphor

The first concept to teach students of all ages is the metaphor of the "behavioral car." Metaphors, as most educators know, are excellent teaching tools. Comparing something that students already understand to something they are not as familiar with can help them acquire or gain insight into new information or concepts. For example, in teaching the vocabulary word *insight,* teachers use the metaphor of a lightbulb being switched on.

---

[1] Durlak, J.A., et al, 2011.
[2] Weissberg, R.P., et al, 2015. Used with permission from CASEL.

The car is a useful metaphor because, while most students may not understand the workings of the internal combustion engine, almost all know that cars need fuel and have a steering wheel, four wheels, and dashboard gauges and lights. That is really all they need to help them understand something that they are not as well-versed in—SEL. The metaphor is concrete enough for kindergartners yet interesting enough for older students.

LESSON

The Behavioral Car Metaphor

Students will learn that controlling our behavior is like driving a car:

- We are constantly *choosing* our behavior (or direction). Everything we do, with few exceptions, is our choice.

- Every choice has a consequence, either good, bad, or neutral (getting us closer, moving us away, or sitting still in terms of reaching our goals or destination).

- Despite hardships, difficulties, and adversity (bad weather, poor roads, or engine problems), people can still achieve success (arrive at their destination).

Time Required: About 20 minutes

Materials Needed: An image of the behavioral car projected as a slide or hung up as a poster. See the thumbnail of handout on page 93.

Deliver the following comments, feeling free to change any language to fit your situation or your own personal style.

As you know, we are trying our best to make our school a place where everyone wants to be and learn. We've all been involved in creating our touchstone and deciding on our school values: [List the values]. Today we're going to start learning some information and skills that will help us achieve our goal.

One of the best ways to learn something new is through an analogy or a metaphor, comparing something we're learning to something we already know. In this case, we're going to compare people and their behaviors to a car and to driving. Even if you've never driven a car, you've seen your parents or others driving since you were little and know enough about cars for our purposes here.

Learning about behavior through this metaphor of driving a car will help us have more control over our own thoughts, words, and actions, which will help us better achieve our own goals ["have a better day" for younger students] and help us get along better and bring alive the values of [list touchstone values again].

Present the image of the behavioral car.

What do we use cars for? Yes, to get to places where we want to go. In a similar way, people use behavior to get what they want: Whether it's opening the freezer for ice cream or studying hard for a test, we use our thoughts, words, and actions to "go where we want to go"—to use the driving metaphor, to reach a desired destination.

Just like sometimes people use their cars for short trips, like to the grocery store or the mall, we all behave or act in ways that get us short-term goals ["things we want right away," for younger students]. These are things like studying for a quiz, grabbing a snack, and texting a friend. Sometimes, we get in the car for long trips, like vacations or visits to relatives. These long trips represent medium or long-term goals, things like getting on the varsity team, graduating or going to college, being a responsible and caring person, opening a successful business, having a successful marriage and happy family, etc. [For younger students: "doing well in school; having good friends; being a scientist, artist, football player, or teacher; and having a happy life."]

Sometimes when people are driving, they get distracted or lost on their way to wherever they're going. People's behavior is like that. Sometimes the things we do, think, or say do not get us closer to the goals we have or things we want. For example, we might want friends but say mean things and laugh at people's mistakes. Or we might want good grades but play video games instead of doing homework.

Finishing

Complete this lesson by stating:

We all agreed that we want to demonstrate [name your touchstone values]. Learning about the behavioral car will help us achieve these values. And it will help each of you achieve your short- and long-term goals.

ACTIVITY

The Iron Fist

Students will gain an understanding that all significant behavior (everything they think, say, and do) is a choice, they can't "make" anyone do anything; and no one can "make" them do, think, or say (or even feel) anything.

Time Required: About 20 minutes

Materials Needed: A one-minute timer

Getting Ready

Explain to students that the activity they are about to experience will teach them an extremely important connection between the behavioral car and their choices. You will discuss this point after the activity.

The Activity

Pair students, assigning partners who are not best buddies and who will, therefore, be less likely to go off task. Ask students to sit next to their partners.

Next, tell them to greet their partner and decide (in no more than a few seconds) who will be partner A in the activity and who will be partner B. Explain that partner A's job is very simple—to make a fist and keep it closed, no matter what, for one minute. Ask them to make their fist now and give you a commitment to keep it shut.

Partner B's job is to persuade partner A to open his fist, using any means possible—almost. The exception is that there can be no physical contact. Encourage students to consider what they have done in the past to get what they want from family members and friends. Some of those strategies might work here. They will need to be persistent and keep trying. If one thing doesn't work, try something else.

Check to make sure everyone understands their role and give them the signal to begin. Observe the different strategies that B partners use to persuade their A partners.

After one minute, give the signal to stop and ask how many B partners were successful in getting their A partner to open their first. If you have gotten a commitment from the A partners, the number of successful B partners will be few. Have a class discussion about what strategies were successful and what strategies people tried that were not successful.

Share the handout "Persuasive Techniques" (see the thumbnail on page 93) and connect the strategies students used with these general persuasive techniques.

Ask students to turn to their partners and each share one thing they learned about choices and behavior from this activity. After about one minute, ask the pairs to share their thoughts with the group. Listen for students to make the following points and highlight them. If they don't bring these up themselves, make sure you draw them out from the students or simply tell them:

- We can't make anyone do anything if they choose not to.
- No one can make you do anything if you choose not to.
- If we open our fist (allow someone to influence us) it is because we wanted something, but it was still our choice.

Finishing

Make connections between what students learned through "The Iron Fist" to the behavioral car metaphor, saying something like:

When people drive real cars, they are constantly adjusting the steering wheel, accelerator, brakes, and so forth as they maneuver through traffic. Similarly, in our daily activity and social interactions, we are constantly choosing what we do and what we say as we maneuver through our day. Our next activity and discussion will show us just how many choices we make every day.

It is important that students understand human beings *choose* their significant behavior. This is essential to their learning the concepts of personal and social responsibility, which you will introduce in the following community meetings. Hold these meetings on consecutive days to help drive home the points that despite the influences and challenges in our lives, we are in control of our behavioral cars, we make our own choices.

COMMUNITY MEETING

"I Have to . . ."

Students will gain an understanding that everything they do, except basic physical functions, is their choice. Choices have consequences (both good and bad). When they choose to obey parents, listen to teachers, and follow other adults it is because:

- They know these adults have their best interests in mind.
- They want to achieve positive consequences.
- They want to avoid negative consequences.

But they are still making the choice.

Hand out copies of the "Things I Have to Do Worksheet" (see thumbnail on page 93) to everyone in class and have them complete the worksheet before getting into the community meeting circle.

Define

Ask students: What are things that you have to do that you have no choice about at school or at home?

Students will list things like go to school, do homework, do chores at home, go to sports practice, breathe, eat, take a shower, go to the bathroom, sleep, play video games, and so on. Record their answers on the board.

Personalize

Go down the list and ask about obvious exceptions to some of the things they said they "have to do." For example:

- Have you ever missed a day of school because you weren't feeling well, or maybe because you went on a family trip?
- Have you ever skipped a chore at home or disobeyed something an adult told you to do?

Of course, many hands go up. You could say, "Well, if you *had* to go to school and had no choice in the matter, we'd all have perfect attendance."

Challenge

- Why, then, does it *seem* like it's not a choice?

Students will inevitably mention getting behind in work, getting in trouble at home or at school, not "being smart," and other reasons. Make the point that these things are called consequences. Ask:

- Are consequences always bad? What's an example of a choice with positive consequences? How about an example of a choice with painful or negative consequences?
- What are the positive consequences of going to school?

Continue through the list you made earlier and discuss whether it is possible to choose each of the things students listed (and the positive and negative consequences involved). It will turn out there are very few things that we have no choice about. (Even eating is an option. But the choice not to eat has dire consequences.) Usually the only items left on the list that one truly *has to* do are behaviors connected to the autonomic nervous system: breathing, sleeping, heart beating, and other autonomic physical functions.

Finishing

After the discussion, summarize what you have discussed about choices and consequences. Ask how this discussion might relate to responsibility? Discuss both personal and social responsibility.

Students will conclude that we do, in fact, choose almost all that we do and say. They will be reminded of the connection between behavior and consequences, both positive and negative. And they may also conclude (with some guidance for younger students) that they may not always intend the consequences of their actions, but whether they are intended or not, people are responsible for their behavior and the consequences.

If students don't make these conclusions, ask questions to draw out these points, telling them if necessary.

COMMUNITY MEETING

Overcoming Adversity

This is a good follow-up meeting to the previous discussion. Students will learn that while everything we do is our choice, not all roads or models of cars are equal. In other words, each person is born into a unique life circumstance. Everyone's personal "Road of Life" is different. Some have more twists and turns than others; some have worn out patches or even huge potholes. While all human beings have equal value, they don't have equal opportunities. However, what they do have in common is a mind and a will. Despite the challenges we face in our lives, we can overcome adversity and achieve success. Despite the car we drive and the roads we may have to drive on, with perseverance and grit we can still arrive at our destination.

Define

- What is adversity?
- What kind of adversity do people in the world experience?
- What can adversity do to people?

Personalize

- Do you know any people—personally or not—who have overcome problems in their lives? Who? What did they overcome? How?
- Can people always control the things that happen to them? What can we control?

If students need help with this question, prompt them toward answers such as "our response, our actions, our words, our *attitude*."

Challenge

- What can we learn about ourselves from this discussion?
- How can the things we discussed today make us stronger?

ACTIVITY

The Contamination Game

In traffic, one driver's choices have the capacity to influence many other drivers. One person's distraction could lead to an accident that creates a massive traffic jam. Similarly, as we journey through our day, in our constant interactions with others, our choices can help keep traffic moving smoothly (everyone working, learning, and getting along) or lead to fender-benders, head-on collisions, and major delays. The following activity helps students understand this point. Students should learn the following points by the end of the activity:

- Whether we are aware of it or not, we influence others through our attitude and behavior.
- One person's behavior or attitude can negatively or positively impact the whole classroom or school.

Caution: Don't tell participants the name of the game until it's over.

Time Required: 20–30 minutes

Materials Needed: One index card for every student; write the number 1 or 2 on each card except one; on that final card, write a 0 (zero)

Getting Ready

Distribute an index card to each student, telling them it's important to keep their numbers to themselves. It's particularly important for the zero card to be kept private, so you may want to give it to a responsible student.

The Activity

After passing out the cards and telling students to keep their numbers a secret for now, explain that when you say "Go!" their job is to walk up to another student and multiply their two numbers together. You may want to demonstrate this with a student. Tell the group that the answer they get will be the *new number* for both of them. Have them write their new number on their card. Next, they should find another student and multiply their new numbers together. Students should do this as many times as possible.

Say, "Let's see who can get the highest number . . . GO!"

As they are multiplying, mill around the room encouraging them to interact with as many people as possible. Of course, 0 x any number = 0, so soon several zeros will be milling about. Encourage them to keep going. Within three to five minutes, everyone in the room will be a zero.

Finishing

Conclude with a group discussion using the following guidelines. This is the most important part of the activity.

- Ask how many people ended up with zero. Have them raise their hands, then ask how many started out with zero.
- Tell them the name of the game.
- Ask: What can we learn about our classroom based on this activity?
- Ask for specific real-life examples (no names) of how the behavior or attitude of one person or group might contaminate the school through a chain reaction. Of course, the main point is that one person's behavior and/or attitude has the capacity to contaminate everyone.

▪ Have students make up a hypothetical chain reaction starting with one student's response to his or her bad morning. Draw a cartoon representation of the chain reaction on the board.

▪ Ask: Does it ever happen in reverse, where a kind act contaminates others? Here you might mention that humans have a universal tendency toward reciprocity, in other words, returning or passing on a kind act. How might a specific kind act create a chain reaction?

▪ Have students make up a hypothetical chain reaction starting with one student getting really good news in the morning. As with the negative example, draw a representation of this chain on the board so students can visualize and compare the two scenarios.

▪ Ask: What could you do today that might have a positive influence on others?

▪ Consider giving an optional assignment to perform a random act of kindness for someone (and not tell that person).

Close this discussion with a pep talk, emphasizing how much impact they, as individuals or a class or a student body, have to make the classroom, the school—even the world—a better place. For dramatic and humorous effect, play some celebratory music, like the theme to *Star Wars* or *Rocky* or the Olympic fanfare.

Connecting SEL to Curriculum

To help students integrate the basic SEL concepts and skills discussed in this chapter, it can be invaluable to connect SEL to the curriculum. This will enhance both SEL and academics. On the following pages are performance tasks that help integrate this chapter's SEL concepts into the ELA and social studies curriculum in ways that satisfy the Common Core State Standards. Suggestions for connecting to other academic areas are also given. These ideas are meant to be a springboard for you to use, modify, and extend, using your understanding of your students and your own creativity.

ELA

Students read a story or view a movie in which the main character overcomes difficult obstacles. Have students write an essay or make a classroom presentation explaining the obstacles the character faced, how he or she overcame them, and what happened next. If you like, have students discuss a difficult obstacle in their own path and how they can overcome it.

Another option is to have students read a story or view a movie in which a character must make a difficult choice. Have students write an essay or make a classroom presentation explaining the choice the character had to make, what was at stake, what he or she chose, and the consequences of his or her actions.

Student presentations can take a wide variety of forms: a panel discussion, a mock TV news report, a multimedia presentation, a mock interview with the character, role-playing the character in a dramatic scene, or role-playing the character giving a speech about his or her story.

Social Studies

Students research a famous historical person who overcame adversity and write an essay or give a classroom presentation about the person that discusses what his or her challenge was, how the challenge was overcome, and what happened as a result.

An alternative is to have students examine the adversity that various countries or groups of people have experienced in history or in the world today and write an essay or make a presentation.

Another option is to have students research a historical figure who faced a difficult and courageous decision, what choice that person made, and what the consequences were. Or write an essay or make a presentation in which the student imagines what might have happened if the person had made a different choice.

For all of these options, student presentations could be made in any of the forms listed in the ELA section.

Other Curriculum Connections

Science. Have students study scientists who struggled to have their new or controversial theories accepted.

Math. Students research a famous mathematician who struggled personally (John Forbes Nash, for example); or students might discuss how what they've learned about overcoming adversity in ELA can help them overcome difficulties in math.

Art. Have students create a likeness of a person who overcame adversity, or a rendering of "overcoming adversity" in any medium.

Music. Each student chooses a famous musician who overcame adversity using their musical abilities. Examples include Stevie Wonder (who was born blind) and Ray Charles (who became blind as a child), Ludwig van Beethoven (who eventually went deaf), John Coltrane (who was addicted to heroin and alcohol), Rick Allen (heavy metal drummer who lost an arm and retaught himself to drum with just one), and Django Reinhardt (who was severely injured in an accident and retaught himself to play guitar).

Final Thoughts About Introducing SEL

If you have led your students through all the activities and discussions in this chapter, students should have learned:

1. We have a choice in all significant behavior.

2. Every choice we make has positive and negative (and neutral) consequences, both natural and imposed.

3. We are, therefore, responsible for the impact our choices have on ourselves (personal responsibility) and others (social responsibility).

This fundamental understanding is crucial to learning to accept responsibility for our lives, both for our successes as well as our mistakes and failures. When students can do that, they are ready to learn about what motivates their behavior, what they have in common with others, and what helps make them the unique individuals that they are. That's what Chapter 8 is about.

Printable Forms

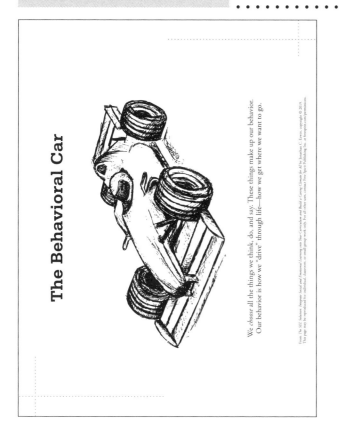

The Behavioral Car

We *choose* all the things we think, do, and say. These things make up our behavior. Our behavior is how we "drive" through life—how we get where we want to go.

Persuasive Techniques

- Asking
- Reasoning
- Telling
- Rewarding (bribing)
- Appealing to the relationship
- Negotiating
- Tricking
- Reverse psychology
- Guilting (shaming)
- Withdrawing affection
- Whining

- Nagging
- Yelling
- Threatening
- Criticizing
- Imposing consequences
- Verbally attacking
- Punishing
- Humiliating
- Physical intimidation
- Physical force

Things I Have to Do

At School	At Home	Other Places

See digital content for full-size reproducible pages

8

The Five Basic
Human Needs
The Fuel for the Car

The Five Basic Human Needs, as explained by world-renowned psychiatrist and educator William Glasser, are the root of all human behavior. An individual's behavior, according to Glasser, is his or her attempt to satisfy the need for *survival* (safety, security, and physical needs), *love & belonging* (acceptance, positive relationships), *power* (competence, knowledge), *freedom* (autonomy), and/or *fun* (play, pleasure).

When members of a school community understand the Five Basic Human Needs, they can better understand their own and others' behavior. Understanding that we are all driven by the same basic needs creates a sense of connection and empathy, helping build a more caring, connected, and compassionate school climate.

When students understand that we are all intrinsically motivated by the Five Basic Needs, students gain other benefits, such as:

- self-awareness

- a better understanding of the internal source of their own behavior

- an appreciation of how human beings are similar in important ways

- an understanding of diverse personalities, talents, abilities, likes, dislikes, and personal identities

- a greater sense of acceptance and empathy

- an appreciation of diversity

- a common language with teachers, which will improve communication, relationships, and problem-solving

In turn, teachers, counselors, and school leaders gain:

- a better understanding of their students' and staff's individual needs

- a common language to use with students and staff for positive, effective behavior or performance management

- specific ways to integrate student-centered, high-interest (it's about them) SEL curriculum into your state standards or the CCSS (Common Core State Standards) at different developmental levels

This chapter connects the Five Basic Human Needs to the behavioral car metaphor and guides teachers, counselors, and principals through the process of teaching the concepts to students and staff. All of the lessons, activities, and community meetings are meant to be completed in the order they appear and can be used with students of all ages (sometimes with modifications as needed) and adults. In fact, before teachers begin to conduct the activities in this chapter, I recommend that principals lead the faculty and staff through them first. This will give teachers clear expectations of how to employ the strategies with their own students, but more importantly, it will help adults in the school get to know one another better, build relationships, gain insight into their own and others' behavior and personalities, and improve communication among staff by sharing a common language.

Introducing the Five Basic Human Needs

Before beginning these lessons, you may want to review what students learned about the behavioral car in the last chapter. Remind them that everything we think, say, and do comes from inside us, and that we choose all of these things. Explain that next they will learn what it is that fuels our car. (For older students and adults, explain that this means the source of our internal motivation.)

ACTIVITY

Stranded

Students will identify the things they think they need in preparation for a lesson on the Five Basic Human Needs.

Time Required: About 15 minutes

Materials Needed: A copy of the "Stranded" handout (see the thumbnail on page 106) for each student; a whiteboard

The Activity

Before the meeting, distribute the "Stranded" handout, read the directions aloud, and have the students complete it. Consider playing some reggae or Hawaiian guitar music in the background while they work. (With older students, you might want to remind them about school-appropriate responses.)

Assign partners or ask students to turn to a neighbor and discuss their lists of the 10 items they would have the genie transport. Give them about five minutes.

Next, discuss the answers as a large group. You might limit responses to one or two items per student. Assign a student to record all of the answers on the board, leaving a little room next to each item. There will be some agreement (friends, parents) and without a doubt, some laughter.

LESSON

The Five Basic Human Needs

After this lesson, students will be able to name the Five Basic Human Needs, define each of them, and give examples of how they meet their needs at school and at home.

Time Required: About 30 minutes

Materials Needed: One copy of the advanced organizer "My Needs Circle" (see the thumbnail on page 106) for each student

The Lesson

Pass out the "My Needs Circle" handout, but ask students not to do anything with it yet. Explain that this is an advanced organizer that will help them understand the information they are going to receive in terms of their own lives.

In this lesson, you will discuss very briefly one of the basic needs, then stop to give students a few minutes to fill out part of the handout. Then you will talk about the next basic need and again give students time to write, continuing like this until you've covered all of the Five Basic Human Needs. Adjust the language and content of these mini-lessons to best fit your audience.

Say:

All human behavior is driven by Five Basic Human Needs. It's like we have five separate fuel tanks that provide all the energy for our behavioral cars.

The first need is to survive, which includes the physical needs for food, water, oxygen, sleep, safety, shelter, and warmth. But human beings are not only concerned with our immediate hunger, thirst, and safety. We think about the future and want to feel a sense of security. We lock doors, protect our valuables, and invest for retirement. Most of us try to eat right and exercise, investing in our health. All of these things give us the sense that we'll be secure in our future. Another aspect of the need for survival is the need for order. Order provides people with a sense of control and well-being. We organize our living spaces, our desks, our lockers, and so on because doing these things helps us feel a sense of order in our lives.

In the Survival rectangle at the bottom of your page, write down the names of some people who have taken care of you physically; taught you how to take care of yourself or get into shape; or have taught you how to organize your room or your locker. Next, in the same rectangle, write down some things you do to take care of yourself physically or financially. Finally, write down a couple of places that feel safe and secure.

Allow a few minutes for students to fill in their handouts, then continue.

The other four needs are not physical—they are psychological needs, which are important to our sense of well-being and happiness. The first is the need for **love and belonging.** This includes the need for positive relationships with family and friends, feeling accepted, being part of a group or community, and helping and caring for others. It's the need for friendship, meaningful relationships, and social acceptance.

In the Love & Belonging quadrant of your needs circle, write down names of people who are important to you at home, at school, nearby, and faraway. Next, write down the things you do with others or to connect with others such as attend a place of worship, have family reunions and celebrations, play on a sports team, play in the band or orchestra, hang out, text message, or use social media. Finally, write down some places where you feel particularly connected, for example, at school, at home, on the playing field, on stage, and so on.

Allow a few minutes for students to fill in their handouts, then continue.

The next need is the need to gain **power.** This need can be misunderstood because people often think of examples of famous figures who abused their power, such as Ghenghis Kahn and Adolf Hitler. However, if humans didn't pursue power, we might still be living in caves—or even be extinct. Think of the need for power as the human need to make positive changes in our world. Power includes curiosity to learn and a desire to feel competent (or to be good at things), to be listened to, to be recognized for our strengths, to feel valued, to make a difference. It is this drive to have an impact on our world that has led us to the scientific, cultural, and technological advances and physical comforts that we enjoy today. Power helps strengthen our self-esteem, gives us a sense of purpose, and allows us to feel personal success. Using this definition of power, other historical or contemporary figures may come to mind: Mahatma Gandhi, Marie Curie, Nelson Mandela, Albert Einstein, Mother Teresa, Bill Gates, Oprah Winfrey.

In the Power quadrant of your handout, write down the names of some people such as parents, family, coaches, teachers, and friends, who have taught you important information, skills, or life lessons. Next, write down things you do that you are good at or proud of, such as being a good student, being a good friend, being good at soccer, excelling in math, or holding a black belt in Tae Kwon Do. Write down some things at which you are trying to get better or improve, too. Finally, write down places or groups where you feel like you make a difference or where you are valued, such as your home, this classroom, a religious organization, a sports team, a dance group or musical organization, or a school club.

Allow a few minutes for students to fill in their handouts, then continue.

The next need is the need to be **free.** This need, which people all over the world have struggled for (and continue to struggle for), includes the drive to be independent, to have autonomy, to exercise free will, to be creative, to move about as we wish, and to be ourselves.

In the Freedom quadrant of your needs circle, write down the names of people around whom you feel free to be yourself. Next, write down things you do that help you feel a sense of freedom or independence, such as playing outside, running, swinging, surfing the Internet, going to the movies, hiking, or going to the beach. Finally, list places where you feel particularly free, such as at home, on stage, in front of a TV, or when reading a good book.

For younger students, who may have a hard time with the concept of feeling free, ask them to list places where they might choose to be, if they could choose anywhere.

Allow a few minutes for students to fill in their handouts, then continue.

The fifth need is to have **fun.** It is the need for play, laughter, and enjoyment. For all mammals, including humans, two objectives are achieved through play—social bonding and learning.

Ask students for examples of animals that play and to guess what life skills they might be learning (hunting, eluding predators, cooperation, social rank).

In the Fun quadrant of your needs circle, write the names of people who make you laugh or who you just enjoy being with, such as family members, friends, and other peers. Next, write things you do that are really fun, such as games or sports you play, movies or TV shows you watch, socializing, and playing with a pet. Finally, write down some places that you think of as fun, such as school, a playground or park, an amusement park, a friend's house, the beach, and your home.

Finishing

Conclude this activity by explaining to students they will have a chance to share what they wrote in their needs circles.

Helping Students Apply the Five Basic Human Needs to Their Lives

The following learner-centered activities provide students opportunities to discover things about others, helping build a more connected climate.

ACTIVITY

Stranded Connection

In this activity, students will connect the things they chose to take with them in the "Stranded" activity with the Five Basic Human Needs. They will understand that while people may not be aware of their needs, per se, needs drive our behavior all the time.

Time Required: About 20 minutes

Materials Needed: Each student's filled-out "Stranded" handout

The Activity

Now that the whole class has a basic understanding of the Five Basic Human Needs, return to their "Stranded" lists and guide them through categorizing the different items they wanted transported in terms of what basic need or needs each item might satisfy. You might begin by taking a few examples from different students' sheets and talking through which of the basic needs the examples satisfy. Then have students go down their lists and write "S" for Survival, "L & B" for Love & Belonging, "P" for Power, "FR" for Freedom, or "FN" for Fun next to each item.

Finishing

Discuss the difference between wants and needs. I may *want* to go to Disneyland, but I don't *need* to go there. What I might need is freedom and fun. Ask, is it possible to have freedom and fun without going to Disneyland? Of course.

Explain that people can choose to be angry and frustrated because they are not getting what they want, but if they choose, they can get at least some of what they need. To meet my need of fun and freedom, I could go to a movie. Is that Disneyland? No, but it meets my needs. For an added bit of fun, and if possible, play the Rolling Stones song, "You Can't Always Get What You Want."

ACTIVITY

Concentric Circles

Concentric Circles is an excellent activity for developing relationships among the various stakeholders in the school as well as for a variety of other purposes. In faculty meetings, the principal can use it for discussing school issues, sharing information, or creative problem-solving. In the classroom, teachers can use it for discussing prior knowledge at the beginning of a learning unit, practicing new skills, reviewing, generating writing ideas, book sharing, and more. For participants, this activity provides opportunities for one-on-one conversations, which builds trusting relationships among members of the group. It also provides people with an opportunity to articulate their thoughts before holding a community meeting, thus decreasing their anxiety about embarrassing themselves ("saying something stupid") in front of their peers.

In this case, you'll be using Concentric Circles to dig deeper into the Five Basic Human Needs.

Time Required: About 15 minutes

Materials Needed: Enough space to have the whole group form two circles, one around the other; everyone's completed copy of the "My Needs Circle" handout

Have your students count off by twos (one, two, one, two) and direct the "ones" to stand in a circle (almost shoulder to shoulder) and turn around so they are facing out. Now direct the "twos" to create an outer circle in which each of them is facing one of the "ones."

1. Give the students a simple direction to greet the partner they're facing, such as "Shake hands with the person you are facing and say 'Good morning!'"

2. Next, give the students an icebreaker-type question or problem to discuss and a time parameter. For example, "For the next two minutes, talk about your favorite things to eat."

3. After a minute or two, direct students to shake hands again and say, "Nice talking with you."

4. Have one of the circles move one to three spaces to their right, and repeat the two steps above.

5. After doing icebreaker-type interactions, shift gears by having the members of the circles discuss how they meet one of the Five Basic Human Needs. Have them refer to their "My Needs Circle" handout if needed.

6. Rotate four more times so that students have a chance to talk about all five of the needs with five different classmates.

Finishing

Afterward, let your students sit down and have a class discussion. Ask the class to share some of the things they learned about their classmates and how the ways they meet their needs are similar and different. Ask students how what they learned today can improve classroom relationships.

ACTIVITY

Musical Circles

If you have less room, or if you prefer a less rigidly structured activity, Musical Circles can be substituted for Concentric Circles. It can be used for all the same purposes, including sharing how students' needs are met.

Time Required: 15 minutes

Materials Needed: Students' completed "My Needs Circle" handout; a way to play music that you can easily start and stop

The Activity

First, ask participants to stand with their "My Needs Circle" handouts in hand. When the music starts,

they are to move (or dance) randomly around the room. When the music stops, they freeze and you hold up two, three, or four fingers. Students are to get into groups of two, three, or four with the people near them. Explain that if they can't find the exact number of people for a group, they can raise their hands and you will find them a group.

Next, explain that you will give them a topic to share with their pair or group. They will have one to two minutes to talk about that topic. Remind students to make sure everyone gets a chance to talk. When the music starts again, they will repeat the process. Emphasize that they are to try to get with *different* people each time.

Start the music, wait a few seconds, and stop it. When students freeze, hold up two to four fingers and tell them to discuss how they met one of the Five Basic Human Needs. They can refer to their "My Needs Circle" handouts. Make sure to allow enough time for everyone in the group to share (a pair might need a minute or two, a group of four would need twice that long).

Repeat the process four times, asking them to share about a different one of the needs each time.

Finishing

Once participants have returned to their seats, ask the group to share some of the things they learned about their peers and how they meet their needs in similar as well as different ways. Ask students how what they learned today can improve classroom relationships.

LESSON

The Quality World— Our Personal GPS

You will teach students that while all human beings are driven by the same Five Basic Human Needs, each person has his or her own way of satisfying those needs. In William Glasser's terminology, all the unique and specific people, places, and things that satisfy a person's needs make up that person's Quality World. In terms of the behavioral car metaphor, we can say that these things are like our Personal GPS, filled with "destinations" (people, places, things, activities) that we've learned will (or we believe will) satisfy our needs. Because Part 2 of this book is centered on the behavioral car metaphor, I use the GPS analogy in this lesson and subsequent activities, but if you prefer, you can use Quality World instead.

Time Required: 15 minutes

Materials Needed: poster or projected image of the "My Personal GPS" (see the thumbnail on page 106)

The Lesson

Explain that the Personal GPS is an individual's ideal world—a map of everything he or she values. Remind students of the things they wrote on their "My Needs Circle" handouts. Those are things they value, and they are like pins or destinations on their own Personal GPS. Show students the image of "My Personal GPS" and point out the different destinations on the map.

Another way of looking at the Personal GPS is like a personal photo album made up of all the people, places, activities, and objects that an individual believes add quality to his or her life (meets his or her needs). But the Personal GPS also includes an individual's values, beliefs, and moral code. All these destinations (or pins) show up on the GPS map. They are all things we've learned will (or we believe will) satisfy our needs.

Characteristics of the Personal GPS:

- Every person, thing, activity, or place in our GPS is something we find highly needs-satisfying.

- The map is dynamic. When we have a new positive experience, we may add a new person, place, or activity to it (a new pin).

- Not everything in a person's Personal GPS is necessarily "Good" or "Right." It just feels good. Someone may find, for example, that people laugh when he makes fun of others. He might come to put "making fun of others" on his Personal GPS.

- We have shorter GPS destinations (like eating a good pizza), and further-out destinations (like becoming a doctor).

- We have superficial pins (like chocolate) and deeper pins like belief systems (such as Democrat, Republican, Catholic, Muslim, vegan, artist, civil rights activist); values (kindness, responsibility, determination); and morals (what is right and wrong).

- Our ideal self is part of our Personal GPS—the person each of us has the potential to become.

Finishing

Acknowledge that right now the concept of the quality world may seem abstract, but after the next activity, it will be much clearer.

ACTIVITY

Personal GPS Collage

Students of all ages will create a visual representation of their Personal GPS and gain a greater understanding about how the Five Basic Human Needs influence a person's personality and behavior (their own and others').

Time Required: 60-90 minutes (This can be spread out over several days)

Materials Required: Discarded magazines, preferably a few dozen that relate to students' interests (such as music, fashion, sports, entertainment, food), poster board, glue sticks, scissors, markers, glitter glue; if you can find a bunch of old maps to use as background, that can be a fun touch

Getting Ready

Before doing this activity with students, create your own Personal GPS to use as an exemplar. (You can use the "My Personal GPS" handout, but it can be inspiring and helpful for students to see their teacher's real-life example.)

The Activity

Direct students to create a collage using words, photographs, pictures, drawings, decorations, and so forth, that is a visual presentation of their Personal GPS. The collage represents the ways they meet their needs for survival, love & belonging, power, freedom, and fun. They can make their GPS look like an actual GPS screen, with destination pins labeled with images like pop-up icons, or they can make a more traditional collage. Some students may prefer to make a Personal GPS book instead of a collage. Students may want to dedicate different parts of their collage to different needs or scatter them about, but they do need to represent all five needs.

Finishing

When they are done, consider having each student prepare a three- to five-minute presentation for the class and set aside time for everyone to give them. Over the next few weeks, have one student share his or her collage at the beginning of class. (**Note:** It is particularly important to maintain an emotionally safe environment for sharing. Many students invest significant meaning in their collages.)

COMMUNITY MEETING

The Five Basic Human Needs and Personal GPS

In this meeting, you will review the concepts of the Five Basic Human Needs and the Personal GPS. It's a good way to check for understanding of how awareness of these concepts can improve students' own lives, their relationships, and the school or classroom climate.

Time Required: About 30 minutes

Define

- What are the Five Basic Human Needs?
- Why are these needs important? What do they do? (Why do I refer to them as fuel tanks?) How do they affect a person's behavior? (Ideally, students will demonstrate an understanding that the needs are the underlying cause of human behavior—they are why we do what we do as human beings.)
- What is the Personal GPS?
- What is the connection between the Five Basic Human Needs and the Personal GPS?

Personalize

- What did you notice about your needs?
- What did you notice about the way other people meet their needs? (Hopefully, students will notice some overlap, but also some differences.)
- What kinds of quality world pictures do we seem to have in common with others?
- What kinds of quality world pictures are different from others?

Challenge

- What are the benefits of understanding the Five Basic Human Needs and the Personal GPS? Consider benefits for yourself and for your relationships with other people.
- What are the benefits of understanding these concepts for our school or classroom climate?

Answers to the challenge questions will vary, but the following points are important to try to elicit. If they aren't brought up by students, even with guiding questions, explain them yourself.

- They help us understand why we do the things we do.
- Understanding why we do the things we do can help us feel balanced.
- It helps us understand why other people act the way they do.
- These concepts help us see what we all have in common.
- When we understand why other people are acting a certain way, it's easier to be accepting of them.
- The needs and GPS also help us see how we're different on the inside, instead of just how we're different sizes, shapes, complexions, clothes, and so on.
- Understanding these ideas helps us get along better and have a more positive climate at school.

LESSON

Responsible vs. Irresponsible Behavior

In this lesson, students will learn that responsible behavior involves words and actions that satisfy their needs but don't compromise others' ability to satisfy theirs.

Time Required: 15 minutes

Materials Needed: Pen and paper

The Lesson

Provide students with the definition of responsible behavior: Behavior that meets your needs (fills your tanks) without hurting you in any way or depriving someone else of meeting theirs (taking their fuel).

Explain that we are all doing the best we can to satisfy our needs and achieve what's on our Personal GPS. But sometimes the things we do to satisfy our needs hurt us or someone else. Give some hypothetical examples:

- A person might feel powerless, so he calls someone a mean name.

- A student wants to chat with a friend (love & belonging) during class, so she spends the class texting or writing notes.

- Someone wants to get out of going to school (freedom), so he pretends to be sick.

For each hypothetical example, ask why this behavior would not be considered responsible. Who does it impact in a negative way? What could this person do to meet that same need in a responsible way?

After discussing these questions with students, ask them to come up with their own hypothetical examples, identifying the need the person in the example is trying to satisfy, and who the irresponsible behavior affects. Again, ask students to identify more responsible behaviors that would satisfy the same needs.

Say: Being human means being imperfect. We all have our irresponsible moments—times when we say or do something that hurts ourselves or others.

Give a personal example here. I might say that when I was in school, sometimes I joked around in class too much [needing fun], which hurt my ability to do my best and distracted others. What I could have done to meet my need for fun in a more responsible way was to save my jokes for lunch and stay focused on the lesson.

Ask students to write about any behaviors (actions or words) they have exhibited at school or at home that might be considered irresponsible. What can they replace that behavior with that is more responsible but that meets the same need? (**Caution:** It's important that teachers discuss their roles as mandatory reporters before students begin sharing their reflections. You never know what students may divulge.)

Finishing

Collect, read, and make (nonjudgmental) comments on students' reflections before handing them back.

ACTIVITY

The Needs and Social Responsibility (or The Needs-in-a-Bag Activity)

This activity is meant to review the Five Basic Human Needs and help students understand that as we interact in the classroom or at school, we are not only responsible for meeting our own needs, but also for helping others meet theirs. This can be done with groups of five or more students. The only limit to the size of the group is the cost of the materials.

Time Required: 20 minutes

Materials: One small brown-paper lunch bag for each participant; an assortment of five different items that might represent the Five Basic Human Needs—these items should be from the same general category. For example, your category could be candy: Lifesavers representing survival, Three Musketeers representing love & belonging, Sour Patch Kids representing power (to make you grimace), Pop Rocks representing freedom (like Independence Day fireworks in your mouth), and Skittles representing fun.

Or if your category is school supplies, they might be small packs of tissues (survival), paper clips (love & belonging—they hold things together), pencils or pens (power—"the power of the pen"), rubber bands (freedom—they're flexible), and funny eraser heads (fun).

You will need enough of each item so every student will eventually have one of all five items.

Getting Ready

Mix the items together and place a random assortment in each of the bags, varying the items and the number of items. One student may get four of one item and one of another; another might receive only two items in the bag while another has eight.

The Activity

Randomly pass out the bags to the students, asking them not to look inside until you give the signal. Their task is to get one of each of the items (make a list on the board) in their bags. (Explain that when the activity is done, if they want to trade items, they will be allowed to do so, but not right now. Also, if you are using edibles as your items, tell students that any eating will take place *after* the activity.)

Explain to students that during the activity they will need to move around the room, talk with one another, and negotiate with each other so they can achieve the task. Set a five-minute time limit and tell them to start.

Carefully observe the different behaviors the students use to achieve their goal. Some students may need to be reminded to keep their hands to themselves and encouraged to negotiate, rather than take. Once it looks like almost everyone has achieved the goal, hold a mini-celebration (like a funny applause and a *woo-HOO!*). You might allow them a couple minutes to trade, share, and eat.

After this activity, immediately hold the following community meeting, or at your earliest opportunity.

COMMUNITY MEETING

Culmination of Personal GPS

In this meeting, students will learn that in order for everyone to meet their needs in the same space, it will take behaviors like communicating, sharing, negotiating differences, and sometimes giving up something they want.

Time Required: About 20 minutes

Define

- We've been studying the Five Basic Human Needs for some time. How might the items we collected in The Needs-in-a-Bag Activity relate? Discuss the meaning behind each item.

- How did we recently define responsible behavior? (Meeting our needs without harming ourselves or preventing others from meeting their needs.)

Personalize

- How was doing this activity like being a member of a classroom? (Try for the answer that they were all trying to meet their five needs at the same time.)

- How did you or others go about getting the five items, which is like meeting our five basic needs? Make a list of the behaviors you and your peers noticed.

Challenge

- Would you describe these behaviors as responsible or irresponsible? Discuss each one on the list.

- How can we use what we know about the Five Basic Human Needs to have a better sense of community (or get along) in our classroom?

- What we are talking about is called social responsibility. How might we define that?

Discuss how being responsible means not only being responsible for your own well-being, but for the well-being of others as well.

Integrating the Concepts into the ELA and Social Studies Curriculums

The assignments and strategies in this section focus on integrating the Five Basic Human Needs and the Personal GPS into the two subjects to which these ideas most logically connect—English language arts and social studies, subjects that focus on human behavior in literature and history. Each of these assignments and strategies satisfy the Common Core State Standards in ways that engage students. A complete list of the standards addressed is provided at the end of the chapter.

Activities for English Language Arts

Report Writing

Have students write a paragraph explaining the meaning of one of the basic needs and the different ways they meet that need in their lives. For secondary students, this could be expanded into an essay on all five needs or extended to include an oral report. You may consider creating a display of the students' needs circles, GPS collages, and paragraphs.

Comparing and Contrasting

Students compare and contrast their needs circle or GPS collage with that of another student. They first create a Venn diagram and then write an essay (or paragraph) using a point-by-point analysis.

Analyzing Film and Literature

Have students read a fictional or nonfiction story or book, or watch a film, and analyze the needs that various characters are trying to meet through their actions or words. This strategy helps students gain a deeper understanding of how these needs drive human behavior, and it also helps them understand character development and motivation.

Since this is a new approach to analyzing fiction, it is important to begin with a guided practice activity as a class.

Time Required: 45–60 minutes

Materials Needed: A short video clip that your class will find engaging, maybe 10 to 15 minutes long, to analyze as a class; copies of the "Analyzing a Character and Theme Through the Five Basic Human Needs" handout (see the thumbnail on pages 106–107) for everyone in the class.

The Activity

Explain to the class that you will be watching a video clip and carefully observing the behavior of one of the characters to determine the need or needs the character is trying to satisfy and what the desired destinations are on the character's Personal GPS. Play the clip until the character does or says something that seems important to the storyline, and pause the clip. While it's paused, discuss the need or needs the character is trying to satisfy and the GPS destination the character seems to be trying to get to. You will hear a variety of answers. To help connect this discussion to the CCSS, ask the students to provide concrete supporting details from the clip to support their responses. Have students record their answers on the "Analyzing a Character and Theme Through the Five Basic Human Needs" handout.

When you're ready, start the movie again and pause once more at an appropriate spot. Once again, engage the class in discussion about the character's needs and GPS. Track these on the first page of the handout, perhaps on a document projector or on the whiteboard. As the story goes on, trace the character's behavior to see if there is a change in the primary needs driving the character's behavior or any significant change in his or her behavior. What does the character value? What does he or she say or do in the video to lead you to that conclusion?

If you are working with older students, you can take this a step further and ask, how does what this character values help us understand the message or theme the story conveys? As a class, look at the second page of the handout and discuss how the observations you recorded on the first page affect what you feel about the character and how the piece's themes are developed. Fill in the character's goals or values on the page, and then fill in the themes of the video.

You can have students complete one of these forms for their own assignment, or explain to them that they can use the form as a guideline when writing their essays. You may also consider having students work in groups ("Literature Circles") if you prefer.

Refer to the sample filled-out handouts (see the thumbnails on pages 107–108) for additional guidance on this assignment (*The Lion King* sample for younger students and *One Flew Over the Cuckoo's Nest* sample for older students). Distributing this sample to students can help them grasp the requirements.

Activities for Social Studies

The same strategies, activities, and assignments described for ELA on pages 102–103 can be adapted to the social studies classroom. Refer to the corresponding assignment in the previous section for more detail on these assignments as well as handouts to use with them.

Report Writing

Students read about a historical figure and write a report about how this person met his or her basic human needs, based on what they have learned. For secondary students, this could be expanded into an essay on all five needs or extended to include an oral report. Another option is to have students create a needs circle or Personal GPS based on what they've learned.

Comparing and Contrasting

Students research two historical figures who relate in some way. For each figure, they create a needs circle or Personal GPS based on what they've learned and compare and contrast them.

Analyzing Historical Figures or Characters from Historical Fiction

Have students read a work of historical fiction or the biography of a famous person and analyze the needs the characters in the story (or the famous person) tried to meet through their actions or words. Use the same process previously explained in "Analyzing Film and Literature" on page 103.

Assessment

The following assessments are appropriate for both ELA and social studies. After students have completed one or more of the analysis assignments, they will need to demonstrate their understanding that:

1. All human behavior is motivated by the Five Basic Human Needs (to survive, love & belong, gain power, be free, and have fun).

2. We call the specific ways people satisfy their needs (through people, activities, things, ideas, and values) their Personal GPS (or their Quality World).

3. By analyzing a literary character's motivation through the lens of the Five Basic Human Needs and the character's Personal GPS (particularly his or her values), the reader can gain an understanding of the author's theme, message, or lesson.

These learning goals can be demonstrated through a variety of performance tasks. Here are some options.

For all students (adjust expectations according to age and development level):

- Have groups create posters or presentations on their character or historical figure.

- Students act out a significant scene and explain their analysis of the scene in terms of how their character's (or figure's) needs and Personal GPS help the reader understand the story's theme, message, or lesson.

- Students develop a multimedia presentation analyzing their character or historical figure.

For primary students:

- Write a paragraph about what need or needs motivated a character or historical figure and what we can learn from him or her.

For secondary students:

- Write character/theme analysis essays on their character, including concrete textual-based evidence to support their analyses.

- Students create a poem or rap song demonstrating their learning and read or perform it for the class.

- Students write a song, create a painting, or choreograph a dance that illustrates their learning.

- Students create a game (or game show) that demonstrates their learning.

- Students develop a social networking page for their character (a made-up site, not a real one).

Aligning to Common Core State Standards

The following table aligns the activities, strategies, and assignments in this chapter with the broad "Anchor Standards" for the Common Core in ELA, which cover all grades. To read more and get grade-specific standards for your grade level, visit www.corestandards.org.

In schools, or anywhere else for that matter, when people are able to meet their needs effectively, they feel good. And when people feel good, they are generally more cooperative and more productive. When they are not able to meet their needs, or they don't know how to in a particular context, they feel a wide range of emotions: frustration, fear, boredom, isolation, and anger, to name a few. These negative emotions often lead to people shutting down or acting out. If people can learn to better manage their emotions, there will be less conflict, fewer disruptions, and less "drama" in schools—not only among students but faculty, administrators, staff, and parents as well.

The next chapter explains how to effectively help others identify and manage their own emotions, identify emotions in others, and respond empathically.

Common Core Anchor Standards for English Language Arts, K-12

Reading

CCSS.ELA-LITERACY.CCRA.R.1
Read closely to determine what the text says explicitly and to make logical inferences from it; cite specific textual evidence when writing or speaking to support conclusions drawn from the text.

CCSS.ELA-LITERACY.CCRA.R.2
Determine central ideas or themes of a text and analyze their development; summarize the key supporting details and ideas.

CCSS.ELA-LITERACY.CCRA.R.3
Analyze how and why individuals, events, or ideas develop and interact over the course of a text.

Writing

CCSS.ELA-LITERACY.CCRA.W.1
Write arguments to support claims in an analysis of substantive topics or texts using valid reasoning and relevant and sufficient evidence.

CCSS.ELA-LITERACY.CCRA.W.2
Write informative/explanatory texts to examine and convey complex ideas and information clearly and accurately through the effective selection, organization, and analysis of content.

CCSS.ELA-LITERACY.CCRA.W.4
Produce clear and coherent writing in which the development, organization, and style are appropriate to task, purpose, and audience.

CCSS.ELA-LITERACY.CCRA.W.5
Develop and strengthen writing as needed by planning, revising, editing, rewriting, or trying a new approach.

Speaking and Listening

CCSS.ELA-LITERACY.CCRA.SL.4
Present information, findings, and supporting evidence such that listeners can follow the line of reasoning and the organization, development, and style are appropriate to task, purpose, and audience.

CCSS.ELA-LITERACY.CCRA.SL.6
Adapt speech to a variety of contexts and communicative tasks, demonstrating command of formal English when indicated or appropriate.

Language

CCSS.ELA-LITERACY.CCRA.L.1
Demonstrate command of the conventions of standard English grammar and usage when writing or speaking.

CCSS.ELA-LITERACY.CCRA.L.2
Demonstrate command of the conventions of standard English capitalization, punctuation, and spelling when writing.

Printable Forms

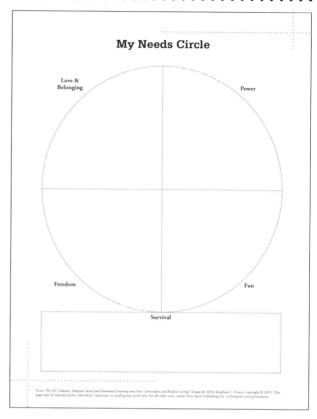

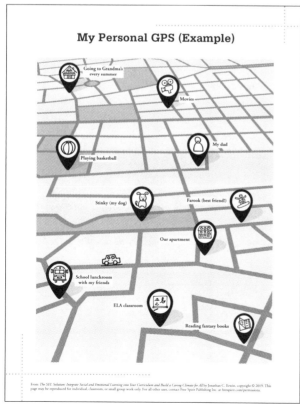

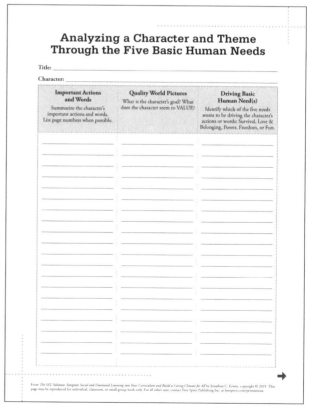

Top-left panel

Analyzing a Character and Theme continued

Deriving Meaning

At the END of the story, in what way does the character's driving need(s) or values (GPS destinations) help develop a message or theme (topic) in the story? Based on the kind of character (sympathetic or unsympathetic, likable or unlikeable, good guy or bad guy), show in the spaces below how your character's needs, goals, or values help develop the story's theme, message, or lesson.

1. If the character is **the protagonist** or another sympathetic character (someone the author intended the reader to like or relate to), then his or her values and needs directly develop a message or theme.

Protagonist's Goals or Values	Theme or Message

2. If, on the other hand, the character is **the antagonist** or another unsympathetic character (someone the author intended the reader to dislike), then his or her goals and values help develop the message or theme by pointing to the opposite of what the protagonist values.

Antagonist's Goals or Values	Identify opposite goals or values	Theme or Message

From The SEL Solution: Integrate Social and Emotional Learning into Your Curriculum and Build a Caring Climate for All by Jonathan C. Erwin, copyright © 2019. This page may be reproduced for individual, classroom, or small group work only. For all other uses, contact Free Spirit Publishing Inc. at freespirit.com/permissions.

Top-right panel

Analyzing a Character and Theme Through the Five Basic Human Needs (Example)

Title: The Lion King

Character: Simba

Important Actions and Words *Summarize the character's important actions and words. List page numbers when possible.*	Quality World Pictures *What is the character's goal? What does the character seem to VALUE?*	Driving Basic Human Need(s) *Identify which of the five needs seems to be driving the character's actions or words: Survival, Love & Belonging, Power, Freedom, or Fun.*
He disobeys rules, ventures outside of the pridelands with his friend Nala, and has to be rescued by his father King Mufasa.	Play, adventure, excitement	Fun, Freedom
Later, after Mufasa is murdered by Simba's ambitious and evil Uncle Scar, Simba runs away into the forest.	To stay alive	Survival
He meets Pumba and Timon, and he learns to eat grubs and have a carefree philosophy "Hakuna matata".	Living day to day with no problems or responsibilities	Freedom, Fun, Survival
Reunites with Nala, who tries to convince Simba to come back to lead the pride. Simba refuses	Loves Nala, but wants to continue the hakuna matata lifestyle	Freedom, Fun, Love & Belonging
After a conversation with wise mandrill Rafiki, Simba returns to the pride, confronts, fights, and defeats Scar (who is actually killed by the betrayed hyenas), restores the pridelands to their former glory, and has a family with Nala	To avenge his father's murder, to retake his rightful place as the Lion King, and restore the pride to its former state of harmony	Power, Love & Belonging

From The SEL Solution: Integrate Social and Emotional Learning into Your Curriculum and Build a Caring Climate for All by Jonathan C. Erwin, copyright © 2019. This page may be reproduced for individual, classroom, or small group work only. For all other uses, contact Free Spirit Publishing Inc. at freespirit.com/permissions.

Bottom-left panel

The Lion King Example continued

Deriving Meaning

At the END of the story, in what way does the character's driving need(s) or values (GPS destinations) help develop a message or theme (topic) in the story? Based on the kind of character (sympathetic or unsympathetic, likable or unlikeable, good guy or bad guy), show in the spaces below how your character's needs, goals, or values help develop the story's theme, message, or lesson.

1. If the character is **the protagonist** or another sympathetic character (someone the author intended the reader to like or relate to), then his or her values and needs directly develop a message or theme.

Protagonist's Goals or Values	Theme or Message
To restore justice and provide a better life for his pride.	Theme: Personal and Social Responsibility
To be a responsible leader.	Message: We not only have a responsibility for our own well-being, but also for the well-being of our families and communities.
To avenge his father	

2. If, on the other hand, the character is **the antagonist** or another unsympathetic character (someone the author intended the reader to dislike), then his or her goals and values help develop the message or theme by pointing to the opposite of what the protagonist values.

Protagonist's Goals or Values	Identify opposite goals or values	Theme or Message
Example: Scar		Theme: Social Responsibility
Values: Power, control, physical pleasures, complete selfishness		Message: Same as above

From The SEL Solution: Integrate Social and Emotional Learning into Your Curriculum and Build a Caring Climate for All by Jonathan C. Erwin, copyright © 2019. This page may be reproduced for individual, classroom, or small group work only. For all other uses, contact Free Spirit Publishing Inc. at freespirit.com/permissions.

Bottom-right panel

Analyzing a Character and Theme Through the Five Basic Human Needs

Title: One Flew Over the Cuckoo's Nest **(Example)**

Character: McMurphy

Important Actions and Words *Summarize the character's important actions and words. List page numbers when possible.*	Quality World Pictures *What is the character's goal? What does the character seem to VALUE?*	Driving Basic Human Need(s) *Identify which of the five needs seems to be driving the character's actions or words: Survival, Love & Belonging, Power, Freedom, or Fun.*
McMurphy "Yessir, that's what I came to this establishment for, to bring you birds fun an' entertainment around the gamin' table. Nobody left at the Pendleton Work Farm to make my days interesting any more, so I requested a transfer, ya see. Needed some new blood. . . . I'll trim you babies like little lambs" (pp. 17)	To escape the hard labor of the work farm and take advantage of the other hospital patients at gambling Values: Self, independence	Freedom, Fun
Fights for patients' rights. Organizes a vote to change the daily schedule so the men on the unit could watch the World Series (pp. 123-128)	To help patients understand that they are strong enough to stand up to Nurse Ratched Values: Individual rights and freedom	Freedom, Love & Belonging, Power
Takes patients on illegal "field trip"—drinking, deep sea fishing, etc. Chief Broom remarks "I noticed vaguely that I was getting good I could see some good in the life around me. McMurphy was teaching me. I was feeling better than I'd remembered feeling since I was a kid and the land was still singing kids' poetry to me" (p. 216.) Here McMurphy is risking being sent back to prison.	To help the patients overcome their fears and learn to enjoy life on their own terms Values: Individual rights and freedom	Love & Belonging, Power
After Billy Bibbit's suicide, McMurphy attacks Nurse Ratched and is lobotomized. Chief Broom suffocates him out of mercy and successfully escapes the mental hospital (pp. 266-272)	McMurphy sacrifices his life for the freedom and rights of the patients Values: Individual rights and freedoms, particularly those on the fringe of society	Love & Belonging

From The SEL Solution: Integrate Social and Emotional Learning into Your Curriculum and Build a Caring Climate for All by Jonathan C. Erwin, copyright © 2019. This page may be reproduced for individual, classroom, or small group work only. For all other uses, contact Free Spirit Publishing Inc. at freespirit.com/permissions.

One Flew Over the Cuckoo's Nest *Example continued*

Deriving Meaning

At the END of the story, in what way does the character's driving need(s) or values (GPS destinations) help develop a message or theme (topic) in the story? Based on the kind of character (sympathetic or unsympathetic, likable or unlikeable, good guy or bad guy), show in the spaces below how your character's needs, goals, or values help develop the story's theme, message, or lesson.

1. If the character is **the protagonist** or another sympathetic character (someone the author intended the reader to like or relate to), then his or her values and needs directly develop a message or theme.

Protagonist's Goals or Values	Theme or Message
Individual rights and freedoms	Theme: Society vs. Individual Rights Message: Individuals, particularly the underdogs, the dispossessed, and those on the fringe of society have the rights to life, liberty, and the pursuit of happiness.

2. If, on the other hand, the character is **the antagonist** or another unsympathetic character (someone the author intended the reader to dislike), then his or her goals and values help develop the message or theme by pointing to the opposite of what the protagonist values.

Protagonist's Goals or Values	Identify opposite goals or values	Theme or Message
Example: Nurse Ratched Values: Conformity to social norms		Same theme and message as above

Understanding Emotions in Ourselves and Others
The Lights on the Dashboard

If school community members support one another emotionally and help one another learn coping skills and empathy, all members of the community would experience unpleasant emotions such as stress and anger less frequently and more frequently experience the emotions that accompany learning and success: personal satisfaction, a sense of being connected, pride, and joy.

This chapter explains how to teach students to identify and manage their own emotions as well as how to identify and adjust to the emotions of those with whom they interact. Like other chapters in Part 2, this chapter has the added benefit that when adults teach these skills to students, the adults become more aware of the skills themselves, helping create a more emotionally stable school climate.

Similar to Chapter 8, all the lessons, activities, and discussions in this chapter are meant to be done in sequence. And like the strategies in previous chapters, if the principal or school leader leads the faculty through these activities and discussions, teachers will better understand how the strategies work. Just as important, the interactive strategies help build relationships, an essential component of climate improvement.

Human Emotions: The Lights on the Dashboard

This chapter elaborates on the behavioral car metaphor, comparing human emotions to lights or gauges on the dashboard of the car. They let us know if things are going well or going awry in our lives. If we know how to respond positively to these signals, we can make effective and responsible choices and keep our car on the road. But before people can respond to the lights on the dashboard, they must understand what they are and what they mean.

Most adults have learned some coping skills throughout their lives—effective ways of controlling impulsive words and actions, dealing with stress, and being able to function in the face of emotional difficulties. (Of course, we can always learn more.) But people are not born with coping skills, and most students still have a lot to learn. Their feelings can often get in their way or drive them to do something irresponsible. Fear and distress not only diminish the capacity to learn (developing brains are particularly sensitive to stress) but also activate the fight, flight, or freeze response, which can lead to all kinds of acting out or shutting down behavior.

If we as educators can first teach students to correctly identify their own feelings—the lights on their dashboards—then we can teach them what they need to know to regulate their own feelings or "give themselves a tune-up." That way they won't be as dependent on parents, teachers, and other adults (mechanics) to intervene.

Teaching Students How to Identify Emotions in Themselves

Before students can regulate their emotions, they need to be able to accurately identify them. The lessons, activities, and community meetings in this section help them do just that.

LESSON

Lights on the Dashboard

Students will review the behavioral car and learn that people's emotions are signals. Emotions light the lights on the dashboard, letting us know how things in our lives are going.

Time Required: 5 minutes

Explain to learners that people, like cars, have signals that help them maintain their balance. Our signals are called emotions. Just as the lights and gauges on a car's dashboard help a driver understand how the car is running, people's emotions let them know how things in their lives are going.

In order to give a car the attention it needs, drivers need to be able to interpret what the gauges are telling them. Sometimes this is easy. For example, we know that if the gas gauge arrow is pointing to E, the car needs gas. But other times, like when the "Engine" light is on, it's hard to know what is wrong, so we take the car to someone who can help. Similarly, sometimes we can correctly identify an emotion—irritation, for example—and we can learn ways to deal with that emotion. Other times, when we're experiencing a strong emotion, we may find that we need to talk to someone we trust who can help us understand our feelings and regain a sense of control. For adults this could be a friend, peer, mentor, or family member; for students it could be a friend, a teacher, a counselor, an administrator, a peer mentor, or a peer counselor.

Tell students that in this unit, they will be learning how to use the lights on their personal dashboards to help them understand their emotions and learn how to deal with them better.

COMMUNITY MEETING

Emotions 'R' Us

In this meeting, students will learn the definition of emotions and develop a vocabulary list of emotions. You will repeat the Personalize section of this meeting seven times in order to cover all seven primary emotions, and you may need to extend this meeting to two or three days to do so. (For older kids with longer attention spans, you can probably cover at least two or three emotions per meeting, whereas with younger students, one or two a day is likely all they can handle.)

Note: There are differing opinions about primary and secondary emotions, with some sources claiming there are six, some claiming four, and some using different terms than the ones appearing here. If you have a preference for another approach, feel free to use it.

Define

- What does the word *emotion* mean?
- When we talk about a person's feelings, what do we mean?
- What are some examples of feelings?

You may need to correct some answers to help students understand the difference between emotions (anger, sadness, joy) and physical sensations (cold), actions (laughing), or thoughts ("That's not fair!"). If students mention something other than a feeling, simply ask, what are you feeling emotionally when you're cold, laughing, or thinking, "That's not fair!" As students come up with emotions, list them on the board.

Before moving on to the Personalize segment of your meeting, take a few minutes to explain the seven primary emotions: love, joy, anger, sadness, fear, surprise, and disgust. All other emotions are combinations or degrees of the primary emotions. (See "Levels of Human Emotion" on page 111.) If students don't come up with all of these, add them yourself to the list and explain these are the most basic emotions.

For older students (fourth grade and up), go on to discuss secondary emotions. Circle one of the primary emotions and try to elicit variations or degrees of it from your group. For example, variations of joy include contentment, satisfaction, bliss, and ecstasy. Encourage your students to use these more sophisticated terms, and challenge them to come to class with new ideas. You might keep an emotional vocabulary word wall and refer to it during community meetings or one-on-one conversations with students.

Personalize

Choose one of the primary emotions to discuss. This example uses *surprise*. Ask:

- What are some words or phrases people use to mean surprised?
- Turn to a neighbor and tell about a time you felt surprised.

Ask for a volunteer or call on a pair to share first. Ask others to follow before moving on to the next questions.

- How do you feel physically when you are surprised?
- What does your face look like when you are surprised?
- What does your voice sound like when you are surprised?
- How long does surprise last?
- What kind of feelings might follow surprise? Why?
- Do you like surprises? Always? Why or why not?

Repeat the Personalize section as needed, perhaps over a few days, until you cover all seven primary emotions.

Challenge

- What are the benefits of having emotions? In what ways are emotions good?
- When might emotions be less beneficial? What are the challenges of feeling emotions?
- What would be better, to have no emotions or not be able to control your emotions

Levels of Human Emotion

Primary emotions	Love	Joy	Surprise	Anger	Sadness	Fear	Disgust
Secondary emotions: Combinations or degrees of the primary emotions	Affection	Cheerfulness	Amazement	Irritation	Suffering	Horror	Nausea
	Lust	Contentment	Astonishment	Exasperation	Disappointed	Nervousness	Revulsion
	Longing	Pride	Shock	Rage	Shame	Alarm	Hate
	Adoration	Optimism		Disgust	Neglect	Shock	
	Fondness	Enthrallment		Envy	Sympathy	Fright	
	Liking	Relief		Aggravation	Agony	Terror	
	Attraction	Amusement		Agitation	Hurt	Panic	
	Caring	Bliss		Annoyance	Anguish	Hysteria	
	Tenderness	Glee		Grouchiness	Depression	Mortification	
	Compassion	Jolliness		Frustration	Despair	Anxiety	
	Sentiment	Joviality		Fury	Hopelessness	Tenseness	
	Arousal	Delight		Hostility	Gloom	Uneasiness	
	Desire	Enjoyment		Bitterness	Unhappiness	Apprehension	
	Passion	Gladness		Hate	Grief	Worry	
	Infatuation	Happiness		Loathing	Sorry	Distress	
		Jubilation		Scorn	Misery	Dread	
		Elation		Spite	Melancholy		
		Satisfaction		Vengeance	Dismay		
		Euphoria		Dislike	Displeasure		
		Enthusiasm		Resentment	Guilt		
		Excitement		Revulsion	Regret		
		Exhilaration		Contempt	Remorse		
		Pleasure		Jealousy	Alienation		
		Eagerness			Isolation		
		Hope			Loneliness		
		Rapture			Rejection		
					Homesickness		
					Defeat		
					Embarrassment		
					Humiliation		
					Pity		

at all? What would the world be like if people had no emotions? What about no emotional control?

- Since we do have emotions, why might it be helpful to know more about them?

- Let's analyze some variations of emotions to see if we can figure out which primary emotions combine to make them OR if they are simply a degree of a primary emotion. For example, rage is a high degree of anger and like is a lesser degree of love, but hurt is a combination of sadness and anger.

ACTIVITY

Feeling Graffiti

Students will generate a vocabulary list of emotions and understand that all are related to one of the seven primary emotions.

This activity is designed for third grade and higher. For younger students, an understanding of the seven primary emotions is sufficient. Primary teachers can go directly to the next activity, "Times When I've Felt . . ."

Time Required: About 20–30 minutes

Materials Needed: Seven large sheets of paper (poster board, chart paper, or sheets cut from a roll of paper about 24" x 36"); markers (one for every four students)

Getting Ready

Write one primary emotion at the top of each of the large sheets of paper and hang them on the wall around the room where students can access them.

The Activity

Briefly review the seven primary emotions with the class, then divide them into groups of four or five and assign each group to a different emotion station. Explain what they will do:

- Each group's job is to write on the poster as many related feelings (stronger, weaker, synonyms, slang) as possible in one to two minutes.

- When you give the signal, the groups are to rotate clockwise to the next poster, read what others wrote, and add to those ideas.

Give each group a marker, and tell them to get started. After a minute or so, signal for the groups to rotate clockwise one poster, read what the groups before them wrote, and add more. Repeat until every group has rotated to every poster, even if all they do the last time or two is read others' thoughts.

While they are at the last poster, go around the room and ask one or two students at each station to read all the ideas on their poster. Watch for teachable moments while this is going on. For example, if the Joy poster says "ebullient," you may need to define it for the class. Or if a poster has a behavior listed instead of a feeling (like "fighting" listed on the Anger poster), you may need to clarify the difference between a feeling and an action or thought.

After all the posters have been shared, have students return to their seats and hold a class discussion based on the following prompts:

- What did we learn about emotions today?

- How many different words do we have in our vocabulary for feelings? Why do you think that is?

- How might it be beneficial to have a good vocabulary for our feelings? For ourselves? How about for our classmates and friends?

Leave up the posters to use in the next activity and to provide a constant peripheral reminder of the vocabulary of emotions.

ACTIVITY

Times When I've Felt . . .

In this activity, students share personal moments related to emotions and read one another's anecdotes. This activity is appropriate for all ages, but students who are too young to write may draw pictures or cartoons of their experiences and share them in a community meeting subsequently.

Time Required: About 20 minutes

Materials Needed: At least seven sticky notes per student; the emotions posters from previous activity; and a classical music selection to play during the activity.

Activity

For each of the primary emotions, have students write a phrase or sentence on a sticky note that describes a time they felt that way. They can use one of the synonyms or other words written on the posters if they prefer. Writing their names on the sticky notes is optional.

Here are some examples to help you and the students think of ideas:

- Love: When I saw my parents after being away
- Fear: When a burglar broke into my apartment
- Joy: When I earned my black belt
- Sadness: When my dad passed away
- Surprise: When I found a $20 bill that I forgot I put in my jacket pocket

Give students about five minutes to complete their sticky notes, then direct them to place their notes on the appropriate posters and return to their seats. Now it's time to conduct a concert gallery review. Put on some soothing or inspiring music (I like to play classical music like Johann Sebastian Bach or Johann Pachelbel), and instruct students to silently move from poster to poster until they have read all the sticky notes.

Finally, to help your group reflect on what they've done and read in the gallery of emotion stories, conduct a brief class discussion focused on the following prompts. Ask students not to identify or try to figure out who wrote which anecdotes. Keep the focus on the content—there is great variety here, and many similarities we all can share.

Ask: What did you learn from this activity?

It might be helpful to have students turn to a neighbor and discuss this before asking them to share in front of the whole class. Hopefully, insightful answers will emerge, including some of the more obvious: *Everyone has feelings. We can't know everything other people have experienced. Some of us have had the same happy, sad, or scary things happen. It can help to see that you're not the only one to experience certain emotions.*

If students don't come up with these answers themselves, ask follow-up questions such as: What do people have in common? Do we always know when someone has an emotional experience? What did you learn about people in this class that you didn't know before?

Ask: How would it benefit the class to learn how to deal with everyone's sets of feelings?

Look for answers such as: *It will help us avoid drama. We can be there for each other. We can give each other a time out (space) when needed.* If these answers don't come out, lead the discussion by asking follow-up questions such as: Suppose someone in the class had a really bad morning.

How would it be helpful for the class to recognize that this person is upset?

Finishing

Explain that it's important that the classroom be an emotionally safe place, and for that to happen, we need to be aware of one another's emotions and give people what they need when they are in an emotional state.

ACTIVITY

Emotional Continuum

Students will learn the degrees of the primary feelings and increase their emotional vocabulary. Later on in this program, when they learn how to regulate their feelings, having this vocabulary will be essential.

Time Required: About 20 minutes

Materials Needed: One copy of the "Emotional Continuum" graphic organizer (see the thumbnail on page 123) for every pair or small group of students

The Activity

Explain to students that when we experience an emotion, some things we think or do will calm us down and help us stay in control, and some things we think or do will increase the feeling, which can lead us to behave irrationally and/or irresponsibly. Having a common vocabulary about emotions can help us all learn to stay in control.

Divide students into pairs or groups of three or four and give each group a copy of the "Emotional Continuum" handout. Tell teams to choose a primary emotion and write it in the center oval. In the oval directly above the primary emotion, they write a related emotion that increases in intensity, and in the oval above *that* one they write another related emotion that increases in intensity even more. In the ovals below, they write emotions that decrease in intensity. When they are complete, groups of students share and discuss their answers.

It's okay if your students struggle to come up with emotions to fill all the ovals. For younger students who may not be able to complete all five ovals, one above and one below would suffice. The point isn't to fill in every oval. What is important is for students to engage in conversations about more and less intense feelings and to learn emotional vocabulary. (For older students, you may even want to add ovals above or below their primary emotion.)

Teaching Students How to Identify Emotions in Others

While it is important to be able to identify our own feelings before we can learn to control them, it is also important to be able to be mindful of and accurately identify the feelings of others with whom we interact. The former helps us perform and function effectively, and the latter helps us perform and function well *as a member of a team or community.* This section provides practices to help students more accurately identify others' emotions through an awareness of context, tone of voice, body language, and facial expression.

LESSON

Driving the Behavioral Car in Traffic

This lesson further extends the car metaphor. Students will learn that people give signals about their emotions, similar to how drivers give signals in traffic.

Time Required: About 10 minutes

Explain to students that in traffic, drivers signal in various ways to let others know what they're doing. Because of turn signals, reverse lights, horns, hand signals, and brake lights, lots of collisions are avoided. Humans send emotional signals as well, though those signals aren't always as obvious as cars. If we learn to better identify other people's feelings, we could avoid a great deal of unnecessary conflict.

Give some examples: If a teacher can spot a student's growing frustration, she can intervene in a manner that will help the student calm down instead of doing something that will push the student's buttons or otherwise escalate the situation. Or, if a student can perceive that a friend is angered by what the student thought was

harmless teasing, he can stop teasing and even apologize, if appropriate, instead of continuing to hurt his friend and possibly damage the relationship.

Conclude this short lesson by putting a finer point on the main idea: When we improve our ability to perceive the emotions of others and learn how to best react to a person who is feeling a strong emotion, then relationships—and the school climate—are improved.

Finishing

On wrapping up this lesson, immediately hold the following community meeting to start making these ideas more concrete.

COMMUNITY MEETING

Reading Others' Signals

The goals of this meeting are to uncover students' prior knowledge of emotional cues and help them understand the importance of identifying them in others.

Ask: Why would it be important to be able to understand what others are feeling?

Answers will vary, as usual, but are likely to include: *It will help us get along with each other. We'll know better how to act around others. So we can help them. So we don't cause drama.*

If they don't bring up these points, ask leading questions, such as: When you're upset, why might it be helpful if others understand how you're feeling? How might it affect our relationships if we understand one another's feelings?

Ask: What "signals" do people give that can help us understand how they might be feeling? How do they signal?

If students don't bring them up, identify the four clues to a person's emotional state: context, facial expression, voice, and body language.

Context. What is going on around the person right now? What is her current situation or recent experience? What's been going on in this person's day or life?

Facial expressions. A person's face can tell you right away what he is feeling. Refer students to the handout "Primary Emotions Facial Expressions" (see the thumbnail on page 123) for some simple examples, or do an Internet search for "emotions faces" or similar terms to find various handouts and charts with more detail.

Voice. This refers to volume, tone, which words the person is emphasizing, and more. To help students understand, demonstrate happy, angry, sad, disgusted, afraid, and surprised ways of saying something innocuous like, "Let's go to the store."

Body language and posture. For example, when people are sad, they tend to avoid eye contact, look down, and slump. When they look up, sit up, and make eye contact, they are likely feeling upbeat. Demonstrate these two emotional postures.

End by telling the class that the next lesson will focus on context and facial expressions.

LESSON

Context and Facial Expressions

This lesson helps students understand more clearly the first two ways of identifying emotions: context and facial expressions. This lesson includes a brief discussion before the facial expressions activity.

Time Required: 20–25 minutes

Materials needed: Copies of the "Primary Emotions Facial Expressions" for each student

Getting Started

Before the lesson, go online and search for "emotions poster." Choose one to project on the whiteboard or print out and project via document camera for the second part of the discussion on facial expressions. Students will be mimicking these expressions, so try to find a poster with plenty of options that is fun but also clear. Many such posters can be found online.

Discussion on Context

Discuss the following prompts, giving students a chance to answer your questions and ask their own.

Ask: What do I mean when I say *context*?

If needed, explain that *context* is the time, place, and/or situation a person is in. It can apply to immediate context—what we're doing right now—and a larger context, like what's going on in a person's life.

Ask: What clues can we get from context that could help us figure out how a person might be feeling?

Discuss several examples, both immediate and larger context. Talk about who the person is

with, how people are interacting with the person, and what kind of activity is happening. Talk about things that might be going on at school, for example, if a big test is coming up that might make someone worried or preoccupied. Talk about things that might be happening at home, in the larger world, and so on that might affect a person's mood.

Discussion on Facial Expressions

Talk about how facial expressions can do the same thing as context—they can give us clues about how a person is feeling. Pass out the "Primary Emotions Facial Expressions" handout, and discuss the characteristics of each face: the shape of the eyes and mouth and the position of eyebrows.

Next, pair up students and project on the board the emotions poster you found. Ask partners to take turns trying to mimic the facial expressions of the emotions you randomly call out. Partners provide coaching and feedback until the "face maker" is successful. Expect lots of laughing, but lots of learning, too.

LESSON

Voice

Students will learn how vocal intonation and inflection can provide clues to a person's emotional state.

Time Required: 15 minutes

Explain to students that it isn't so much *what* we say but rather *how* we say it that matters. One of the things we can infer from a person's voice is their feeling state.

Ask students: How can the way a person says something give us clues to his feelings?

If they don't mention them, bring up volume, pitch, and inflection (tone of voice).

Ask: Can two people say the same words and mean different things?

Ask for examples. You could provide one first, such as saying "Nice haircut!" first sarcastically, then sincerely.

Now write a nonsense word or random phrase on the board and have the whole class say it in unison showing the emotion that you call out. The meaning of the words are not important, only the vocal expression. Some examples of words or phrases:

- Snickerdoodle

- Red beans and rice
- Yadda yadda yadda
- Peas and carrots
- It's impossible
- What do you think?
- I like you

Next, call out different emotions one at a time, pair them with a random phrase, and ask individual students to say the phrase with that emotion. Occasionally go beyond primary emotions and mix in more nuanced ones, such as content, excited, irritated, furious, peaceful, and terrified. Coach students if their performance doesn't match the emotion. ("Try sounding sad again without giggling in the middle.")

LESSON

Body Language

Students will learn how body language provides clues to a person's emotional state.

Time Required: 20 minutes

Hold a class discussion about body language. Do the students know what it is? In what ways do our bodies communicate information? Ask for examples.

Talk about different aspects of body language—gestures, posture, how close you stand to others, the speed at which you move, where you're looking when you talk, whether you're leaning forward or away, what you do with your hands, and so on.

Go through the primary emotions and ask students what type of body language might communicate each. Have a student volunteer express the body language characteristics the class comes up with (or do it yourself if no one volunteers). For example, if you're talking about sadness, the person might hang her head, look at the ground, hands in pockets, and move slowly.

ACTIVITY

I Have a Feeling

Students will practice identifying the emotions of others using various cues.

Time Required: 30 minutes

Materials Needed: One index card for each student, each with a different emotion written on it

The Activity

This activity is great for all ages. With younger students, stick with primary and more straightforward feelings. For older students, include more challenging emotions.

One at a time, invite students to come up and pick a feeling card out of a hat or bowl, read it silently, and hand the card to you. Their task is to say the words "I have a feeling," and only those words, while expressing the emotion on their card. They may say the phrase as many times as they want, using vocal clues (volume, pitch, inflection), facial expressions, and body language.

Give each student about 10 seconds (that's usually plenty of time). When the time is up, let the group guess what the emotion is. (Tell them not to guess while the student is still performing.) If they guess right, ask what gave away the emotion—facial expression, voice, or body language. If the student struggled to convey the emotion, ask the other students for ideas of what might have made the emotion more obvious.

Finishing

Emphasize the point that, in this activity, students were exaggerating the cues they were giving, but in "real life," the cues may be subtler. The cues are still there. It's up to each of us to be sensitive to others' emotions in the school or classroom setting.

Communicating Emotions on Electronic Media

Young people today are regularly communicating via electronic media—texting, messaging, commenting through social media and other apps, emailing, and more. Even kids as young as preschool use devices and computer games that allow for them to communicate with others.

Electronic communication has lots of benefits, but it's also fraught with challenges. One of those challenges is that when we communicate using only text or images, we don't have the benefits of vocal intonation, facial expression, body language, or context. Because of that, electronic communication can easily be misinterpreted. For example, the message "u need help" might be interpreted a few different ways. It might be a sincere question: "Do you need help?" It could be a joke: "You need help! LOL :-)." Or it could be sincere advice. "I really think you need to seek help." If it is meant as a question or a joke but is interpreted as unsolicited advice, it's easy to see how this could lead to hurt feelings or even conflict. Nearly everyone who uses electronic communication has had an experience in which one side or the other has misinterpreted the message. Even emoticons and emojis can be misconstrued.

Another issue regarding electronic communication is that it tends to be less empathic due to the fact that people aren't communicating face to face. Students don't immediately see the direct impact of their words, which can lead to insensitivity or even cruelty. While most electronic communication is happening outside of the school setting, educators know that students bring those extra-curricular interactions to school with them, which can have a direct impact on the school climate. So it's worth our while to address these issues.

COMMUNITY MEETING

Electronic Communication and Emotions

Because even students as young as preschool are using computer games and could be exposed to social media, this meeting is relevant for all ages. I have included appropriate Personalize and Challenge questions for younger students, but you may want to adjust these or add other questions for your particular group.

Define

- What does the term *electronic communication* mean?
- What ways do people communicate electronically?

Personalize

- How do you communicate electronically?
- We've been discussing the importance of being able to identify how others are feeling. How do you figure out how someone you are texting, for example, is feeling?
- How do you express your feelings?
- Have you ever had your feelings hurt while texting or communicating through social media? Was it intentional?
- Have you ever hurt anyone's feelings while texting or communicating through social media (intentionally or unintentionally)?
- Has electronic communication outside of school ever caused problems (or drama) for you in school?

Personalize for Younger Students

- Do you ever play games with other people using a computer, phone, or other device?
- Do you send messages on a phone, tablet, or computer?
- Have you ever sent or received a mean message from someone on one of these devices? Do you think it's okay to be mean if you can't see each other?

Challenge

- What should we keep in mind when we are communicating electronically to prevent misunderstandings, hurt feelings, and drama?
- What are some specific ways we can make sure we are understood by those we are texting?
- What are some specific ways we can make sure we don't misinterpret others?

Challenge for Younger Students

- Can you tell what a person is really thinking when she or he sends you a message online? Why or why not?
- What can you do to make sure you don't hurt someone's feelings online?

MINI-LESSON

Electronic Communication and Emotions

This lesson is designed to immediately follow the previous community meeting. It's most appropriate for students in fourth grade and higher.

Lesson

In order to improve your emotional understanding when using electronic communication, keep the following in mind:

- You are communicating with a human being who has feelings and moods. You can't see the person, but he or she is there.

- You can't see the situation or context the other person is in. Ask. (Where are you? How is it going? Everything good?)

- Choose your words carefully. Ask yourself if they could be interpreted in different ways.

- Conversely, never assume that your first interpretation of someone else's words is correct, especially if they seem unusually hurtful or out of character. Ask questions for clarification.

- Use emoticons and emojis to communicate your intended meaning and feelings. Although imperfect, they help.

- Use and understand texting shorthand. When people text, they try to be as brief as possible. Some people might not want to take the time to type all the words it would take to address emotional concerns. But, using texting shorthand makes it possible to be both sensitive and efficient.

- Be extra kind to everyone you communicate with. You never know what they are going through.

Emotional Intelligence, Social Responsibility, and School Climate

Creating and maintaining a positive school climate doesn't require everyone in the learning community to be best friends. But a positive school climate and culture *does* require community members to be socially responsible. That means we are working and learning cooperatively, caring about one another's well-being, and helping each other when necessary. At the very least, social responsibility means behaving in ways that do not hurt others.

If we use the ability to pick up emotional cues and accurately identify how a person is feeling, we can avoid behaving in ways that will inflame a situation. For example, if a teacher can discern that Mai Lin is feeling highly stressed or agitated, he would understand that right now might not be a good time to put her on the spot during class. If Jaden realizes that his science teacher is feeling pressured to get all the lab equipment out for class, he may realize that now is not the time to ask about his grade.

These situations may seem like "no brainers." But many people with brains—students *and* adults—frequently miss or ignore emotional cues and inadvertently do or say things that make matters worse.

Now that students have begun to learn how to identify emotions in themselves and others, the material in the following activities focuses on how to adjust our behavior in ways that maintain and even improve the classroom or school climate.

COMMUNITY MEETING

Social Responsibility and Emotions

Students will learn that how we respond to others' emotional states can have a positive or negative impact, and that we have a social responsibility to try to help.

Time Required: 15 minutes

Define

We've been learning about how to identify others' emotions. What are some of the cues we can use to figure out how someone might be feeling?

Personalize

- What signals do you think you give when you're feeling a strong emotion? (Take time to gather several examples of both negative and positive strong emotions.)

- When you are feeling really emotional, what do you need from people?

Challenge

- Why would it be good to understand how others are feeling?

- What kinds of things can we do when someone is really upset?

- What are some things we can do to make things worse? Better? Keep them the same?

Attuning Behavior to Others' Feelings

Students will learn a simple five-step process for attuning their behavior to others' feelings. This lesson is meant to immediately follow the previous community meeting.

Time Required: 10 minutes

Materials Needed: A poster, projected image, or copies for each student of the "Attuning Our Behavior to Others' Feelings" handout (see the thumbnail on page 123)

Pass out the handout or point to the poster and go through the five-step process, giving examples as you address each step. Here are the steps:

Attuning Our Behavior to Others' Feelings

1. Notice the situation.

2. Observe the person's facial expression, voice, gestures, body language, and actions.

3. Identify the feeling or feelings you observe.

4. Ask yourself: What kind of behavior do I need around me when I'm feeling that way?

5. Behave that way.

For example, you might tell students:

I walk into the classroom and see a student sitting at his desk, fidgeting and tapping his pencil fast and hard, his face tense and angry-looking. I immediately can tell he is very frustrated or angry. I ask myself, what do I need when I'm feeling that way? When I'm very upset, I need someone to check in with me in a private place. So I could ask him to step into the hall and ask, "Are you doing, okay? What do you need right now?"

Adjusting yourself to others' emotional state is a skill that takes practice. Therefore, the next activity involves participating in a role play that is both fun and gives students practice.

Behavior Role-Playing

Role-playing in a safe, supportive environment allows students to practice socially responsible behavior in situations they might encounter in school.

Time Required: About 20 minutes

Materials Needed: A few copies of the handout "Role Playing: Attuning Behavior to Others' Feelings" cut up into slips with one scenario on each slip; you'll need one scenario for each pair of students (if your class is large, you may end up with several pairs doing the same scenarios; see the extension option at the end of this activity)

Activity

Start by pairing up students and distributing a scenario to each pair. Have each pair perform a brief (one minute or so) role play of their scenario for the class—twice, switching roles the second time.

After each role play, discuss as a class how person A expressed an emotion and how person B reacted. This feedback may lead to improved performances when the roles switch.

As a variation or extension, consider having students make a list of scenarios they might experience in school and use those for role-playing.

Integrating the Understanding of Emotions into the Curriculum

Feel free to tailor these assignments to your grade level and particular situations, making them more or less complex, focusing on content or techniques you're already covering, and so on.

Activities for English Language Arts

Narrative Writing

Expanding on the "Times When I've Felt . . ." activity on page 112, assign a daily journal prompt that begins, "Tell about a time you felt _____," focusing on a different emotion each time. If students can't come up with an example for a particular emotion, you might allow them to write twice about an emotion they have an easier time with.

After you've gone through several emotions (at least the seven primary emotions), ask them to choose one and develop it into a first-person nonfiction narrative.

As an option or extension, consider having students create a storyboard or comic strip of their experiences, or even a graphic novel. Another way to extend the activity is to publish their stories in a class book or journal or on a website.

Compare and Contrast

Assign students to write an essay, write a poem, create a poster, develop a collage, or make a digital presentation comparing and contrasting different emotions. It can be interesting to compare similar but different emotions, such as jealousy and envy or irritation and anger. Or students might be more interested in comparing very different emotions, such as joy and fear or surprise and contentment.

A variation is for students to focus on or include their own behavior when experiencing the emotions they're analyzing.

Character Analysis

Have students write an analysis of the emotional life of a character in a fiction or nonfiction book or short piece. How do readers know what a character is feeling? How does the character's context affect his or her emotions? How do the character's emotions change over the course of the story? Students could compare the emotions of two characters, or compare a character to themselves, focusing on a time when they felt similar emotions.

Activities for Social Studies

Character Analysis

Students research a historical figure or contemporary figure in the news and write a character analysis like the one described in the previous ELA section that considers the figure's emotions and the effect those emotions may have had on important decisions the person made.

Write to Someone in the News

Have students research a person in the news who has undergone trauma or other difficult experiences and write a letter or an email to that person expressing empathy. You might refer to the "Attuning Our Behavior to Others' Feelings" handout (see the thumbnail on page 123). Have students think of times when they felt an emotion similar to this person and ask themselves, What kind of behavior do I need when I'm feeling that way? Their answer can guide the content of their letter.

If a personal letter is impractical because you can't find an address, or for other reasons, students could write a letter to the editor of a news website or post an "open letter" on your class website.

Common Core State Standards (CCSS)

The table on page 121 aligns the activities, strategies, and assignments in this chapter with the broad "Anchor Standards" for the Common Core in ELA, which cover all grades. To read more and get grade-specific standards for your grade level, visit the Common Core website at www.corestandards.org.

Other Subjects

Science

Middle and high school students might research and report on information about emotions: the brain and emotions; evolution of emotions; emotions in animals; emotions and learning; clinical depression, bipolar disorder, or other emotional disorders.

Music

Orally, in writing, or as a panel discussion, students share music that creates various emotions and explain how musical components such as instrumentation, tempo, and volume help elicit that emotion.

Art

Create a visual representation of different emotions: a drawing, an abstract painting, a sculpture, a mosaic, a collage, or something else.

Health

Research and report on how emotions affect our physical health.

Common Core Anchor Standards for English Language Arts, K–12

Reading

CCSS.ELA-LITERACY.CCRA.R.1
Read closely to determine what the text says explicitly and to make logical inferences from it; cite specific textual evidence when writing or speaking to support conclusions drawn from the text.

Writing

CCSS.ELA-LITERACY.CCRA.W.1
Write arguments to support claims in an analysis of substantive topics or texts using valid reasoning and relevant and sufficient evidence.

CCSS.ELA-LITERACY.CCRA.W.2
Write informative/explanatory texts to examine and convey complex ideas and information clearly and accurately through the effective selection, organization, and analysis of content.

CCSS.ELA-LITERACY.CCRA.W.3
Write narratives to develop real or imagined experiences or events using effective technique, well-chosen details, and well-structured event sequences.

CCSS.ELA-LITERACY.CCRA.W.4
Produce clear and coherent writing in which the development, organization, and style are appropriate to task, purpose, and audience.

CCSS.ELA-LITERACY.CCRA.W.5
Develop and strengthen writing as needed by planning, revising, editing, rewriting, or trying a new approach.

Speaking and Listening

CCSS.ELA-LITERACY.CCRA.SL.4
Present information, findings, and supporting evidence such that listeners can follow the line of reasoning and the organization, development, and style are appropriate to task, purpose, and audience.

CCSS.ELA-LITERACY.CCRA.SL.6
Adapt speech to a variety of contexts and communicative tasks, demonstrating command of formal English when indicated or appropriate.

Language

CCSS.ELA-LITERACY.CCRA.L.1
Demonstrate command of the conventions of standard English grammar and usage when writing or speaking.

CCSS.ELA-LITERACY.CCRA.L.2
Demonstrate command of the conventions of standard English capitalization, punctuation, and spelling when writing.

Final Thoughts on Emotions

It is easy to think, because of kids' rapid physical development during adolescence, that their cognitive and emotional development are keeping pace. But that is not the case. While young adults reach their peak height by around age 21, the prefrontal cortex continues to develop until approximately age 24. And what happens in the prefrontal cortex—reasoning, analysis, evaluation—has a huge impact on the brain's emotional center, the limbic system. One of the SEL skills in which adolescents seem particularly lacking is in identifying the emotions of others.

Deborah Yurgelun-Todd, director of the Cognitive Neuroimaging Laboratory at the University of Utah, did a well-known study in which she asked teenagers to look at a picture of a face and identify the emotion they saw. Of the adults who looked at that picture, 100 percent saw fear. But of the teenagers, only half saw fear; the rest saw anger, confusion, shock, sadness, or something else.

Teens' inability to read others' emotions, especially during a time when their brains are producing more dopamine than they ever will again (which amplifies already intense feelings), can have devastating results: Suppose an angry student verbally abuses another student during lunch. The abused student may be signaling *fear* with all he's got, but if the abuser misinterprets his expression as anger, it may serve to increase his own anger and aggressive behavior, leading to more verbal or even physical abuse.

Younger students, even more egocentric than teenagers, are just beginning to develop the ability to understand their own feelings. Teaching them emotional awareness and the ability to both regulate their own feelings and attune themselves to others can serve to accelerate their emotional development, providing them with skills that will help them both in school and later in life.

If students learn the vocabulary of emotions and develop the skills to identify them in themselves and others, they can learn to regulate their own behavior, alone or when "in traffic," to return to the behavioral car metaphor. In the next chapter, the car takes on additional meaning as it helps us learn about self-control and self-regulation—the "keys" to success in life, however one measures it.

Online Resources

Collaborative for Academic, Social, and Emotional Learning (CASEL)
www.casel.org
This organization conducts and publishes research on SEL and provides resources and training.

Edupics.com Coloring Page Facial Expressions
www.edupics.com/coloring-page-facial-expressions-i8896.html
This link is for a coloring page of facial expressions for primary students, but many other fun coloring pages and activities are available at the site.

Facial Expressions Quiz
www.greatergood.berkeley.edu/quizzes/ei_quiz
This website offers an interesting online test you might want older students to try individually or as a class. It shows a series of emotional facial expressions and you try to identify the emotion. After each question, there is an explanation of each expression.

Printable Forms

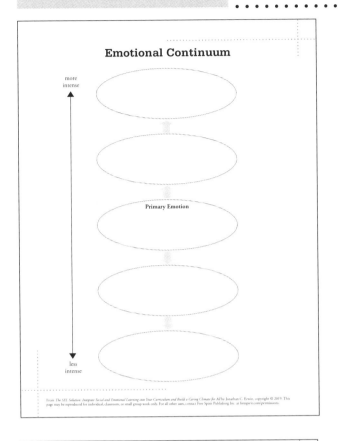

Emotional Continuum

more intense

less intense

Primary Emotion

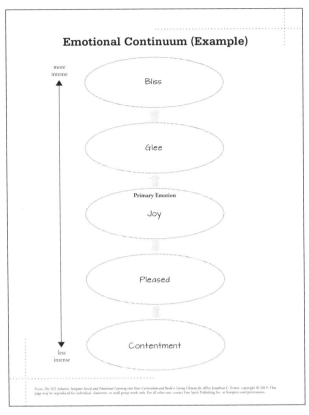

Emotional Continuum (Example)

more intense

less intense

Bliss

Glee

Primary Emotion

Joy

Pleased

Contentment

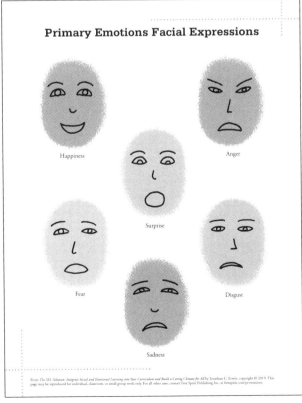

Primary Emotions Facial Expressions

Happiness

Anger

Surprise

Fear

Disgust

Sadness

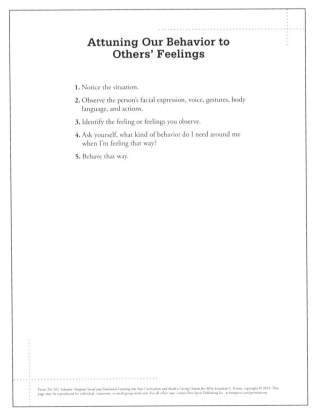

Attuning Our Behavior to Others' Feelings

1. Notice the situation.
2. Observe the person's facial expression, voice, gestures, body language, and actions.
3. Identify the feeling or feelings you observe.
4. Ask yourself, what kind of behavior do I need around me when I'm feeling that way?
5. Behave that way.

See digital content for full-size reproducible pages

Role Playing: Attuning Behavior to Others' Feelings

Scenario 1
A: A student frantically looking for something in his notebook
B: Another student really needs to borrow a pen

Scenario 2
A: A student looks upset when she gets back a test
B: Nearby student who got an A

Scenario 3
A: A student who was just yelled at by the teacher in front of the class
B: Partner in science experiment

Scenario 4
A: A student who had a big argument with a parent before school
B: Partner in cooperative learning activity

Scenario 5
A: A student who was just yelled at by a monitor in front of other students in the cafeteria
B. A lunch companion

Scenario 6
A: A student whose parents are going through a divorce
B: A classmate who sits next to Student A

Scenario 7
A: A teacher is highly frustrated by class disruptions
B: A student in this teacher's class

Scenario 8
A: A student who was recently embarrassed on social media
B: A friend who doesn't know about it yet

Scenario 9
A: An athlete or band musician who is nervous and excited about an upcoming game or performance
B: A peer who is not interested in that sport (or band)

Scenario 10
A: A student who is surprised and disappointed by a low grade on an assignment
B: The teacher who just handed back the assignment

Self-Regulation
The Four Wheels of the Car

Being aware of emotions and being able to label them is an important skill, but unless people understand how to regulate their emotions—especially when they are running high—simply identifying them is of little value. This chapter provides specific information and skills that students and adult members of the school community can use to lower stress, reduce anger, restrain impulses, and calm themselves down—self-regulation skills.

Self-regulation skills can improve individual performance by helping students focus, pay attention, and stay on task. They can also improve the school and classroom climate, because when people are able to control themselves and their emotions more effectively, there are fewer conflicts and, therefore fewer disruptions. This helps maintain a sense of safety and order and positive relationships. Once again, the behavioral car is a useful metaphor.

The Four Wheels of the Behavioral Car

Just as cars have four wheels, humans have four components to their behavior. These four components stem from William Glasser's concept of "total behavior." Typically, when people think of behavior, they are thinking of behavior we can directly observe—someone's actions. The concept of total behavior expands the definition of behavior to include a person's thoughts, feelings, and body state (or physiology). When a person engages in any action, she is also thinking something and feeling something, and her body's physiology (heart rate, blood pressure, breathing, brain chemistry, and so on) responds accordingly. For example, a student may raise his hand to answer a question in class. When he does that, he may be thinking, "I know this answer." He may be feeling anxious but confident. And his physiology might respond with shallow breathing, a slightly elevated heart rate, and muscle tension.

The four components of total behavior go together like the four wheels of a car. When one of the wheels goes in a certain direction, the other three follow along. Since we have the most direct control over our actions and thoughts, those two components are represented by the front wheels of the car, the wheels the driver has direct control over. The back wheels—feelings and physiology—follow along behind.

What this suggests is that if we can effectively control the front wheels of our behavioral cars, our thoughts and actions, we can also indirectly control our feelings and our physical responses, despite the situation we may be experiencing.

For example, if a student calls me an inappropriate name, I can choose my thoughts ("Calm down, you know how to handle this") and my actions (take a deep breath and invite the student into the hall for a brief conference) instead of losing my temper. As a result, my feelings will be calm and confident, and while I may experience a slightly elevated heart rate and tension, I can remain relatively relaxed.

If, instead, I let my back wheels take over, I might behave in a way I would regret later. In other words, if I let feelings of anger and humiliation trigger an adrenaline rush, those parts of my behavior might drive my thoughts to those of retaliation, and my action might be to say something hurtful back to the student—or perhaps even worse.

This chapter explains how to teach students and adults a powerful concept: how to self-regulate and gain self-control—how to "drive themselves" effectively and responsibly. Although I will be referring to the behavioral car, remember, it's the concepts and skills that are important, not the metaphor. If the extended metaphor of the car doesn't appeal to you, create a different way of teaching the self-regulation skills in this chapter.

That being said, the following process is one I have used successfully hundreds of times to teach kindergartners through adults.

Teaching the Concept of Total Behavior

The activities in this section are carefully sequenced to help learners understand the concepts, personalize them, and finally gain the skills to apply them to their lives. They don't all have to be done within the same day or even the same week, but they are designed to be carried out in the order they appear.

A learner's understanding of the concept of total behavior will help him or her develop self-control and personal/social responsibility. This understanding will better equip the stuent to behave in ways that align with the school touchstone values. The social-emotional skills students will learn include

- self-awareness

- metacognition, the ability to be aware of and consider one's own thoughts

- self-regulation and impulse control

- anger and stress management

LESSON

The Four Wheels of the Car

Through this lesson, you will help students understand the four components of total behavior, which components we have direct and indirect control over, and how our choices influence the different components.

Time Required: 30-40 minutes

Materials Needed: Poster or slide of the "Behavioral Car: Four Wheels" handout and copies of the "Four Parts of Total Behavior" handout (see the thumbnails on page 139) for every student

For younger students, you may want to break this slightly extended lesson into smaller chunks or do a brain break or energizing activity in between components.

First, pass out the "Four Parts of Total Behavior" handout to the class. While students are looking at the handout, project the "Behavioral Car: Four Wheels" handout on the board, pointing out the four wheels of the car. Show students how the four parts of behavior on their handout correspond to the wheels. Explain the definition of each of the four components (parts) of total behavior, relating them to the four wheels of the car: acting and thinking are represented by the front wheels, while feelings and body state are represented by the rear wheels.

Give the following comments (but you might consider replacing my examples with your own):

When we think of behavior, we typically think of actions, what someone is doing. The idea of total behavior is more than just what people are doing: it also includes their thoughts, feelings, and body state. All four of these components of total behavior are present all the time and change from moment to moment. We are often more aware of one part than others, but our total behavior always includes all four parts. For example, if I am running, the most obvious component is the "doing" component—the action. But I am also thinking something, maybe like, "What a beautiful spring morning!" Along with that action and thought, I feel an emotion, too—perhaps a sense of well-being and exhilaration. The physiological component would include elevated heart and breathing rates, sweating, and endorphin production. All four components would be, in this slice of time, my total behavior of running.

When one component changes, the other three change as well. For example, if my thought changes from "What a beautiful spring morning!" to "Oh, no, here comes that steep hill," my actions, feelings, and physiology will change accordingly. I may begin to run slower, my feelings may change from well-being to dread or maybe determination, and my heart will be pumping faster and harder.

Whatever my behavior, one of the four components will be more prominent than the others. Whichever component is the most prominent is the one I usually focus on—and label the behavior after. For example, in the running example, the most obvious part of the behavior is my action, which is why I label it "running." But if I am meditating, the most prominent component of total behavior is the thinking component. I am focusing on a single thought or an image. While there is little action, I am still doing something: I'm sitting. Calm and peacefulness are the dominant feelings, and my body state slows down: my heart rate decreases, my breathing is slow and deep. This is the total behavior of meditation.

If feeling, or emotion, is the most apparent component (for example, if I am extremely angry), the other components are present as well. My body state may be tense and flushed. My brain chemistry is affected, and my blood pressure may become elevated. I might be thinking something like, "I can't believe he said that!" And my actions may include pacing back and forth and venting to anyone who will listen. While all four components of my total behavior are affected, in this case I am most aware of my feelings.

I usually digress a moment when explaining this scenario and discuss some of the choices other people might make when they are angry. A teenager might punch a wall, a shy person might just sit quietly and internalize the anger, and someone else might go for a long walk. The point to make is that even though feelings are powerful influences on our behavior, we still have choices (control) over our actions.

Finally, if I am sick to my stomach, the most prominent component of total behavior is my body state: My nausea has my full attention. My thinking may be, "Oh, please make this go away." I am probably feeling upset and sorry for myself. And my actions are to lie down and try to sleep. So, like the other examples, we name the behavior of the moment, being sick, by the most prominent component, which in this case is body state.

ACTIVITY

Think Red

This activity is an effective and enjoyable way to help learners of all ages experience total behavior and learn the basics of self-regulation. It should be completed soon after the previous lesson. Students will learn that:

- All four wheels of their behavioral cars are operating (turning) all the time.
- They have the most direct control over their actions and thoughts (the front wheels).
- They can indirectly control their feelings and body state (back wheels) through effectively controlling their thoughts and actions.

Time Required: About 15 minutes

The Activity

Begin this activity by asking learners to stand up at their desks. Explain that they are going to be a part of an experiment on total behavior. You are going to ask them to control each of the four components of total behavior they just learned about, and their job is simply to do their best to follow your directions. Also, explain that it is important that they do this with their eyes closed and without talking. Once they all have their eyes closed and are quiet, give the following directions, waiting three to five seconds after each step.

Thinking

First, I'm going to ask you to control your thinking. Think red; try to see the color red in your mind, maybe think of something red.

Wait three to five seconds. **Now think green; try to see the color green in your imagination.**

Again wait three to five seconds. **Stop thinking green.**

Feeling

Now I'm going to ask you to control your feelings. Keeping your eyes closed, try to feel angry. Pause. **Feel sad.** Pause. **Stop feeling sad and be happy.** Pause.

Giggles may follow some of the directions. There's no need to stop the activity. Bring that behavior into the post-activity discussion: What were you thinking when you giggled?

Physiology

Next, I'm going to ask you to control your body state. Again, keeping your eyes closed, **raise your heart rate.** During the pause, some students may start running in place. That's okay—they are simply complying with your directions. **Lower your cholesterol.** Expect some chuckles, maybe a comment or two about diet. **Sweat profusely.** Pause. **Now stop sweating.**

Doing

Now, I'm going to ask you to control your actions. **First raise your right hand.** You won't need much of a pause between these directions. **Lower it. Touch your nose. Stop touching your nose. Open your eyes, and sit down, please.**

Ask the students to return to their seats and hold the following discussion.

CLASS DISCUSSION

Think Red Activity

Follow up the Think Red activity with this discussion right afterward. This will help students understand the concept of total behavior, giving them the foundational understanding necessary to self-regulate effectively.

Once again, project the "Behavioral Car: Four Wheels" handout, and review everything you asked students to do.

Point to the thinking wheel: **First, I asked you to think red, think green, and stop thinking green.** Next, point to the feeling wheel: **Then I asked you to feel angry, feel sad, and stop feeling sad and be happy.** Point to the body state wheel: **I asked you to raise your heart rate, lower your cholesterol, sweat, and stop sweating.** And finally, point to the actions wheel: **And lastly, I asked you to raise your hand, touch your nose, open your eyes, and sit down.**

Of all four parts of total behavior: doing, thinking, feeling, and physiology, which are the easiest ones to control?

Usually, the students will say *doing* or *thinking.* Respond with: Yes, it's really easy to raise your hand, touch your nose, and open your eyes. And it's pretty easy to think of something red or green. If students say *feeling* or *body state*, ask them *how* they got that feeling or changed their body state. The answer will include an action or

a thought. Respond with something like, That's interesting. We're going to talk about that more in just a minute.

Next, go on to explain that the front two wheels are labeled *acting* and *thinking*. Those are the wheels that the driver—us—has most direct control over. When a person is driving, she turns the steering wheel, and the front two wheels change direction. The back wheels follow along.

Ask: What did you do when I said stop thinking green? The answers will vary, but may include, *I went back to red*, or *I kept thinking green*, or *I thought black.* Make the point that different people may think different things but we never stop thinking. Whether we are aware of it or not, the thinking wheel is always spinning, even when we sleep.

Ask: Was anyone able to feel angry or sad or happy when directed to?

Usually, most students raise their hands. Ask one of them (if someone identified feeling as the easiest wheel to control, call on that student, otherwise call on anyone with their hand up): How did you do it? Students will almost always say that they thought of someone or something that "makes" them mad or sad or happy.

Respond: Exactly! Our thoughts drive our feelings!

Ask: How many of you were able to raise your heart rate? Some students will raise their hands. Ask, How did you manage that? Students will respond with answers such as, *I ran in place*, or *I held my breath*, or *I thought of something that stressed me out.* Point out that they once again were able to *indirectly* control a "back wheel" behavior (the body state) by directly controlling one of their front wheels—by doing or thinking something.

Before concluding, ask students where do people sit when they drive—in the front seat or the back? The answer is the front, of course. Ask what would happen if people drove from the back seat. The students will say, *They would crash* or *They'd go off the road.*

Elaborate on that metaphor: But people too often drive their behavioral cars from the back. They let their feelings or their physiology drive their front wheels. Share an example with the students. Feel free to use mine if you don't have any anecdotes of your own. I tell participants I once heard an adult say, "I'm in a bad mood, so I'm not responsible for anything I say or do today." This is an example of someone letting their feelings (bad mood) drive her actions and simultaneously relieve herself of any responsibility for them. The students will laugh, but most will get the point.

Next ask: What wheel would represent anger? Students will see (or point out) that anger is a back wheel (feeling) behavior. Ask: What might happen if someone lets anger drive his behavioral car? It's easy for students to come up with examples of ineffective and irresponsible actions if people allowed the back wheel behavior of anger to drive their whole car.

Finally, direct the students to turn to a partner and summarize what they have learned about their behavioral cars through this activity. After a minute or two, ask them to share their conclusions with the class. Points that should be emphasized include the following, which you may want to write or type on the whiteboard.

- Total behavior consists of four parts (wheels): doing, thinking, feeling, and physiology.
- We have the most control over our front wheels—doing and thinking.
- We have indirect control over our back wheels—feelings and physiology.
- We drive our behavioral cars most effectively when we concentrate on "front wheel" behavior.
- It's not a good idea to try to drive our cars from the back seat. When we let our feelings or physiology drive our behavior, we often do things that are ineffective or irresponsible. In other words, we crash our cars.
- And the main point: If we don't like how we're feeling (emotionally or physically), we should change what we're *doing* or *thinking*.

Finishing

At the end of the discussion, you might issue each student a keychain and tell students their assignment for the next day is to find a key for it, one from home that no one needs anymore. This usually is not a difficult assignment; most families have old keys lying around. You could pick up a few blank keys from a local hardware store to give to students who can't find one at home. They can clip it to their backpacks as a concrete reminder that they are in control of, and therefore responsible for, their behavior. Another idea is to issue each student a behavioral driver's license, ideally with their picture on it. Use your judgment and understanding of your students to decide which symbol to use (or whether to even use one).

COMMUNITY MEETING

The Behavioral Car Keys/ Driver's License

This meeting will help drive home the point that we all choose our behavior. In other words, we have the keys to our behavioral cars. However, even though we are driving our cars, we sometimes allow others to influence our behavior. They are acting as navigators, and that's okay if we trust that the navigators have our best interests in mind.

Time Required: 20–30 minutes

Materials Needed: students bring their keys or drivers licenses (optional)

Students are learning the final part of the behavioral car metaphor, so this meeting opens with a basic review of the car before moving into the new material. Ask:

- Who drives your car?
- When we're driving our cars, where are we trying to go?
- What do our destinations represent in our car metaphor?

Draw from students or make the point that our destination might represent a short- or long-term goal. Remind them that we all have our own Personal GPS—our goals and values are our own. But when driving, sometimes we get directions from people who may know the roads better than us. Similarly, in life we sometimes get advice and guidance from others.

Ask: Who do you allow to direct your car at school and at home? In other words, who gives you advice and guidance and helps you reach your goals?

Students will list people like parents, teachers, coaches, and other adults. Ask them why we let these people "navigate" for us or—for younger students—simply make the point that we choose to listen to them, obey rules, try to meet their expectations, and let them be our navigators because we can trust that they have our best interests in mind. Students will likely mention that if they don't follow the directions of these navigators, they will suffer consequences like getting bad grades or having a privilege taken away. If they do mention consequences, let them know that you will discuss that soon.

Next, ask students who they should *not* let navigate their cars (who they should not take guidance and advice from). If you don't hear the following answers, ask questions to prompt them or provide them:

- People who are trying to make us angry, sad, afraid, intimidated, or upset.

- People who are trying to pressure us into doing something we know is wrong or irresponsible.

- People who don't care about us.

- People we don't trust.

- People we don't know.

Make an explicit connection between the behavioral car and school climate by asking: How can we connect the idea of choosing trustworthy navigators to being in school and "driving your car" through your day? How can we use the concept of driving your own car to make the classroom or school a better place to be and learn?

Reiterate that we all drive our own cars—nobody can take our car keys away from us! But we all need help from others who have more experience and knowledge than us, and those who want what is best for us. It's important to make sure we can trust the people we let influence our behavior (our navigators).

At this point, the students have completed the behavioral car metaphor. Hold a brief review of everything they've learned so far. Simply ask them in what ways they have learned that people are like cars. Answers should include that people, like cars:

- are heading in a direction in life; they can move forward or backward, spin their wheels, go off the road, crash, and so on

- are constantly making choices, adjusting to the road

- can get hurt or hurt others if they're not careful

- have five fuel tanks, the Five Basic Human Needs

- have a Personal GPS, their Quality World pictures

- have lights on the dashboard, their emotions

- most importantly, are the drivers of their own behavioral cars, they hold the keys, and no one can take away their keys without their permission

If students don't give all the desired responses, ask leading questions, such as,

- What is the behavioral car's fuel?

- How does GPS relate to the car?

- Do we have gauges or warning signals? What are they?

- Who holds the steering wheel of your behavioral car?

Consider holding a short ceremony in which you bestow the students their car keys or driver's licenses. Simply have them hold up their keys or licenses and say: Congratulations, you've all just earned your behavioral driver's licenses (or car keys)! No one can take your keys away from you.

Self-Regulation: Maintaining the Behavioral Car

When emotions are running high, people need coping skills—self-regulation skills—to calm themselves down so they can work or learn, and so they don't say or do anything they will regret. This section provides specific stress, frustration, and anger-reduction strategies that are useful for both adults and students.

Every car, even the most finely engineered vehicle in the world, needs an occasional tune-up for optimal performance. If cars don't get the maintenance they need, they do things that we don't like. They run sluggishly, make strange noises, and eventually may break down completely. The parallel to students (and adults) is remarkable. When a car is driven hard, it overheats, breaks down, and may need maintenance or repair. The human equivalent of being "driven hard" is feeling distressed, highly frustrated, or angry. When we are feeling that way, we often do things we don't like: We stop working, cause conflict, disrupt the learning environment, and sometimes become violent.

Teaching students how to tune up their own behavioral cars (manage stress and anger) may take a little time initially, but in the long run, it leads to a healthier life for students and an improved climate at school, so the time investment is worth it.

The best time to teach these skills is during a planned unit, *not* when a student is already stressed, angry, or acting out in class.

COMMUNITY MEETING

Stress

Students will learn the definition of *stress*, discuss their own stressors—both environmental and self-induced—and begin to identify self-regulation strategies.

Time Required: 15-20 minutes

Define

- How can we define *stress*?
- What kinds of things cause stress?
- What emotions do people experience when they are stressed out?

Personalize

- What kinds of things create stress for you?
- How does stress affect you emotionally?

Challenge

- What can people do to reduce their stress?

Follow this meeting immediately with the next activity.

ACTIVITY

Self-Inflicted Stress

Students will learn that when they are feeling stressed, the things they do or think can serve to either increase or decrease their stressful feelings.

Time Required: About 15 minutes

Materials Needed: A copy of the "Accelerating Thoughts" handout (see the thumbnail on page 139) for each student

With students still in a community meeting circle, share the following information.

Since we know that it is our thoughts that drive (or steer) our feelings, it makes sense that certain kinds of thoughts are accelerators: They intensify stressful emotions like fear, embarrassment, powerlessness, and hopelessness. We can't control the stressful events in our lives, but we can control how we respond to them. Many people choose (without realizing it) thoughts that only serve to increase their stressful feelings. Choosing to think these things is like stepping on the car's accelerator, revving up our emotional engines to the point of overheating.

Pass out the "Accelerating Thoughts" handout and go over it together. Then invite students to write in their journals for about five minutes on the following prompts:

- Can you think of a time you chose any of these accelerator thoughts?
- What was the situation?
- How did those thoughts make you feel?
- Did your thoughts come true?

After five minutes, get the class's attention again and discuss what they just wrote. Ask for volunteers to read their entries or just talk about them.

Finishing

Explain to students that what they have been doing is thinking about thinking—for older students, you may want to introduce the term *metacognition*. This is a very important skill. If we are aware of our thinking, we are better prepared to avoid accelerating thoughts and make better choices. While fear, embarrassment, powerlessness, and hopelessness are clearly emotions that we want to be able to control, the emotion that often leads to the most destructive behavior is anger.

COMMUNITY MEETING

Anger

While the previous activity is still fresh, hold this community meeting to help students learn thoughts to avoid when they are angry and specific strategies for regulating anger and maintaining self-control.

Time Required: 10 minutes

Define

- How would you define the word *anger*?
- Are there different kinds of anger, or different levels?

Personalize

- How do you feel physically when you are angry?
- Can you feel anger coming on?
- What kinds of things have you seen people do when they are angry?

Challenge

- What are some things you do to calm yourself down when you are angry?

Follow the meeting immediately with the next lesson.

MINI-LESSON

Anger

This lesson will help students understand the points raised in the preceding community meeting.

Time Required: About 10 minutes

Materials Needed: A copy of the "More Accelerating Thoughts: Anger" handout for each student

Say:

Just as some accelerating thoughts can increase our own fear, embarrassment, and other negative feelings, some thoughts can accelerate or inflame our anger—adding fuel to the fire, so to speak.

Distribute the "More Accelerating Thoughts: Anger" handout. These thoughts not only accelerate a person's own anger, but also serve to validate or affirm his or her resulting angry behavior. The following comments correspond to the sections on the handout. Feel free to use your own words or make adjustments to the speech for your situation.

Always or Never Thinking

If someone in a conflict thinks, "This person is always rude to me," it places all the blame for the conflict on the other person and seems to rationalize or validate an equally mean or rude response. Also, *always* or *never* thinking is rarely, if ever,

accurate. (It would be impossible for anyone to always be mean to another person. They have to sleep sometime.)

Labeling

Labeling may be the most dangerous of accelerating thoughts. At its worst, historically, labeling has been used to dehumanize the "other." During times of war or conflict, nations often dehumanize or demonize the enemy, which provides the rationale to kill them. If people think of the "other" as individual human beings—with families, friends, and dreams—it becomes much harder to pull the trigger. Similarly, when we think of someone as a "complete jerk" or other nasty label, we not only accelerate our anger, we give ourselves an excuse for being cruel or hurtful in our response to them.

Fairness Worries

Fairness is a wonderful value to encourage. However, humans made up this idea—it doesn't exist in nature. Life is not fair. Focusing on the unfairness of things we can't control not only increases our frustration but also our feelings of powerlessness. And these feelings often lead us to try to regain a sense of power, which when fueled by anger, can easily lead to destructive behavior.

Provide an opportunity for learners to reflect on their insights by having them write in their journals for about five minutes on the following prompts:

- Do you ever have accelerating thoughts when you are irritated or frustrated?
- How do they make you feel?
- Have you ever done anything irresponsible or destructive when you feel that way?

After five minutes, ask for volunteers to read or talk about what they wrote. Continue the discussion by asking the following questions:

- What kind of words or actions result if we let accelerating thoughts and feelings continue?
- What might be the consequences of these actions?

Explain that it is much harder to manage anger once it reaches this point. It is more effective to focus our energy on transforming initial trigger thoughts. If people can learn to recognize their anger, understand it, and regulate it through their thoughts and actions, they can transform anger into something constructive.

LESSON

The Tune-Up Process

This lesson is intended to help students learn a simple three-step process for regulating their feelings in everyday situations. It involves both direct instruction and activities. For younger students, break up the lesson into shorter segments, perhaps dividing the "Breathe, Relax, and Think" section into two lessons. For older students, complete the entire lesson and follow it immediately with the Tune-Up Practice activity.

Time Required: 40 minutes

Materials Needed: A copy of the "Calming Thoughts" handout (see the thumbnail on page 140) for every student, soothing music or relaxing soundtracks (like ocean waves or rain, often found on meditation or sleep apps) for the relaxation exercise

Tell students:

To take effective control of our feelings and not let them drive our behavioral car in a direction we may later regret, we can do a simple "tune-up." Tuning up our behavioral car is a three-step process. In terms of the car analogy, we:

1. Shut down the engine

2. Let the engine cool down (relax, breathe, and think)

3. Restart the engine

Step 1. Shut Down the Engine

Explain that the first step in the process is to recognize our feelings and stop the thoughts that are creating or increasing our stress. Our physical signals are like the warning lights on the dashboard of our cars, letting us know we are getting into an emotional state.

Ask students to identify where in their bodies they feel tension when they are stressed or angry. Do their shoulders tighten up, or do they feel tension in their jaws? A student's "hot spot" might be in his forehead, neck, abdomen, or legs. When we learn to identify these physical signals, we can then effectively interrupt our thoughts and turn off the ignition of an angry or stressed behavioral car by deliberately using self-talk. We do this by saying to ourselves words, phrases, or imperatives like "Chill!" "Stop and think," and "Relax!"

Step 2. Let the Engine Cool Down (Breathe, Relax, and Think)

Once we have interrupted our stress or anger, the next thing to do is to relax ourselves physically. It is easy to maintain or increase our anger or stress if our bodies are hot and tense. It is important, therefore, to learn how to breathe and relax properly. Once relaxed, it's necessary to choose a thought that will help maintain a more relaxed physical and emotional state. Explain that shallow breathing or chest breathing does little or nothing to relax tension. Deep, abdominal breathing—breathing with the diaphragm—is what works.

Breathing Exercise. Have students practice by placing one hand on their abdomen and the other on their chest. (They may lie on their backs on the floor.) When they take a deep breath, their stomachs should expand before their chests. Have them practice this natural breathing a few times so that they can do it automatically.

Relaxation Exercise. After they have practiced breathing, lead students through a guided relaxation or guided imagery exercise. Here's a simple one in which students tense and relax different muscles, but you can use others that you're familiar with.

Tell students to lie on their backs, sit with backs straight and legs crossed, or sit at their desks with their backs straight and feet on the floor. Have them close their eyes. With soothing instrumental music playing, and a calm, soothing voice, take them through the following steps:

1. **Breathe in, breath out. Make sure you're breathing the way we just learned: slowly and deeply.** (Continue this for one to two minutes.)

2. **I am going to have you tense up different parts of your body, hold the tension for a few seconds, and then relax and try to let all the tension go. Keep breathing slowly, deeply, and naturally throughout this exercise.**

3. **Tense up your feet. Try to curl your toes as tight as you can.** (Students hold for three to five seconds). **Relax your feet. Let all the tension flow out of your toes.**

4. **Breath in, breath out, and relax your feet.**

Repeat steps one through three for legs, stomach, shoulders, arms, hands, and finally face. Have students tense each body part, then relax.

While they are still sitting or lying quietly, direct students to scan their bodies again for tension and repeat the tightening and releasing process on any tense areas. Then have students return to their seats and share the following calming thoughts that they might choose from to help regulate their feelings when they are angry or stressed. Say:

Once we've relaxed and calmed down our body state, it's important to get into the front seat of the car immediately and choose a thought that will help us remain calm and in control. What thoughts have you used in stressful situations to calm yourself down?

Get responses from volunteers, and write them on the board. Tell them that if these thoughts work to help them stay calm, they should feel free to keep using them. Pass out copies of the "Calming Thoughts" handout and explain that this is a list of many other ideas they can also try. Ask students to choose a couple of the statements (or one that the students listed on the board) that they think will help them remain calm and feeling in control.

Step 3. Restart the Engine

Explain that once a person has done the first two steps, she can now restart and return to normal driving. This simply means returning to whatever activity she was involved in before the emotional issue, only now she can do it while maintaining emotional control.

Students will have a chance to practice this process in a safe environment in the next activity.

ACTIVITY

Tune-Up Practice

Through this activity, students will practice using the tune-up process so that it comes easier when the situation is real.

Time Required: 20 minutes

Materials Needed: Blank index cards (one per student)

The Activity

1. Pair students with a partner with whom they will be comfortable, but not buddies (so they will be less likely to go off task).

2. Have them each share with their partner something that someone has said that really irritated them (at school or home)—but don't name names. Explain that they will be using those two situations (or triggers) to practice tuning up. It's important to emphasize this is not an opportunity to tattle on or talk about others behind their backs. No names or references to specific people are allowed.

3. Review the tune-up process: Start by shutting down what you're doing and stopping your negative thoughts. Second, relax and breathe—use positive thoughts to help settle yourself. Finally, restart your engine by returning to the situation you were in before the tune-up.

4. Direct everyone to write on their index card a three-step tune-up script for their own irritating situations, including the specific thoughts and actions they will use to take their foot off the accelerator, relax, and restart.

5. Have everyone practice their scripts by having their partner act as the person who has provoked them in the past. The first students would then *say aloud* the thoughts and practice the relaxation strategies they have determined will help them. Then students act out the other partner's script, with the first student now playing the role of the antagonizer.

6. Suggest to students that they may want to use their index card as a bookmark or tape it to their desk or locker for a few weeks as a reminder.

After the pairs have practiced both scripts, explain that so far the emphasis has been on self-talk, or our thoughts. But we all have two front wheels on our cars—thoughts and actions—and we can also use actions to decelerate (or accelerate) our emotions.

Ask students to share things they do when they are angry or stressed to help them calm down. List those ideas on the board. Next share these other effective actions that students might find useful, depending on the situation.

- getting away from the situation, such as by going outside for a three-minute breathing break

- talking to a peer

- talking to a parent, friend, teacher, counselor, social worker, or administrator

- finding a quiet spot

- taking a walk or doing some kind of moderate exercise
- listening to music
- drawing or coloring
- writing in a journal
- going to the "chill out" area in the classroom
- doing something you love to do
- spending some time with people you trust
- going somewhere that has special meaning to you
- doing something you are good at
- improving yourself in some way: working out, practicing an instrument, playing a sport, trying something new

COMMUNITY MEETING

The Front Wheels

Students will discuss the importance of effectively controlling the front wheels of their behavioral cars (thoughts and feelings). They'll learn what situations are best for using thoughts and what situations are best handled with actions.

Time Required: 20 minutes

Define
- What are the four wheels of the car?
- What do we consider the front wheels? Why?

Personalize
- Have you ever let your feelings or body state drive your behavior? Tell about it. What happened?
- If you were able to choose a front wheel behavior (action or thought) in that situation, what might have you done or thought differently? What do you think the result of that behavior would be?
- Which is easier for you to control, your actions or your thoughts?

Challenge
- When is it better to focus on changing your thoughts, and when is it better to focus on changing your actions?

- Are there situations where it's harder to change one than the other? Give examples.

In summary, sometimes it can be more effective to do something physical to help us control our back wheels. But sometimes, because of the situation we're in, we can't take a walk or listen to music. When we're in school, at work, or in some other more destructive situation, it's better to focus on controlling our thoughts. If students don't make these points, make sure you do.

ACTIVITY

The Traffic Circle of Life

This cooperative group activity helps students understand that in any situation, they always have a choice and every choice has a consequence.

Time Required: 30–40 minutes

Materials Needed: A copy of "The Traffic Circle of Life" handout (see the thumbnail on page 140) for every pair or small group; a projected version of "The Traffic Circle of Life" handout

Note: Consider making laminated traffic circles so you can use them year after year. Just have the students write on them with erasable markers or transparency pens.

Getting Ready
Before the activity, prepare brief (one sentence) anger-inducing scenarios for each pair or small group to respond to. You might write them on note cards and pass them out, or simply keep a list and tell the groups verbally.

The Activity
Show students "The Traffic Circle of Life" image and explain the metaphor it describes:

Every minute of our lives, we are making choices. Every situation we encounter is like a traffic circle. Each exit off the traffic circle represents a different choice, and each exit takes you to a different destination—in other words, each choice has a different consequence or result.

Divide students into pairs or small groups and give each group a scenario that a person might respond to with anger or frustration. One scenario might be, "Bella just called you stupid." The pairs or groups then generate three to four different possible choices of total behavior, one for each of the exits on the traffic circle. Next to each exit, the students identify all four components of total behavior *in the following order:* thoughts, feelings, body state, and actions involved for each choice. Encourage students to include both irresponsible and responsible choices on their traffic circles.

For example, one behavior a student might choose is to respond to Bella by calling her a name. Next to the first exit the students would write:

> Thinking: "I can't stand her. She is always so nasty."
> Feeling: Angry
> Body State: Hot, tense, heart beating fast
> Acting: Calling Bella a jerk

Another choice or exit might be:

> Thinking: "No one calls me stupid and gets away with it."
> Feeling: Angry and embarrassed
> Body State: Hot, tense, adrenaline rush
> Acting: Punching her hard on the arm

Another exit might be labeled:

> Thinking: "I'm not going to let Bella drive my car."
> Feeling: Calm
> Body State: Cool, relaxed
> Acting: Focusing on schoolwork, ignoring Bella

After the students have generated their choices, ask them to identify the destination where each one might take them and label it on the "Destination" box on the handout with a name that sounds like a destination. In other words, what might the natural or imposed consequences of each choice, or exit, be? In the first example given, the choice might result in the teacher doling out consequences, so the students might name that destination "Trouble with Teacher Town." The second destination might result in harsher consequences, so the name of the destination could be "Suspensionville." The third choice may result in the student feeling strong and in control of himself. Maybe the students would call this "Coolburg."

After the small groups have predicted the likely outcome or consequence of each choice, have them identify the exit that has the best chance of taking them where they want to go. Have each group share their scenarios, their different choices, and the destination they agreed on.

This activity teaches students in very concrete terms that choices exist in any given situation.

Even if it seems like the world is conspiring against us, or we find ourselves in extremely difficult circumstances, our response (where we drive our behavioral car) is ultimately our choice. The activity also provides students with the opportunity to practice, in a safe way, deliberately analyzing the probable consequences of various actions.

Integrating Total Behavior Concepts into ELA and Social Studies

Teachers can help students connect the concepts in this chapter to ELA and social studies in numerous ways tho satisfy the CCSS.

Activities for English Language Arts

Choice Stories

The concept of total behavior provides a natural springboard for first-person nonfiction narratives. Students know about and are interested in the topic—it's all about them. Assign students to write a few paragraphs or an essay about a time they allowed their back wheels (powerful emotions or physiology) to "drive" their choices. Have them analyze the outcomes of the choices they made. Then have them discuss an alternative choice they might have made if they had been in the front seat of their behavioral car and hypothesize what might have been the results.

For prewriting, hold a short discussion, brainstorming choices and results in a hypothetical situation. For example, you could share a less effective choice you made in your life and have students brainstorm other choices you might have made and predict consequences of each.

For a variation, have students write about a time when they caught themselves *before* they allowed their feelings to drive some irresponsible or destructive behavior, and how they were able to take more effective control. Ask them to discuss both the results of the thoughts and actions they chose and what might have been the consequences of the initial "back wheels" impulse.

The Road Not Taken

When students personally connect to characters and events in literature and history, the curriculum comes alive. After students read about a difficult decision faced by a character in a short story or novel, present the students with Robert Frost's poem, "The Road Not Taken," which is easy to find online.

Lead a class discussion in which you help students make connections between what they have learned about making choices (the behavioral car) and what the poem's persona has learned about choices in life. Discuss the difficult choice the person or people in your reading faced, the choices they made, and their consequences.

Here are some options for writing assignments.

- Students write about the decision faced by the fictional character in the class reading, the choice he or she made, and the results or effects of that choice. Discuss alternate choices the character may have made if he or she had been able to drive from the front seat, and the possible consequences of those choices.

- Students write about a difficult choice they may have to make that might subsequently make "all the difference" in their lives. Have them discuss how they will use their front wheels to make that choice.

- Write a prediction of the choices a literary character might make during the reading of a novel or short story, analyzing their possible results. Explain whether the character is choosing to be guided by front wheels (thoughts and actions) or back wheels (physiology or body state.)

The final drafts of any of these narratives or essays might be published on a class website or blog. For high school kids, you might create a class Facebook page (set privacy settings so only other members of the class or grade can see the page). Students would orally present their stories or papers individually or in panel discussions. Audience members might have an advanced organizer or questionnaire to complete during or after each oral presentation to help them practice focused listening skills. Alternatively, students could give electronic or multimedia presentations or make a video set to music. This could be extended into a speaking and listening assignment.

Another option is to have students turn their story into an ebook. Many educational apps are available for doing this on computers and tablets. One that I love is My Story: Storybook Maker for Kids and the Classroom at www.mystoryapp.org or you can find it in the App Store.

Research and Report

Helping satisfy the CCSS's emphasis on nonfiction, students might be assigned to do some research on health-related topics such as those in the following list. This assignment works well in physical education, health, or science classes as well as ELA.

- the physical, mental, and emotional effects of stress
- psychosomatic illness
- panic attacks
- cognitive behavior therapy
- stress reduction
- SRI antidepressants
- benefits of meditation
- major causes of stress

Have students gather information on one of these topics and develop a written and/or oral report, presentation, live or video skit, video documentary, or website dedicated to mind-body health issues.

Activities for Social Studies

The previous ELA assignments are also relevant in the social studies classroom. Instead of focusing on fictional characters in "The Road Not Taken" assignment, students will focus on a historical or contemporary figure, analyzing his choices and the consequences of his actions, discussing other choices he may have made, and predicting those results.

Common Core State Standards

The table on page 138 aligns the activities, strategies, and assignments in this chapter with the broad "Anchor Standards" for the Common Core in ELA, which cover all grades. To read more and get grade-specific standards for your grade level, visit the Common Core website at www.corestandards.org.

Common Core Anchor Standards for English Language Arts, K–12

Reading

CCSS.ELA-LITERACY.CCRA.R.1
Read closely to determine what the text says explicitly and to make logical inferences from it; cite specific textual evidence when writing or speaking to support conclusions drawn from the text.

CCSS.ELA-LITERACY.CCRA.R.2
Determine central ideas or themes of a text and analyze their development; summarize the key supporting details and ideas.

CCSS.ELA-LITERACY.CCRA.R.4
Interpret words and phrases as they are used in a text, including determining technical, connotative, and figurative meanings, and analyze how specific word choices shape meaning or tone.

CCSS.ELA-LITERACY.CCRA.R.5
Analyze the structure of texts, including how specific sentences, paragraphs, and larger portions of the text (e.g., a section, chapter, scene, or stanza) relate to each other and the whole.

CCSS.ELA-LITERACY.CCRA.R.10
Read and comprehend complex literary and informational texts independently and proficiently.

Writing

CCSS.ELA-LITERACY.CCRA.W.1
Write arguments to support claims in an analysis of substantive topics or texts using valid reasoning and relevant and sufficient evidence.

CCSS.ELA-LITERACY.CCRA.W.2
Write informative/explanatory texts to examine and convey complex ideas and information clearly and accurately through the effective selection, organization, and analysis of content.

CCSS.ELA-LITERACY.CCRA.W.3
Write narratives to develop real or imagined experiences or events using effective technique, well-chosen details, and well-structured event sequences.

CCSS.ELA-LITERACY.CCRA.W.4
Produce clear and coherent writing in which the development, organization, and style are appropriate to task, purpose, and audience.

CCSS.ELA-LITERACY.CCRA.W.5
Develop and strengthen writing as needed by planning, revising, editing, rewriting, or trying a new approach.

Speaking and Listening

CCSS.ELA-LITERACY.CCRA.SL.4
Present information, findings, and supporting evidence such that listeners can follow the line of reasoning and the organization, development, and style are appropriate to task, purpose, and audience.

CCSS.ELA-LITERACY.CCRA.SL.6
Adapt speech to a variety of contexts and communicative tasks, demonstrating command of formal English when indicated or appropriate.

Language

CCSS.ELA-LITERACY.CCRA.L.1
Demonstrate command of the conventions of standard English grammar and usage when writing or speaking.

CCSS.ELA-LITERACY.CCRA.L.2
Demonstrate command of the conventions of standard English capitalization, punctuation, and spelling when writing.

Printable Forms

Behavioral Car: Four Wheels
You have the keys!

(Wheel labels: Feeling, Acting, Body State (Physiology), Thinking)

Four Parts of Total Behavior

Acting
What we do and say

Thinking
Our focus, attention, thought processes, perceptions, and self-talk

Feeling
Emotions such as sadness, joy, love, and anger

Body State (Physiology)
Basic body functions such as heartbeat, blood pressure, breathing, and body and brain chemistry

Accelerating Thoughts

These kinds of thoughts can accelerate emotions such as fear, embarrassment, frustration, and hopelessness.

Fear of failure
- I'll never be able to . . .
- I'm not any good at . . .
- What if I can't do it?

Fear of how others will react
- What will everyone think of me if . . .
- I'll look stupid (unskilled, funny, incompetent, and so on) if . . .

Feeling trapped
- I'll never get out of this mess.
- Nothing I do will help.
- I don't have any good options.

Hopelessness
- My whole day (or week or life) is going to be ruined if . . .
- There goes my future.
- I might as well give up now.
- What's the use?

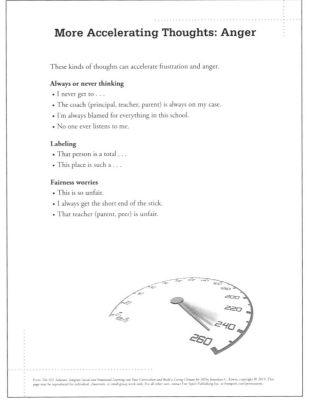

More Accelerating Thoughts: Anger

These kinds of thoughts can accelerate frustration and anger.

Always or never thinking
- I never get to . . .
- The coach (principal, teacher, parent) is always on my case.
- I'm always blamed for everything in this school.
- No one ever listens to me.

Labeling
- That person is a total . . .
- This place is such a . . .

Fairness worries
- This is so unfair.
- I always get the short end of the stick.
- That teacher (parent, peer) is unfair.

• • • • • • • • • • • • • • • • See digital content for full-size reproducible pages • • • • • • • • • • • • • • • •

Calming Thoughts

- It's not worth it to lose my temper (or to stress out).
- In a month from now, who will know the difference?
- Who is driving my car right now? Is that what I want?
- I have the keys to my car.
- Stay in the front seat.
- Whatever. (Thought, not said aloud!)
- Don't sweat the small stuff.
- Stay calm and carry on.
- Stay cool and don't be a fool.
- Getting stressed (or angry) will cost me _____.
- I'm annoyed (mad, worried), but I can stay calm.
- Getting upset or angry won't help.
- Strong people control themselves.
- Stay chill.
- I can stay in control.
- It's going to be okay.
- Isn't it interesting how this person is trying to make me angry (afraid, feel bad)?
- I'm not going to let him (this situation) get the best of me.
- Getting upset or mad only gives her what she wants.

The Traffic Circle of Life

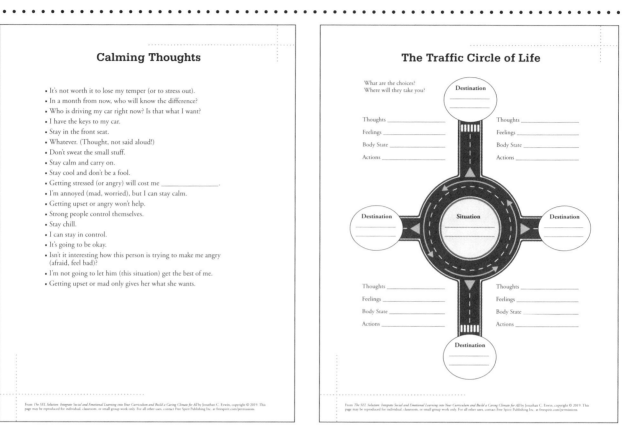

What are the choices?
Where will they take you?

Destination
_____
_____

Thoughts _____
Feelings _____
Body State _____
Actions _____

Thoughts _____
Feelings _____
Body State _____
Actions _____

Destination
_____
_____

Situation
_____

Destination
_____
_____

Thoughts _____
Feelings _____
Body State _____
Actions _____

Thoughts _____
Feelings _____
Body State _____
Actions _____

Destination
_____
_____

OPTIMAL CONDITIONS

Creating a
Needs-Satisfying
Environment

11

Addressing the Needs for **Emotional Safety and Connectedness**

The school climate will continue to improve and sustain itself if everyone in the school—particularly teachers and school leaders—intentionally create and maintain a needs-satisfying environment. That environment includes classrooms, hallways, the main office, faculty and staff meeting rooms, sporting and other extracurricular event locations, and everywhere else associated with the school.

The Internal Profile and the Hierarchy of Basic Needs

When I say "needs-satisfying," I'm referring to the Five Basic Human Needs discussed in Chapter 8. In that chapter, students learn how all human behavior stems from one of five needs—the needs for survival, love & belonging, power, freedom, and fun.

All human beings are motivated by the same Five Basic Human Needs, but due to a combination of genetic variations and environmental influences, we each have our own individual internal profile, or hierarchy of needs. For example, one person—we'll call him Barry—may have survival as his primary driving need, with love & belonging second, fun third, power fourth, and freedom last. Barry's internal profile is partly based on genetics and partly on his environment. His strong need for survival may have been influenced by his living conditions, for example, moving frequently or experiencing domestic violence. His low need for freedom may be partly based on the fact that he has little adult

supervision. Whatever the reasons, Barry's internal profile and personality will most likely look much different from a person—we'll call her Bridget—whose most intense needs are freedom and power, followed by fun, love & belonging, and survival last. Bridget was born with a predisposition to a certain internal hierarchy of needs, but her environment has also influenced it. For example, her high need for freedom might be the result of strict parenting or a restricting home environment.

Considering his internal profile, driven primarily by survival, Barry is unlikely to be a risk-taker. He is probably cautious, prompt, reliable, well organized, and dependable. He may seem a bit rigid at times, but if you need something organized, Barry is the person to go to. Bridget, on the other hand, who is primarily driven by freedom, is much more likely to take risks. She may not be well organized, but she is a creative problem-solver. She may not seem like a team player at times, but if given a task and some autonomy, she will work well independently.

The concept of the internal profile makes sense if you think of people you work or live with. Consider the wide range of temperaments among children of the same parents. Then consider the range of personalities in a classroom or on a faculty. If we were all driven by equal amounts of the same five needs, humans wouldn't display such an incredible variation in behavior and personality. The important thing to remember, in terms of creating a needs-satisfying environment for those we teach or supervise, is to intentionally address all of the needs. That way, despite the disparate internal profiles of those we work with or teach, everyone will have the opportunity to meet their needs in responsible ways.

However, even though each individual has his or her own internal profile, I believe that organizations like schools must have a more universal hierarchy in order to best function. At school, that hierarchy is:

1. Survival
2. Love & Belonging
3. Power
4. Freedom
5. Fun

1. Survival

For any school to function effectively, there must be a sense of safety and order. While building relationships might help a person feel more safe, most people are unwilling to start new relationships if they are fearful of being teased, embarrassed, criticized, or physically harmed. In order to move on to addressing the need for love & belonging, leaders and teachers must adequately address the need for survival by making the classroom and the school at large feel safe, ordered, and reliable.

2. Love & Belonging

When I ask students and teachers what they think is most important in a teacher or a school leader, the number one answer is, "We want them to care about us as individuals." People not only want to feel cared about by their teacher or supervisor, they also want to feel accepted by their peers. And they want to feel as if they fit in to the larger group. When we address this need by creating conditions under which people feel cared about and connected, we begin to address the next need, power, which is directly related to job performance and student learning and achievement.

3. Power

The purpose of schools is to empower students and to provide them with the knowledge and skills to be successful in college, the work world, and in life. If school leaders and teachers empower their staff and students in ways that help them learn useful information, do their jobs more efficiently, feel a sense of importance, and be successful, then they will be inspired to work harder and learn more. When this happens, staff and students can be given more choices and autonomy.

4. Freedom

The more successfully (and responsibly) people are learning and working, the more freedom and autonomy they can handle. By providing autonomy, choices, and novelty, people will feel less trapped or confined in their roles, and creativity flows.

5. Fun

Fun is the sense of joy and pleasure that comes along when all the other needs are met. When a school has successfully addressed the other basic needs, fun is a natural by-product. But the need for fun can also be addressed intentionally through encouraging play. When we've achieved this stage of climate improvement, the school will be a place of joy that people will feel as soon as they enter it.

Teachers, coaches, drama directors, principals, department chairs, and others who manage groups of students or adults have a responsibility to provide these basic needs. This chapter explains how to do so, starting with survival (by providing structure and safety) and love & belonging (by building connections among themselves, their students, and members of the various groups they work with). The next chapter explains how to address the other three needs.

Address All the Needs

I don't want to give the impression that a needs-satisfying environment is achieved in a lock-step manner—by first focusing *only* on safety and order, then *only* on creating a sense of caring and connectedness, and so on down the hierarchy. Doing that would mean ignoring four other basic needs at any given time, which would lead to a lot of dissatisfaction, acting out, and irresponsible behavior.

I am suggesting, however, that the emphasis be first on safety, then on connectedness, then on empowerment, and finally on freedom and fun—but also keeping in mind all of the needs. When the school has reached an acceptable level of safety and order (survival), continue to address those needs, but move up the hierarchy and place a greater emphasis on creating connectedness and building relationships (love & belonging), then on empowerment, and finally on freedom and fun.

Providing Structure and Safety

As part of the need for survival, people need to feel both physically and emotionally safe. Structure helps provide that sense of safety and order. Most schools already have a great deal of structure built into the day: arrival and dismissal times, schedules of all kinds, bells, cafeteria procedures, and so on. And most good teachers have lots of procedures for accomplishing practical tasks in the classroom: passing back papers, getting a lunch count, lining up, putting away materials. School districts also provide codes of conduct for students, written contractual agreements with teachers and administrators, and other elements that create structure and safety.

People vary in the amount of structure they need to feel a sense of safety and order. Some prefer a little, some a lot! I prefer less structure but quickly learned, as a teacher, how important it is to others. Once, as a first-year teacher, I was assigning my eighth graders what I considered to be a fun creative writing assignment. One girl raised her hand impatiently as I was talking.

"Yes, Stacey?" I said.

"How would you like our heading on the paper?" she asked.

"I don't care," I told her. "Just make sure your name is on the paper."

Stacy looked perturbed, which confused me a little bit, but I went on explaining the assignment. Almost right away, up went Stacey's hand again.

"On the right side or the left? Our heading?" she asked with an attitude that only an eighth-grade girl can deliver.

Now feeling a little irritated by the interruptions, I said with a less-than-patient voice, "I don't care, Stacey, as long as I know it's your paper."

Now she was rolling her eyes all over the place and ready to spew venom at the thought of this incompetent teacher who doesn't even know how he wants his heading! But before she could ask another question, an insightful student named Jarrell came to my rescue: "Hey, Mr. Erwin, why don't you just have us do our heading the way Mr. Doostam has us do it?"

"Perfect! Yes! Thanks, Jarrell. You okay with that, Stacey?"

Whew!

In retrospect, I realize that Stacey probably had a high survival need, and if I had addressed it right away, the interruption to my assignment would not have occurred. She was starting to get under my skin, and she was clearly frustrated with me. If Jarrell hadn't bailed me out, I can picture Stacey saying or doing something resulting in a Stacey-getting-kicked-out-of-class scenario. When people perceive their needs being thwarted, they often act out.

Adults, too, need structure. In my workshop evaluations, adult learners have complained about not having a written agenda posted during a workshop, about my varying from my agenda, and about not strictly following my slides in the same order as the packet handout. Other times, in graduate courses I've taught, I often gave students a wide range of options in terms of how they might demonstrate their learning. More than once, I have had students ask: Could you please just tell me what to do? In each case, the adults were not receiving the degree of structure they felt they needed.

Several strategies explained in previous chapters can increase the sense of safety and order: 1) the community meeting provides an effective structure for safe communication; 2) the touchstone values are developed to provide people with an emotionally safe place to learn and work; 3) the social contract clarifies behavioral expectations for students and adults; and 4) SEL provides people with coping skills, decreasing the likelihood of violent or mean behavior.

The following activities are specific ways principals, adults, and other school leaders can increase a sense of safety and belonging through clarifying roles, replacing destructive relationship habits with *caring habits*, intentionally connecting with those they supervise or teach, and facilitating community building activities.

ACTIVITY

My Job/Your Job/Our Job

Every member of the school community will have a clear understanding of his or her responsibilities.

Time Required: About 30 minutes

Materials Needed: One copy of the "My Job/Your Job/Our Job" handout (see the thumbnail on page 150) for each participant (including the leader)

One of the best ways of alleviating fear and anxiety and increasing a sense of emotional safety is to make sure everyone in the school has a clear understanding of his or her roles and responsibilities and the roles and responsibilities of those with whom they interact. Role clarification addresses the need for survival as well as for love & belonging. It builds relationships through eliminating the anxiety of the unknown and minimizing conflict.

Any two people or groups who work together, but who have different roles and responsibilities, will benefit from filling out the "My Job/Your Job/Our Job" handout: teachers and students; principals and teachers; principals and assistant principals; special education and regular education co-teachers; coaches and players; teachers and paraprofessionals; and so on. Whenever there is a role differential between two people at school, it can be valuable to do this activity. You can do it any time, but it's best when done early in the year, like within the first two weeks of school.

Here's the process. It works if you're working one-on-one or in a group setting such as a teacher with students. The person who has the greater positional power takes the lead in the activity and meeting.

Begin by having each individual complete both sides of the "My Job/Your Job/Our Job" chart, then hold a group discussion in which you create a new chart document as agreement on roles is reached. You can do this electronically, on the whiteboard or a computer screen, or by hand.

Begin with the "Our Job" section—your shared responsibilities. One at a time, discuss the items on that section of people's charts, asking for consensus on each item that it is a shared responsibility. Once a consensus is reached on an item, add it to the new document. (In a group situation, you don't need to go through every item on every student's chart, because there will likely be plenty of overlap. Ask if everyone is satisfied with what's on the chart or if anyone has something to add.)

Do the leader's job next (you can decide whether you call this "My Job" or "Your Job" on the handout), and do the student's or subordinate's job last. Continue to the second page of the handout and follow the same process.

As you go through the three sections of the chart, you may have differences of opinion on certain items. When that happens, try to negotiate them as you go. For example, if students say it's the teacher's job to make class fun, the teacher might explain that she can't *make* anyone have fun, but she would be willing to write that it's her job to create lessons that are engaging and interactive.

If an item becomes a sticking point and can't be resolved, don't let it hold up progress. Table that item and return to it at the end of the discussion—it might clear up simply by going through the rest of the sections. Revisit these items at the end of the discussion and try again to resolve them using all the information on the sheet. Sometimes, differences can be clarified by referring to the school district's job description or student handbook, which should have clear parameters explained.

If differences can't be negotiated and they are not clearly spelled out anywhere, table those items and complete the charts based on points of agreement. Set a time (maybe a month out) to revisit the document and discuss whether the differences are having a negative impact on either the relationship or performance. If they're not, simply keep the document as it is. If they are, the leader may have to assert his or her authority and explain what she needs to include on the chart, as long as what she needs is reasonable and doesn't violate any contracts.

Print or make a copy of the final document for each member to keep. If both parties have agreed on all items on the chart, this document will reduce the likelihood of misunderstanding, conflict, and redundancy or gaps in areas of responsibility. Everyone will be clear about what is expected of her or him and what to expect from those she or he works with. This creates a sense of emotional safety and order and helps avoid relationship issues later on.

Building Connections

This section focuses on specific strategies you can use to create a greater sense of connection among various stakeholders in the school community.

Healthy Boundaries/ Healthy Relationships

According to the neighbor in Robert Frost's poem "Mending Wall": "Good fences make good neighbors." Similarly, among the many subgroups that exist in a school community, clear boundaries make healthy relationships. Where and how do we set the boundaries? I'm not referring to legal or ethical boundaries. Every educator is well aware (or should be) of those already. Instead, I'm referring to boundaries within our working relationships. It is up to school leaders and teachers to take the initiative to set up healthy boundaries.

Providing those you teach, manage, or lead with the following information helps them learn appropriate information about you as a person—in other words, what is in bounds. Telling people what you will and won't do for them lets them know what is *not* within boundaries. Sharing this information not only sets healthy boundaries, it helps students (or teachers) get to know you in a way that will strengthen the relationship.

Through your actions and words, think about ways you can share the following information during appropriate times.

Personal Information: Who You Are

What roles do you fill other than your role at school? Besides being a teacher, coach, or principal, are you also a brother, sister, mother, father, son, or daughter? Are you a music fan? Are you a reader, an amateur astronomer, a musician? Have you had other jobs? What information about yourself would you be willing to share that might improve students' (or others') perception of you as a person? (Also, consider what information about yourself is inappropriate to share.)

Character Information: What You Stand For

Which of the touchstone values are most important to you, and why? What other values or principles inform your teaching, counseling, managing, or coaching?

Here it is important to be sensitive. Focus on universal values such as honesty, respect, responsibility, empathy, or fairness—values that are relevant to the school and classroom. Avoid religious, political, family, or social values that might be controversial or alienate some people.

Students will primarily learn about your values by observing you and your interactions with others. However, community meetings based on touchstone values will give you an opportunity to discuss what the values mean to you through sharing life experiences.

Expectations

Be clear with your students, faculty, parents, or staff about the following. (Some of this is covered in the "My Job/Your Job/Our Job" activity on page 144.)

What you will ask them to do. What are your behavioral, character, academic, performance, or professional expectations? What will be required on a daily, weekly, per semester, or yearly basis?

What you will not ask them to do. This might include busywork, wasting time in meetings, or managing their peers.

What you will do for them. Include things like explaining directions in different ways, listening to them, letting them retest or redo assignments to achieve mastery, providing resources, and asking for their input or opinions.

What you will not do for them. You might mention lending money, giving rides to school, allowing them to break school rules or district policies, listening to complaining without a suggested solution, spoon-feeding them, and doing their work for them.

What you will do with them. This might include learning, discussing, exploring, playing learning games, and team-building activities.

What you will let them do on their own. This would include things like expecting them to work out conflicts for themselves before coming to you; requiring them to use resources to answer some of their questions before you give them the answers; and expecting them to come to you with questions about assignments or for extra help if they don't understand something or if they missed the directions to an in-class activity.

The best way to deliver these expectations to students is directly, by explaining them, and by providing them in writing. Consider using the "Positive Boundaries/Positive Relationships" handout (see the thumbnail on page 151) to clarify all of this information for yourself and your students/subordinates. You might post it in your room.

Friends vs. Buddies

Some people may misperceive this chapter's personal, relationship-oriented approach to teaching and managing as a sign that you want to be considered students' buddy. To avoid this misperception, share the following table and explain to students (or your faculty) that as a teacher (or coach, principal) you want to be their friend but not their buddy. If you are the school leader, ask your faculty and staff to share this same information with students.

When I am a friend, I:	When I am a buddy, I:
• truly care about students and/or staff as individuals • want what is best for students and staff • will listen to students and staff • will help students and staff • will encourage and support students and staff • will keep people accountable This results in *independence* for students and staff.	• socialize excessively with students or staff • make excuses for people • overextend: do things above and beyond for students and/or staff • say things like, "Do it for me" • allow irresponsible or inappropriate behavior This results in *dependence* for students and staff.

It's important that the individuals we teach or supervise like and respect us but also understand that we will not be taken advantage of or enable irresponsible behavior.

Community Building

While it is essential for you to develop trusting relationships *with* your students, athletes, staff, and so on, it is equally important to facilitate positive relationships *among* the people you supervise. Community meetings, touchstone development, and teaching social-emotional skills provide a good foundation for positive relationships among different stakeholders. Use the following activities in classrooms, sports practices, faculty meetings, chorus rehearsals, parent-teacher organization meetings, and other environments as ways of facilitating connection and communication among members of the group.

Concentric Circles

This activity is described in detail on page 97 for teaching students the Five Basic Human Needs. But it is a flexible activity that can be used to help develop a sense of structure and safety, too. It is an excellent way to develop relationships among members of the faculty, students in a classroom, members of a sports team, parent groups, or any other group. In faculty meetings, you can use it for discussing school issues, sharing information, or creative problem-solving. In the classroom, you can use it for discussing prior knowledge at the beginning of a learning unit, practicing new skills, reviewing, generating writing ideas, book sharing, and more. The only requirement is that you have enough space.

After reading the basic setup and directions on page 97, consider using Concentric Circles first as an icebreaker and get-to-know-you activity. After participants are comfortable with the structure, you might use it for academics or problem-solving, for example, having students review content or quiz one another. Or have students discuss books they've read and share what they liked about them, which helps everyone learn about other books they might want to read. Concentric Circles also makes an excellent brainstorming process that you can follow up with a community meeting to discuss the ideas that emerged.

If you're using Concentric Circles as an icebreaker or team-building exercise, here are some topics to consider:

- Things you do for fun
- Your favorite kind of music (or favorite song or group)
- A favorite food or dessert
- People you respect or admire
- A favorite movie, television show, YouTube series, book, game, and so on
- Something you wish people knew about you
- Something you are proud of
- A gift you would like to give the world
- Something you are grateful for
- Something you would do every day if you were independently wealthy

Musical Circles

This activity accomplishes the same goals as Concentric Circles and is a good alternative if you have less room. It is described in detail on page 98. Like Concentric Circles, use it as an icebreaker and relationship-builder, then use it for problem-solving, information sharing, or academics.

Do You Know Your Neighbors?

This activity gets people moving and laughing, helps them learn about one another, and is a lot of fun. Typically after this game, people are more relaxed but energized, so you can then get down to more serious business in a meeting or the classroom.

Time Required: 15 minutes

Materials Needed: A circle of chairs, one fewer than the number of people participating (including yourself)

The Activity
With participants sitting in circle, stand in the middle and say:

This is a game that helps you get to know others in the group a little better, share some things you enjoy, and see what you have in common with others. The person in the middle starts. It is very likely that each of you will be in my spot here in the middle at some point, so you all need to know what to do.

Then begin the game. Here's how it works:

The person in the middle turns to someone in the group, calls that person by name, and asks, "Do you know your neighbors?" (While explaining the game, you might demonstrate: "Sasha, do you know your neighbors?") That person simply introduces the people on either side of her. (Sasha says, "Yes, this is Tamiko, and this is David.")

Then the person in the middle asks the same person, "Is there anyone else you'd like to know?"

That person has to say yes (or the game is over and everyone is sad). She describes the kind of person she'd like to know by naming a criterion that is true about her. For example, Sasha might say something like, "Yes, I'd like to know anyone who likes soccer," "Yes, I'd like to know anyone who has a dog," or "Yes, I'd like to know anyone who has been to Disney World." The criterion can be

anything the speaker has, does, enjoys, might like, or has done—as long as it is true about the speaker (and appropriate for school).

Once the person being addressed states her criterion, she and everyone who fits that criterion has to get up and move to a different (empty) chair in the circle. People are not allowed to sit in the chair right next to them (they have to move at least two chairs away from where they started). The person in the middle will also try to get to a chair, meaning one person—a new person—will be left without a seat. That person will stand in the middle and will start from the beginning by asking a random person if he knows his neighbors.

Before getting started, you may want to do a practice round. Using the previous example, it might go like this:

You: Sasha, do you know your neighbors?

Sasha: Yes, they are Tamiko and Darnell.

You: Thank you. Is there anyone else you'd like to know?

Sasha: Yes, I'd like to know anyone who likes pizza.

You: Okay, everyone who likes pizza move to a new chair.

You and the students all try to find a new seat, leaving one person left in the middle. Now you're ready to begin, with that middle person acting as the starter. Play the game until time runs out or you sense the group has had enough (usually about 5–10 minutes).

I have used this game with ages five to adult, and everyone seems to really enjoy it. It breaks the ice, encourages laughter, increases energy, and helps students learn about one another. Here are a few hints and observations that might help you conduct the activity:

- With primary students, I've found that many of them want to be the center of attention, so they don't try to get to a chair and just stand around in the middle. You may want to emphasize that they have to do their best to get a seat.

- With middle and high schoolers (boys in particular), you will want to emphasize safety, saying something like, "This is not a full contact activity. Try *not* to run into anyone or knock anyone out of a chair."

- With all groups, explain that one of the objects of the game is to find things you have in common with others, so choosing a criterion that is unusual may leave you standing alone (for example, "someone who likes to get up at 5:00 a.m. on Sunday mornings and run 10 miles").

- With all groups, it sets a great example and sends a positive message if you and any other adults in the class participate.

For more community-building books and websites, see the list of resources on page 81.

Final Thoughts About Emotional Safety and Connectedness

As educators, there is so much demanding our time and attention that it seems difficult to justify playing games or doing team-building activities. (What if a board member walked in?) It may seem counterintuitive to spend time discussing who does what job or playing "Do You Know Your Neighbors?" when you have a mile-wide curriculum to teach or 100 observations to conduct.

But, like the other basic human needs, the need to feel safe and socialize is not something people can turn off while at school and turn back on at home. They're not the five basic *wants*, they're driving *needs*. If we don't structure the environment so people can meet these needs responsibly at school or in the classroom as a regular part of their day, then students or followers will figure out less-than-responsible ways to meet these needs, usually at others' expense. The time spent on these seemingly soft skills and attending to students' needs yields solid results.

Printable Forms

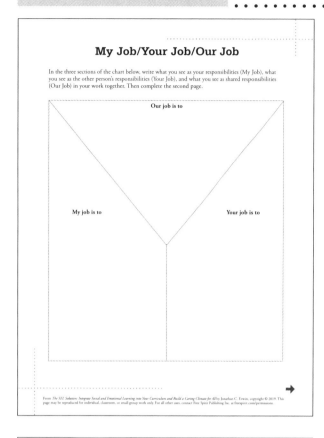

My Job/Your Job/Our Job

In the three sections of the chart below, write what you see as your responsibilities (My Job), what you see as the other person's responsibilities (Your Job), and what you see as shared responsibilities (Our Job) in your work together. Then complete the second page.

Our job is to

My job is to

Your job is to

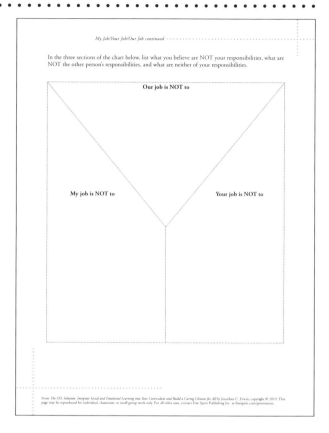

In the three sections of the chart below, list what you believe are NOT your responsibilities, what are NOT the other person's responsibilities, and what are neither of your responsibilities.

Our job is NOT to

My job is NOT to

Your job is NOT to

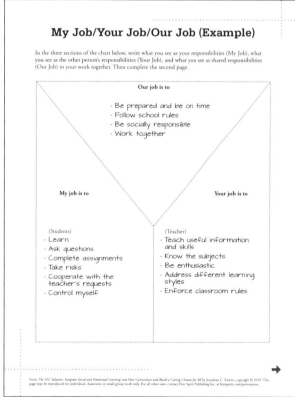

My Job/Your Job/Our Job (Example)

In the three sections of the chart below, write what you see as your responsibilities (My Job), what you see as the other person's responsibilities (Your Job), and what you see as shared responsibilities (Our Job) in your work together. Then complete the second page.

Our job is to

· Be prepared and be on time
· Follow school rules
· Be socially responsible
· Work together

My job is to

(Students)
· Learn
· Ask questions
· Complete assignments
· Take risks
· Cooperate with the teacher's requests
· Control myself

Your job is to

(Teacher)
· Teach useful information and skills
· Know the subjects
· Be enthusiastic
· Address different learning styles
· Enforce classroom rules

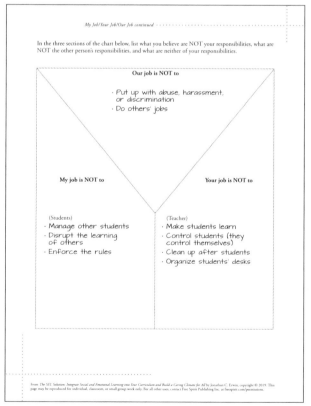

In the three sections of the chart below, list what you believe are NOT your responsibilities, what are NOT the other person's responsibilities, and what are neither of your responsibilities.

Our job is NOT to

· Put up with abuse, harassment, or discrimination
· Do others' jobs

My job is NOT to

(Students)
· Manage other students
· Disrupt the learning of others
· Enforce the rules

Your job is NOT to

(Teacher)
· Make students learn
· Control students (they control themselves)
· Clean up after students
· Organize students' desks

See digital content for full-size reproducible pages

Positive Boundaries/
Positive Relationships

Who I am	What I stand for

Positive Boundaries/Positive Relationships continued

What I will ask you to do	What I won't ask you to do

What I will do for you	What I won't do for you

What I will do with you	What I will let you do on your own

12

Addressing the Needs for **Power, Freedom, and Fun**

Chapter 11 focused on how to create the conditions under which students and adults could satisfy their needs for survival and love & belonging in the school setting. This chapter will explain how school leaders and teachers can enhance the school climate through addressing the needs for power, freedom, and fun by empowering, liberating, and encouraging play among those they supervise, coach, or teach.

If teachers and leaders in the school are consistently using community meetings and the community has developed a touchstone, the school is already taking important strides at empowering people. For this reason, and because adults in schools already enjoy positional power and a certain degree of autonomy that comes with it, more of this chapter will be devoted to helping those who often perceive themselves as less powerful and more controlled in school—students. However, everyone in a leadership position will benefit from using the Four Decision-Making Modes (pages 153–155), a model for empowering people, while making it clear when decisions are shared and when they are made by the leader. In addition, many of the activities and games listed later in the chapter can be used in professional development sessions as well as faculty, department, PTO, and staff meetings to encourage play and liberate adults from the stressful routine of the workday.

Power Issues

Many educators are reluctant to "give up" their power to students or the adults they supervise. The logic involved in this kind of thinking is faulty. The kind of power I'm discussing is personal power—the power of learning, achievement, and success—it isn't something someone can give up. It is only something one can strive for oneself or encourage or discourage in others. Power is not a commodity, like a pie, it is not as if one person having a slice of power takes away from someone else having some. That is scarcity thinking. One person's achievement, competence, or recognition does not take those things away from someone else. We can all learn, achieve competence, and receive recognition for our successes.

I'm not suggesting that we turn the school over to the students. The principal is still the authority in the school, the teacher in the classroom, and the coach on the court or field. There will still be rules, procedures, and accountability. What I am suggesting is empowering adults and students in ways that help us all satisfy our human needs and achieve more together. The power need, when not satisfied, can lead to all kinds of irresponsible and antisocial behavior, from disruption to meanness, bullying, insubordination, vandalism, or violence. Providing an empowering climate prevents many of these behaviors.

Empowering All

Shared decision-making can be a highly effective and empowering practice when done well, but it is sometimes misperceived by those involved in the decision-making practice. Sometimes people involved can become resentful if the leader makes a decision that the decision-making team didn't agree was their first choice. That may have been because the leader was simply seeking advisement from the team, not turning over the decision to the team. Or misunderstandings or resentment can also occur if the leader makes a decision without consulting the team.

In both of these cases, misperception and the subsequent bad feelings can be avoided if everyone in the decision-making process knows:

1. which decisions are team decisions and which decisions are solely the leader's

2. who makes and is responsible for the final decision

Knowing and using the Four Decision-Making Modes helps keep those roles clear.

The Four Decision-Making Modes

One of the most effective ways of increasing people's sense of personal power is simply to listen to them and involve them in decision-making whenever possible. When you have decisions to be made or projects to tackle, be deliberate about which mode you are using, and be clear with your group about which mode you are using. There are four modes to choose from.

Mode 1. The Leader Decides

Mode 1 decisions are made by the leader alone without any input from subordinates. Situations that call for Mode 1 decisions are those involving safety and immediacy. The superintendent decides when to close schools on snow days, for example. The teacher decides how the furniture is arranged in the classroom. The coach decides when to cancel practice. Other decisions that call for Mode 1 involve non-negotiables such as meeting times, observation times, discipline decisions, seating assignments, and assigning homework or duties.

People may not always agree with your Mode 1 decisions, but they do appreciate your ability and courage in making them in a fair and timely manner. If you see all decisions as Mode 1 decisions, however, you risk being perceived as a dictator or micro-manager. Whenever possible, empower students or staff using one of the higher decision-making modes.

Mode 2. The Team Advises

Mode 2 decisions are still made by you, the leader, but not until you have elicited input from the group you're working with. It's important that you emphasize that you will be making the final decision, but you want to hear ideas, concerns, questions, and suggestions from the group first so you can make the best-informed decision possible.

Mode 2 is useful when you want to listen to your staff, class, team, or club, but there is a sense of urgency or it's impractical to form a committee and come to consensus. Examples are a teacher asking for suggestions for service learning projects or educational field trips, or a coach asking for input on new uniforms or a new team logo. A principal might ask the faculty for suggestions for improving the release time procedure, ideas for celebrating completion of the school touchstone, or suggestions for additions to the next meeting's agenda.

Mode 3. The Whole Team Decides

In a Mode 3 decision, the leader, once explaining clear parameters (time, budget, legal, and so on), becomes an equal part of the team or committee that will come to consensus on the decision. It's important that when using this mode you do not rely on positional power to sway opinion. Otherwise, team members may perceive the committee as simply a ruse that only appears to share decision-making power, while in reality you have already made the decision. This results in distrust and resentment. While you have as much right to make suggestions as anyone else on the team, it's important to focus on listening, inviting ideas and concerns, raising concerns if the discussion begins to go outside the parameters you set at the onset, and encouraging consensus.

Mode 3 is suited for situations like setting or revising school policies and procedures (such as a cell phone policy); researching and possibly adopting a new school schedule; deciding on the class trip; deciding on a class pet; choosing classroom themes for the year; parents choosing fund-raising events; and a team choosing which invitationals to compete in. When you and your team reach a Mode 3 consensus-based decision, the team experiences a sense of accomplishment, pride, and ownership in its decision.

Mode 4. The Leader Delegates the Decision

A Mode 4 decision is when the leader delegates a decision to a committee, department, or team. Clearly explain the budgetary, time-related, or other parameters of an acceptable decision ahead of time, and then support whatever decision the committee makes. Mode 4 is suited for decisions that are specialized in nature or may be long, extended projects. Mode 4 is also suited for decisions such as curriculum planning and development; project and program development (such as a stop-texting-while-driving initiative); and event planning.

Any of the examples listed in Mode 3 could also be Mode 4 decisions. In deciding whether to make a decision in Mode 3 or 4, consider, 1) the time commitment you would be making to the team in Mode 3, and 2) your willingness to support whatever decision a committee will make. This requires a high degree of trust. While it is a risk to allow others to make a decision for which you as the leader will ultimately be held accountable, Mode 4 is a powerful way to develop the trust of others. In trusting people to make responsible decisions within acceptable guidelines, you will be perceived as a leader who treats others as professionals or as responsible students.

To better involve everyone and empower them, try to use Modes 3 and 4 as often as possible. But not all decisions are appropriate for delegating or sharing.

Misunderstanding the decision-making mode can lead to relational and attitudinal problems. For example, a team of people may think they are in Mode 4, believing they have the power to make the final decision. If they subsequently realize they were just an advisory committee—that they

Four Decision-Making Modes

Mode	Decision-Maker	Example Situations
Mode 1 The Leader Decides	The leader makes the decision on her or his own.	Issues of immediacy or safety Discipline issues Setting meeting times Assigning duties The day's agenda
Mode 2 The Team Advises	The leader asks for input from others but makes the final decision.	Agenda for meetings Ideas for a class trip Topics for community meetings Suggestions for conference day themes or topics Suggestions for improving the release-time procedure
Mode 3 The Whole Team Decides (including the leader)	The leader is an equal part of a team or committee that makes the decision by consensus.	Cell phone policy Conference day planning Creating or changing the school schedule Choosing PTO projects for the year Students and teacher choose themes for the school year Revising the discipline policy
Mode 4 The Leader Delegates	The leader delegates the decision to a committee or team, providing clear parameters.	Any of the examples in Mode 3 Social event planning Field day planning Door decorating contest Creating a character education event

were in Mode 2—and the leader ends up making a different decision, people on the committee will most likely be angry and resentful, and trust will erode. If, however, they knew ahead of time they were only making recommendations, they might be more likely to support the final decision.

If you're a principal, explain the different decision-making modes at the beginning of the year in a faculty meeting. Post the modes in meeting rooms and refer to them whenever you are in a decision-making situation, always reminding team members what mode they are in and alerting the team if the mode changes. You might have to change the mode, for example, if the one you initially choose ends up not being practical.

Teachers don't necessarily need to teach the four modes to students, but they should be conscious of explaining how much voice students have in any particular decision.

Empowering Adults

Here are other ways for principals and school leaders to help adults in a school gain personal power.

Acknowledge their presence. This seems like a no-brainer, but I have heard from hundreds of educators, parents, and teachers that one of their pet-peeves is when they meet a school leader in the main office or hallway and the leader doesn't even say hello. It probably is unintentional. The school leader probably has a hundred things on his mind and may be rushing to deal with the latest crisis. Unfortunately, people can't read the leader's mind and often end up feeling disrespected, or worse, invisible and unimportant. When leaders simply make eye contact and say, "Good morning!" or "How are you, Mrs. Jones?" staff, students, and parents feel as though they count.

Provide professional development. All teachers and staff need opportunities for learning and increasing their effectiveness. Offering opportunities for professional development is essential to a school's success.

Create a cadre of experts. Create teams of experts on various topics (literacy, character

education, technology integration, and so on), invest in professional development in their area of expertise, and involve them in training their colleagues. This approach to professional development enables staff and faculty members to take on a greater leadership role and have a greater impact on the school. It also saves the school money in the long run, because instead of paying for outside consultants and trainers, the school will have its own trainers—a team that understands the unique strengths and challenges of their school.

Provide recognition. I hesitate to suggest this, because it can easily turn into "Teacher of the Month" or something similar. That kind of singled-out, one-winner kind of recognition usually does more harm than good. If one person out of a faculty of 100 teachers, for example, is recognized each month, that means there are 99 losers each month, which can demoralize those who are doing an outstanding job and never "win." It also might create resentment toward the winner (brown-noser, suck-up). The best kind of recognition is done one-on-one and involves specific positive feedback. A principal might come into a teacher's classroom after school and say, "I walked by your class today while you were setting up for cooperative learning groups. The way you provided directions was very clear." Or the assistant principal might tell a cafeteria monitor, "I appreciate how you handled the situation with the kid who threw the cupcake. You really maintained your cool." The president of the PTO might call a volunteer and express her appreciation of the high quality job she did on the yearbook. This kind of recognition is far more meaningful than a Teacher of the Week trophy.

Empowering Students

Ironically, while the mission of schools is to empower students to succeed upon graduation, students often perceive themselves as powerless while in school. The following are ways of helping students satisfy their need for power by:

- giving them a voice: having their ideas and questions valued

- allowing students to generate some of the curriculum
- involving students in the development of their own assessments

Giving Students a Voice

Students spend a lot of time listening to adults: parents, teachers, coaches, club leaders, and so on. It is crucial for students to become good listeners. Effective listening skills are essential for following directions, learning, collaborating, building and maintaining relationships with family and friends, and for all other social interactions.

But, like all of us, students don't only need listening skills; they also need to be listened to. Being listened to sends an important message that they are valued and their ideas deserve respect, which in turn provides students with the opportunity to have an impact on their world. Additionally, being listened to builds and maintains important relationships. We enjoy being with people who listen to us; we avoid people who interrupt, criticize, or act as if we have nothing important to say.

Why then, don't many educators listen to students? The short answer is "Time!" It takes time to listen to students, time that would cut into what is already a packed school day. Teachers feel enormous pressures to cover the mandated curriculum and continually increase their students' performance, particularly on state and other standardized tests.

I sympathize with the pressures teachers feel today. Although listening to students does take time away from things like direct instruction and independent practice, it can accelerate students' learning and achievement[1] and provide support for and enhancement of the policies and programs already in place. Additionally, listening to students increases students' sense of community and personal importance, helping create a positive climate. The potential benefits far outweigh the costs.

Creating the touchstone and holding community meetings are two important ways of listening to students. Allowing students to help develop curriculum and assessments are two others.

[1] Loehr, P., 2011.

Student-Generated Curriculum

Through listening to and valuing students' questions, teachers can achieve three important goals: 1) showing students we care about them, 2) tapping into their intrinsic motivation to learn, and 3) making the curriculum, which is often dictated by the district, state, or federal education departments, meaningful to students on a personal level.

Two ways to encourage student-generated curriculum are: 1) to listen to and value students' spontaneous questions, and 2) to create structures such as the KWL and Beyond KWL that invite students to discuss what they already know about topics—and what they *want* to know (see page 157).

Valuing Spontaneous Questions

Sometimes questions happen spontaneously. As a teacher, be mindful of listening to students' spontaneous questions, keep a record of them, and think of ways the questions can be incorporated into lessons or learning units. You might be surprised how engaged students become when you not only listen, but help them find answers to their own questions. An experience I had as a curriculum coordinator shows how this can happen.

It was a rainy spring morning, and I was observing a fourth-grade classroom in Watkins Glen, New York. As the students were entering the room and settling into their seats, one student asked, "How come worms are all over the sidewalks and streets on rainy days?" Many teachers, in their zest to get to their lesson plans and cover the mandated curriculum, might have pretended not to hear the question or responded with a vague, "I don't really know, but let's turn to page 159 in our math books." This teacher, however, responded differently.

"That's a wonderful question!" she said. "Has anyone else ever wondered about that? I have!" Most students' hands went up. "Let's find out! Are there any other questions you have about worms?"

"Yeah," responded one boy, "Why are there worms, anyway? They're so gross!"

"What do they eat?" asked another student.

After listening to and writing down their questions about worms, the teacher told the class that they would start a science unit the next day that would answer all their questions. She went home that night and modified her lesson plans in a way that addressed her students' curiosity about worms, working their questions into a unit on ecosystems and the life cycle, a unit that was already part of New York state's mandated science curriculum. Just think how much more interested the students were in this unit than if she simply had them read the chapter in the science book and answer questions on a worksheet.

Use students' spontaneous questions to create engaging lesson plans. If the timing isn't right to address a particular question, keep a question board in the room to post students' questions, and return to them at an appropriate time.

KWL

As teachers we can't always count on spontaneous questions from students, but we can invite them. One way to do this is through the well-known KWL strategy. Before a new learning unit, check for prior knowledge by asking students what they *know* about the topic (the K). Then stimulate curiosity by asking what they *want* to know about the topic (the W). During the learning unit, we can make sure we answer (or even better, make sure they answer) the questions they generated. Finally, as a formative assessment, ask students in small groups what they have *learned* about the topic (the L). As each small group reports, the class engages in review, clarification, correction, and preparation for the summative assessment.

While the KWL strategy is well-known, many teachers do not practice it because it takes up instructional time. However, taking the time to find out what students already know about a topic can reduce redundant teaching and provide mental "hooks" to attach new information to. Asking, "What do you want to know?" increases student motivation to learn, which will, in turn, increase the amount and depth of the subsequent learning.

Beyond KWL

When working with older students (fifth grade and higher), sometimes asking, "What do you want to know about Medieval England (or the three levels of government, or Spanish culture, or quadratic equations)?" is met with resounding silence—or the response, "Nothin'." So instead of asking that, challenge them: "Let's see how many questions we can come up with regarding this topic." You can even turn it into a friendly competition between cooperative groups to see which group can come up with the most or most interesting questions. Consider handing out or posting the "Question Starters" handout (see the thumbnail on page 165) to help students come up with a variety of questions.

Once students have generated their questions, list all questions on the board. As a class, categorize and prioritize the questions. (Add your own questions to the list if students didn't ask all of the "right" questions in terms of the required curriculum.) Assign different groups of students to find the answers to certain questions and report back. When students teach each other, they feel like they are making a significant contribution to the class (power).

Student-Developed Assessments

Educators know the importance of providing clear expectations to students about what they are to know and be able to do and how their performance is going to be evaluated. One way of helping students understand these expectations is to involve them in developing the assessments. The following activity shows one way of doing this.

ACTIVITY

Inquiring Minds

Inquiring Minds is a way of engaging all students in a group-reading assignment and involving them in developing their own assessments. This activity works well with students who can read fluently, typically third graders and up.

Time Required: 30–40 minutes

Materials Needed:

- A laminated piece of card stock shaped like the letter X or a large plus sign positioned in the middle of the group; one "leg" of the X is labeled "Reader," another "Inquirer," the third "Answerer," and the last "Helper"

- A short reading assignment

- One piece of paper per group

- The "Question Starters" handout (see the thumbnail on page 165)

Getting Started

Arrange students into groups of four at a table or with desks facing together. If you have an odd number of students, have one group of three and you act as the Helper when they need you.

The Activity

Place the X in the center of each group's table so each leg of the X is pointing at a different student. Provide all the "Inquirer" students with a copy of the "Question Starters" handout. The "Reader" of each group reads a section of the text (just a paragraph or two), and the Inquirer develops a question based on the reading and writes it on a sheet of paper (the answer sheet). The Inquirer then passes the paper to the Answerer, who comes up with an answer and confers with the Helper to make sure they agree. Then they share the answer with the other two group members, and if everyone agrees, the Answerer writes down the response on the answer sheet.

The Helper not only helps the Answerer, but can also help the Reader, who might need assistance with some of the vocabulary, or the Questioner, who might need assistance coming up with a good question.

After this first round of reading, the Helper turns the X one place to the right, so that the Inquirer is now the Reader, the Answerer is now the Inquirer, and so on. Continue reading the assignment and repeat the process.

Once the reading assignment is completed, consider having the groups quiz one another or the whole class using the questions they developed.

To ensure that students follow the process with integrity and generate questions that are appropriate and sufficiently rigorous, you will want to engage students in guided practice until you are satisfied they are ready to work independently in teams.

Finishing

Collect the questions the students developed and use them to create a formative or summative assessment. This saves you time developing quizzes and tests and ensures the students have learned what they are expected to know for the assessment.

Collaborative Criteria

Give students a voice in developing the criteria for a summative assessment, providing them with a sense of power and clarifying academic expectations. This strategy is not designed for multiple choice or short answer tests, but for reports, multimedia presentations, panel discussions, poster presentations, skits, and other student-centered, performance-based assessments.

All grade levels can participate in creating collaborative criteria. Even kindergartners can be engaged in what they think a good poster, book share, or *All About Me* book and presentation look and/or sound like. You may need to ask more clarification questions with them such as *What would I be seeing?* and *What would I be hearing?* These will guide them to appropriate criteria.

After giving students an assignment, tell them they are going to help create the rubric or checklist on which they will be assessed. Explain that this will help clarify for everyone what is expected of them.

Begin by having students discuss with a partner for one to two minutes what they believe makes a high-quality presentation (or essay or whatever you have assigned). What criteria do they think is important to include on the rubric? After two minutes, invite each pair to suggest criteria they came up with and discuss each one as a class. List points of consensus on the board. If they have not included important criteria, explain that as the teacher and expert, you will be adding additional criteria you think are important. Add them to the group's list and explain why.

When you develop the rubric or checklist for the assessment, include the students' criteria.

Teachers can listen to students regarding other kinds of performance assessments as well, asking things like: What does a high-quality homework assignment look like? What are the characteristics of a high-quality essay or story? What does a high quality lab report look like and include? Teachers can always add criteria that are important to standards and understanding the unit, but listening to students' ideas helps them gain a clear understanding of the expectations and gives them some ownership in the process.

Collaborative Criteria Example

For the students' summative assessment at the end of an 11th-grade humanities unit on the 1930s, I assigned a 15- to 20-minute presentation that would demonstrate their understanding:

of the social, political, and economic conditions of the 1930s

of the plot and characters of Steinbeck's *The Grapes of Wrath*

that art (in this case literature) is often shaped by the times in which it is created

that the times are sometimes influenced by art

Students could work individually, with a partner, or with a group, and their presentation could take any of several forms: a formal speech, a song or rap, a work of art accompanied by an explanation of its meaning, a skit, or any other creative way that might demonstrate their understanding.

I gave students the opportunity to develop the criteria by telling them, "You will be an audience member for all of these presentations. What characteristics would make watching and listening to these presentations enjoyable?" The students brainstormed a list, and we came to consensus that:

The presentations would clearly demonstrate the students' understanding of the content.

The presentations would appear to be well-organized.

All members of groups or pairs would take an equal role in the presentations.

Presenters should be audible and clear.

The presentations should emotionally or actively engage the audience.

The presenters should not simply read their speech or scripts—they should be able to make eye contact with the audience and/or one another.

I then made a grading rubric based on these criteria. During the several days the students worked on their presentations, sometimes in class, I was able to meet with each presenter and group of presenters to help them address each of the criteria on the rubric. Listening to the students and getting their input paid off. The final presentations included formal speeches, paintings with explanations of how the paintings demonstrated their understandings, songs and raps that students composed, and a game show *Family Feud*-style, which had the Joad family from Steinbeck's novel on one side playing against the California fruit growers on the other. In general, these presentations were more engaging and of a much higher quality than I'd experienced in the past when all the criteria came from me.

Liberating

The need for freedom, independence, and autonomy is a powerful force. If people feel manipulated or controlled, oftentimes they feel an urge to resist in order to regain their independence, resulting in behaviors like avoidance, absenteeism, rule breaking, acting out, or withdrawing. This is true for adults and students. Freedom may be one of the most difficult needs to meet in a school setting: School employees or students are required to be at work or in class for a certain number of hours; while in school, their schedules are set for them, they have rules and protocols to follow, and they have lots of tasks to accomplish.

However, within the restrictions of a structured school environment, school leaders and teachers can liberate their staff and students in ways that will address their need for independence, autonomy, and novelty.

Liberating Staff and Faculty

Here are some general strategies leaders can use to help the adults in the school community fulfill their need for freedom.

Suggestion Box

Provide a place where staff can make suggestions for improving current practices or offering solutions to school problems. No complaints are allowed unless accompanied by a solution.

Open-Door Policy

If school leaders keep an open-door policy whenever possible, it provides staff with access to the leader within their highly structured schedules. As the school leader or teacher, establish and communicate to staff or students the criteria for what constitutes an appropriate "drop-in" in order to avoid unnecessary distractions.

Regular Social Gatherings

Provide opportunities for faculty and staff to have fun together in their free time. Hold monthly events, building in as much novelty as possible to involve as many faculty and staff as possible: bowling parties, softball games, board game night, sledding or skiing in winter, pool parties, picnics, hiking. Consider forming a committee to survey the staff, come up with interesting events, and create a schedule. Not only does this provide novelty and fun, it frees people from their work roles and helps teachers, custodians, secretaries, school leaders, and others see one another as human beings. (These should not be mandatory; that would negate the purpose. Instead, focus on making the events fun and people will want to come.)

Emphasize Autonomy

Whenever possible, avoid telling people how to do their jobs. It is the leader's role to communicate expectations clearly and then to trust staff to be competent, responsible professionals. It is the responsibility of teachers, assistant principals, and staff members to know how to do their jobs. Of course, if they ask for help or are not achieving quality results, then suggestions and coaching are in order.

In addition, leaders can help liberate their staff by encouraging play. See the "Encouraging Play" section on pages 162–165 for games that will enliven meetings and help people enjoy a break from the daily stresses.

Liberating Students

Since we are not likely to change attendance laws or let students choose to attend only their favorite classes, we can liberate students within the structure of the school day by providing choices and integrating novelty and play into the classroom. This way we can help them meet their needs for freedom and fun *and* keep them in school.

Awareness

One way to help students meet their need for freedom is by helping them understand how much of what they do every day is a choice. You can do that by conducting the "I Have To . . . " community meeting on pages 88–89. When students understand that almost everything they do is their choice, it helps them feel a sense of both liberation and personal empowerment.

Choices

When offering choices to students, it's important to keep students' developmental levels and ages in mind—provide fewer choices for younger students, more choices for more mature students. Also, it is important to discuss that with freedom comes responsibility. For example, freedom to choose where to sit comes with the responsibility to behave in your chosen spot. Consider providing students with choices regarding:

- where they sit
- collaborative or cooperative learning partner(s)
- homework assignments
- literature
- writing topics
- work they publish
- what is included in their portfolio
- room decor (consider providing wall space in the room for their art, photos, posters, and so on)

Choices in Assessment

In including student voice though the "Collaborative Criteria" activity described on pages 158–159, students are both empowered and liberated from the traditional teacher-centered approach. As the teacher, however, you are responsible for making sure the rigorous standards for the class are kept in place. Criteria that address those standards are not negotiable. In that respect, students have little choice.

What they can choose, however, is *how* they demonstrate what they have learned. If a student is a strong writer, he might choose to write a traditional essay to demonstrate his understanding. Another student, musically skilled, could choose to write and perform a song. A group of students might choose to work together to develop a skit that meets the criteria. The table below lists a wide variety of assessment options you might offer students.

When providing assessment choices to students, keep in mind the following:

- Some skills and information can only be assessed in certain ways. For example, learning to write a persuasive essay can really only be authentically assessed through writing a persuasive essay.

- Make sure the choices you offer students satisfy your grade-level standards.

- Start gradually. Offer two or three choices to younger students (and to older students when you first introduce this new approach).

- Do not simply present the list of options in the table and ask students to choose. Only let students choose from a list of assessment strategies that will address standards. Older students (fifth grade and up) can be provided as many as a dozen choices.

- Tell students that if they're interested in an option not on your list, they will need to discuss and clear it with you first.

Of course, offering choices for every unit isn't practical. Sometimes only one method demonstrates a certain skill (solving quadratic equations, for example). But whenever assessing declarative knowledge (information) as well as some procedural knowledge (skills), providing developmentally appropriate choices allows students to play to their strengths and be liberated from the one-size-fits-all assessment.

Assessment Options

advertisement	documentary	oral report
advice column	drawing	painting
animation	editorial	pamphlet
artifact collection	electronic storybook	parody
autobiography	essay	photo essay
bar graph	experiment	pie chart
bill of rights	field manual	play
blog	flow chart	poem
book jacket	gallery	poster
book report	game	puppet show
brochure	game show	rap song
campaign speech	graph	report
cartoon	graphic organizer	review for newspaper
CD or DVD cover	guidebook	role play
celebrity profile (historic figures)	illustration	scrapbook
chart	interview	sculpture
cinquain	journal	short story
classification system	keynote	skit
classified ad	learning centers	soap opera
collage	letter to the editor	social media profile page
comic book	lyrics	song
commercial	memorandum	speech
crossword puzzle	mnemonic device	TV newscast
debate	model	video
demonstration	monologue	visual aid
dialogue	mural	year (or decade) in review
diary	music	yearbook
digital slideshow presentation	newsletter	
diorama	newspaper	

Novelty

Research tells us that the brain thrives when ritual (such as routines, procedures, predictability) is mixed with novelty. Novelty gets and helps keep the students' attention, breaks up the tedious routine, and creates curiosity—the optimal state for learning.

Here are some ways to bring novelty into the classroom:

- Teach in or from a different location. You might do a lesson from a different part of the room, take the students outside, or conduct a lesson in a different part of the school.

- Play music in the classroom for a variety of purposes, for example, as background for a warm-up or journal writing activity, to celebrate individual or class successes, to celebrate special days, to energize students, or to inspire creativity.

- Use a variety of instructional strategies to address different learning styles, including direct instruction, cooperative and collaborative learning, kinesthetic learning, videos, computers, and learning games.

- Take field trips.

- Change students' seats when you begin a new learning unit.

- Use a variety of seating arrangements. Form follows function: a circle for class discussions, desks facing forward in rows for direct instruction, desks pushed together in pairs for collaborative learning, and four desks facing each other for cooperative learning.

- Insert an energizer or guided stretch break into a lesson.

- Invite a guest speaker.

- Hold theme days: 1980s day, dress in school colors day, dress backward day, slippers day, dress like a business executive day, crazy hair day, funny hat day, or other fun, appropriate ideas you come up with.

- Use a variety of attention-getting signals like a hand clap, wind chimes, call and response, music, and so on.

Encouraging Play

Like all mammals, humans play. The purpose of play is rooted in our need to bond with members of our species (love & belonging) and our need to learn (power). Laughter and play, aside from helping us build and maintain relationships and learn, also help reduce stress. Unlike the other needs, the activities in this section can be used with equal ease with adults or students. The following are some tried-and-true activities that are fun for all ages and guaranteed to generate lots of laughter.

ACTIVITY

The Name Game

Participants will learn one another's names in a fun and memorable way.

Time Required: 15–20 minutes

The Activity

Participants first choose a word that describes them that begins with the first letter (or sound) of their first name. They might choose an adjective (Enthusiastic Elena), a sport they enjoy (Soccer Sasha), a food they love (Doritos Darnell), an activity they enjoy (Xbox Xavier), or any other interest that relates to them (Rappin' Rivera, Shopping Charmaine, Movie-loving Mai Lin). Give them a few minutes to come up with their describing word and encourage them to talk to a partner or two about what they might choose. Emphasize that the word they choose should have positive connotations.

Once everyone has chosen their descriptor, explain how the game works: One person (the adult leader) will start by saying his descriptor and his name (I use Jelly Belly Jelly Bean Jon, just to give them a challenge). The person to the leader's left goes next, saying the leader's descriptor-name and adding her own (Jelly Belly Jelly Bean Jon, Tap Dancing Tamiko). The person to her left continues, saying the first two descriptor-names and adding his own. This goes on until the last person in the circle has the challenge of repeating everyone's descriptor-name. To be fair, I encourage the adult leader to finish by doing the same.

Participants, especially those toward the end of the circle, may groan when they hear the directions. Explain that you're not going to hang them out to dry—if they need help, they are allowed to ask for help. Some people reach for paper and pencil, which I allow, but I do encourage them to try to do without.

Finishing

After the game, to enhance the purpose of this activity, ask students how they were able to learn and remember so much new information in such a short period of time. Students' answers will include: repetition, using visual imagery, the use of alliteration, active listening, feeling accountable, and the fact that it was fun. Explain that they can use these same strategies in their academic classes to remember class content.

ACTIVITY

Electric Eyes

This game provides a quick break for students and gives them practice in making eye contact.

Time Required: 5 minutes

The Activity

Electric Eyes can be done in less than five minutes from beginning to end or extended by playing multiple rounds. Start by having everyone stand in a circle. When you say, "Look down!" everyone looks at the floor. When you say, "Electric Eyes!" everyone is to look at someone's eyes. Repeat. Each time you say "Electric Eyes," participants can choose to look at the same person's eyes or someone else's. When two people make eye contact, they are both "out." They sit down or step back, while the people in the circle continue. Tell those who are out that their job is to watch the players and make sure they are following the rules. One of the best things about this game is it's as much fun watching (once you are out) as it is playing.

Close up the circle slightly each time people leave. Continue until you end up with the final survivor (or two if there are an even number of participants).

Finishing

Hold a discussion about eye contact, asking questions like:

- How does it feel to make eye contact?
- Did anyone feel uncomfortable making eye contact? Why do you think that is?
- When making eye contact with someone, when does it become uncomfortable?
- When is it important to make eye contact? Why?

ACTIVITY

Group Juggle

This favorite activity not only is a great energizer, it also leads to a discussion about cooperation.

Time Required: 15–20 minutes

Materials Needed: Five soft balls or small stuffed animals (Koosh balls, stress balls, and beanbags work well; avoid using a bouncy ball)

The Activity

Have participants stand in a circle with their hands in front of them. Call out the name of another participant in the circle, make eye contact with that person, and toss him the ball or stuffed animal. After catching the ball, that player calls the name of another player, makes eye contact with that person, and tosses the ball to her. After players throw the ball, they put their hands behind their backs so it will be clear who has not caught the ball yet.

Continue the process until everyone has caught the ball. The ball is then tossed back to you (or whoever was the first player). Once the pattern is established, the first player starts again, this time following the first ball with a second one to the same participant, and the group completes the juggle with both balls. The third time, add a third ball, and continue to add balls each time through. The challenge is to see how many balls the group can have going at one time.

Variations

- With a set number of balls (six, for example), time how long it takes the group to complete the juggle once. Then do it again and see if you can beat that time. Discuss as a group and try various ways to improve the time.
- Once all the balls are in play, the leader shouts, "Switch" and everyone reverses the order of the pattern (if you threw me the ball, now I throw it to you).

Finishing

Immediately after the game, hold a class discussion asking students:

- What was our goal? What did we do that helped us achieve our goal?

- Is there anything that we did that got in the way of achieving our goal?

- What could we do to improve the process?

- How is playing this game like life? How is it like being in school or being a member of a family? Can you think of other analogies?

- What attitudes and behaviors help us make this game successful? Where else could those attitudes and behaviors be useful?

- How can we use what we learned through this activity to make school and our classroom a better place to learn?

ACTIVITY

Balloon Teams

This activity will get the students laughing while demonstrating the importance of cooperation and interdependence. (**Caution:** This activity cannot be used in a school or classroom in which a student is allergic to latex.)

Time Required: 10 minutes

Materials Needed: One large (helium quality) balloon per group of three students

The Activity

Have participants form groups of three, and give each group a balloon to blow up. (For younger students, provide inflated balloons.) Have the groups of students form circles, facing inward, hands joined. The object of the game is to keep the balloon up in the air without letting go of hands. They can use any body part to keep the balloon afloat.

To add an extra challenge, give the groups a second balloon. Or give them directions like "Heads only," "Elbows only," or "Hands only."

Finishing

Afterward, hold a discussion about what made the groups successful. One point that participants may bring up is the importance of being flexible and resourceful in our attempts to achieve goals. Also, participants may mention that different people accomplish similar goals in diverse ways.

ACTIVITY

Balloon Juggle

This activity can be used simply as an energizer or can be extended as a team-building activity. You may want to let your neighbors know ahead of time they'll be hearing some loud pops. (**Caution:** This activity cannot be used in a school or classroom in which a student is allergic to latex.)

Time Required: 10–15 minutes

Materials Needed: One large (helium quality) balloon per participant.

Gather the group in a standing circle and explain the game: You are going to toss a balloon into the circle, and their job is to keep it up in the air as best they can. If a balloon hits the ground, simply pick it up and put it back into play. After the group goes for a while (maybe half a minute) with one balloon, add a second balloon and tell them they have to keep them both in the air. Then, after another few seconds, add a third balloon. Keep introducing one balloon at a time until you have the same number of balloons as students in the game.

Extension

Place folded slips of paper inside each balloon with discussion topics like those listed in "Suggested W.H.I.P. Sentence Starters" on page 32. After you've introduced all the balloons into the game, stop the action and have students pair up (possibly with someone who has the same color balloon). Pairs go somewhere in the room, pop their balloons, and answer the questions inside. This way the activity turns into another great team builder.

You can also use this as a review activity by putting questions about content in the balloons.

Finishing

Bring participants back to the circle to discuss their questions and answers.

ACTIVITY

Group Knot

This popular group challenge is guaranteed to create laughter as it teaches about cooperation and leadership.

Time Required: About 15 minutes

The Game

Have an odd number of students stand in a circle. With younger students, five students is best—they're more likely to be successful. With older students, seven or nine students is a good-sized group. If your class or group is larger, you can have two or more groups going simultaneously or, if space is limited, have teams take turns.

Ask everyone in the group to reach out and grab two other hands. They should not hold both hands of the same person, and they should not hold the hand of someone directly next to them. One person must leave their right arm out and one person must leave their left arm out.

Next, direct the group to untangle, without letting go of hands, so that the students are standing in a straight line. Carefully observe their behavior as they work to solve their dilemma.

Finishing

Hold a discussion, asking students:

- What behaviors helped the group solve the problem? Did any behaviors slow you down?
- Did leadership emerge? How?
- What enabled you to be successful (or prevented you from success)?

The discussion following this game might also use the group knot as a metaphor: Make the point that in life we sometimes get ourselves into difficult situations, but with patience, cooperation, and help from others we can resolve our problems.

Final Thoughts on Empowering, Liberating, and Encouraging Play

People who help us achieve our basic needs become part of our Quality World (or Personal GPS, see Chapter 8). We trust them, hold them in high regard, and allow them to influence us. When students, teachers, staff, and school leaders are able to satisfy these needs in responsible ways in the classroom and at school, everyone's behavior tends to be more personally and socially responsible. Less time is spent addressing discipline or performance issues, and more time can be devoted to learning.

Printable Form

Question Starters		
Who . . . ?	What . . . ?	Where . . . ?
Who might . . . ?	What was . . . ?	Where might . . . ?
Who would . . . ?	What were . . . ?	Where could . . . ?
Who seemed . . . ?	What if . . . ?	Where do . . . ?
Which . . . ?	What could . . . ?	Where would you find . . . ?
Which might . . . ?	What might . . . ?	Where might you look for . . . ?
Which could . . . ?	What facts . . . ?	Where in the text . . . ?
Which were . . . ?	What can . . . ?	Where do you see . . . ?
How . . . ?	Why . . . ?	Can . . . ?
How might . . . ?	Why might . . . ?	Can you list . . . ?
How would . . . ?	Why do . . . ?	Can you name . . . ?
How do . . . ?	Why should . . . ?	Can you explain . . . ?
How is . . . ?	Why are . . . ?	Can you describe . . . ?

See digital content for full-size reproducible pages

A Social-Emotional Approach to **Behavior Management**

No matter how positive your school climate is or how well all members of the community use social-emotional skills, human beings will, at times, make mistakes and behave irresponsibly. Many behavior management (or discipline) systems rely heavily on external control, punishing students through denying them privileges, isolating them in school, assigning detention, suspending them, and so on. Having reasonable consequences for irresponsible behavior is important, but relying on consequences alone to change behavior is not enough. Effective behavior management should always have an educational component. Consequences in and of themselves do not teach anyone a better way to behave.

This chapter does not prescribe a complete discipline program (that would be a book unto itself), but it does share useful conferencing tools and other strategies based on your school's touchstone and social-emotional concepts that you can use with students and adults when behavior management is necessary.

The chapter centers on three main approaches to classroom and other behavior management that can be used in conjunction together as well as fit in with many other behavior management systems you may already have in place. The three approaches are:

- **The Process for Positive Change (PPC),** a long-term strategy for helping people become internally motivated to improve behavior

- **Restorative Discipline (RD),** an extension of the PPC that focuses on situations in which one person needs to repair damage he or she has done to someone else

- **The Solving Circle,** a simple, practical conflict resolution process

What these three approaches have in common is that they:

- are non-punitive, which helps maintain the relationship between the teacher and student or the administrator and staff member

- have an educational component—the student or staff member learns to replace an unacceptable behavior with a more responsible one

- make use of the SEL concepts and skills taught in Part 2 of this book

These three approaches can be used by anyone in the school whose role is to manage students or adults. While the first two approaches may seem to be geared toward older students or adults, this chapter provides ways of modifying them for use with younger students. The third approach, the Solving Circle, is used the same way for any age.

These strategies can also be used in a wide variety of contexts and can be used for both minor infractions (forgetting to do homework, arriving late to school two days in a row, or being unprepared) and more chronic or serious behaviors (chronic name-calling, failing academically, spreading rumors, being frequently absent, not fulfilling work duties).

Very serious infractions like violence, chronic insubordination, drug or alcohol use, vandalism, or harassment need to be dealt with seriously using superintendent's hearings, parent involvement, mandated counseling, and/or law enforcement involvement. The strategies in this chapter are not designed to address those kinds of infractions.

The Process for Positive Change (PPC)

Based on William Glasser's Counseling with Choice Theory, PPC is a simple yet highly effective way of helping people learn more responsible, productive behavior. It is also a process an individual can use to set personal or professional goals and improve their efficacy in achieving them. It can even be used by groups of people (such as classes, faculties, parent groups, sports teams, drama casts, and academic departments) as a process for continuous improvement: to identify shared goals and achieve them effectively and efficiently.

The emphasis here, however, is on how the Process for Positive Change can be used in schools as a behavioral management protocol. Though it can be used in a variety of contexts, including adults working with other adults, to keep things simple, I use the term *teacher* for the person who is using the PPC to counsel someone and the term *student* to refer to the person being counseled.

Why PPC Works

PPC is based on the following premises:

1. **People are doing the best they can.** This does not mean that they can't do better; it simply means that, in general, human beings don't intentionally cause problems for themselves. Given the knowledge and social-emotional resources at their disposal, they are doing their best at the time to satisfy their very real, legitimate needs.

2. **All effective discipline involves learning.** This premise follows from the first. If people are doing the best they can and are still breaking rules or being disruptive, they need to learn new behaviors that are acceptable in a school context.

3. **Coercion doesn't work.** Traditional discipline involves a significant amount of coercive

behavior, such as threatening consequences, humiliating students (publicly at times), yelling, nagging, criticizing, using sarcasm, punishing, and lecturing.

Another popular coercive technique is bribing, most often known as rewarding. Rewards can be as destructive as coercion to our goal of encouraging students to learn and behave responsibly for the right reasons. In his now famous book *Punished by Rewards*, Alfie Kohn does a meta-analysis of the research on the effectiveness of reward systems and concludes that rewards:

- Damage relationships, increasing the power differential between the authority figure and the students or staff.

- Decrease intrinsic motivation, creating the mindset of "What are you going to give me if I comply?"

- Decrease interest in what we are trying to get people to do. Rewards feel manipulative and create cognitive dissonance. "There must be something inherently wrong with what they are asking me to do if they have to offer me a reward to do it."

- Decrease productivity (learning) and creativity. In his *New York Times* best-selling book *Drive,* Dan Pink shares research underscoring this point: A large-scale study at the London Institute of Economics analyzed dozens of studies of pay-for-performance plans and concluded that incentives result in a negative impact on overall performance.

- Punish. When a promised reward is withheld, it has the same effect as a punishment.

Instead of being another coercive tool (extrinsic motivator) aimed at controlling people, PPC is a conferencing approach that focuses on placing the responsibility for an individual's behavior on the individual and empowering that individual by involving him or her in the solution. When PPC is used effectively, behavior change results not because the person is going to get a reward or avoid punishment, but because the process helps her or him choose a behavior that is in itself needs-satisfying. No external reward is necessary; the internal reward is enough.

In addition, PPC:

- encourages personal and social responsibility

- enhances a sense of emotional safety in the school

- maintains or improves the relationship between the teacher and student

- can be taught to students and adults as a tool for self-regulation and self-efficacy

In general, PPC involves asking people to examine what they want in a given situation or to prioritize what they want. This is done in a private conference after a behavior incident at a time when neither the teacher nor the student is upset. Depending on how emotionally charged the situation was, that might be minutes, hours, or up to a whole day after the inciting incident. Once the student has a clear and compelling vision of what she wants (her Personal GPS destination in this situation), she is asked to "look in the mirror"—to undergo an honest self-examination of her behavior. Next, she is asked to evaluate her behavior in terms of her destination vision and make a plan for positive change (or continued success).

The Conferencing Environment

Before attempting to address the concern at hand (whether it's a performance, academic, or behavior issue), it is essential to establish a positive conferencing environment, one that:

- sets clear roles and goals

- establishes trust

- creates an emotional safety zone

- expresses optimism

Here are some ways you can establish that kind of environment:

- Hold the conference in a private space and assure confidentiality. (With students, in some cases it might be necessary to explain mandated reporter guidelines.)

- Hold the conference when both parties are calm, not during "the heat of the moment."

- Sit down with the student ideally at a table or with no furniture in the way (not from behind a big desk).

- Make a personal connection with the student. If your relationship with the student is already strong, this can be as easy as asking about something you know he is interested in such as a sports team he likes or a club he's interested in. If the relationship is not as strong, or is new, ask questions that relate to the student's Five Basic Human Needs. For example:

  - Who are some of your friends here at school? (love & belonging)

  - Tell me about your family (love & belonging)

  - What are some things you are good at? (power)

  - What's your favorite subject? (power)

  - What do you like to do when you're not in school? (freedom)

  - What's fun for you? (fun)

  - What are some things you like to do? (this could bring out any need)

- Make statements that set a noncoercive, positive tone. For example:

  - We're here to solve a problem, and I'm sure that we can work things out so that we are both satisfied with the results.

  - I'm not interested in punishment or consequences. I'm interested in a solution to a problem. (If the student is unresponsive or uncooperative, you might ask, "If we could work this out without having to look at [detention, suspension, a letter of reprimand], would you be interested in that?" If still unresponsive or uncooperative, you may have no choice but to administer consequences.)

  - If you are willing to work this out with me, I believe we can come up with a solution to this problem pretty easily.

  - I want you to know that I'm not yelling at you. I'm here to help you solve a problem. (This is useful with younger students, who tend to think that when an adult speaks to them about discipline they are being "yelled at.")

The Conferencing Environment

Set roles and goals

Establish trust

Create a safe zone

Express optimism

PPC: Four General Questions

Once you have established a positive, comfortable environment, it's time to conduct the four steps at the heart of PPC. Answer all of these questions in order.

Question 1. What do you want (or need)?

This question is rarely asked as simply as that. Frame it in the context of the problem: What kind of grade do you want in math? How do you want your fellow faculty members to perceive you? What kind of person do you want to be in this difficult situation?

These questions tap into the source of the student's motivation, his or her Personal GPS (see Chapter 8). It is important to help students get a clear mental picture of what they really want in this situation and how achieving this goal will add to the quality of their life. Without a compelling vision, behavioral change, already difficult, becomes close to impossible.

The questions can also help the student identify his or her goals. Let the discussion and the situation guide you. The situation might call for short-term goals, like grades; longer-term goals, like graduating; or life goals, like being a responsible person. It's not necessary or appropriate to ask all of these questions. The point is to have the students articulate a vivid picture of what they really want in the situation you're discussing and how achieving that goal will make their lives better.

Here are some question starters you may want to consider at this stage:

- What do you want in terms of _____?
- What kind of grade would you like in _____?
- How do want to be treated by _____?

- What do you hope to accomplish in _____?
- How would you like _____ to be?
- Draw me a picture of how you would like _____ to be?
- How would your life be better (at home, at school, in the long run, in the short run) if you achieved this want?
- What kind of person do you want to be?
- What kind of student (teacher, employee, athlete, cast member, school leader) do you want to be?
- What is it you *don't* want? (Then flip the answer to a positive. For example, if the student doesn't want people saying mean things to her, you can say, "So, are you saying what you want is for people to be nice to you, or to leave you alone?")

Another approach to asking about the students' wants is to refer to the touchstone. Since everyone in the school was involved in developing the touchstone, you might use it as leverage, asking one or more of the following, depending on the situation:

- When we developed the touchstone, we all committed to (your list of values). What does (the relevant value) look like in this situation?
- Do you still value being (one of the touchstone values)?
- At this school, we believe in (one of the touchstone values). What would being (that value) look like in this situation?
- What is it that you wanted that you were trying to get by (problem behavior)?

This final question is very useful for teachers when dealing with disruptive student behavior. If we can identify what a misbehaving student is trying to achieve, we can help that student find a more appropriate way to accomplish it.

If the student has learned about the Five Basic Human Needs, you can ask, What is it you need that you were trying to get by (problem behavior)?

We can't always get the specific thing that we want. However, as the Rolling Stones accurately sang, "You can't always get what you want. But if you try sometimes you'll get what you need." Sometimes the student's stated want is unattainable or unacceptable. But, if we can discover the underlying need driving the behavior, we can help people substitute the unattainable want for one that satisfies that same need. For example, Jordan may come to realize that all her attention-seeking, class-clown behavior is aimed at meeting her need for power. She wants to feel important and loves the impact her jokes have. Another way Jordan might meet the need for power in class in a responsible way is to tutor other students when she finishes her work. This way she can feel both a sense of importance and like she's making a difference.

Other questions that help students clarify their wants revolve around feelings:

- How do you want to feel in this situation?
- How will you feel if you achieve this goal?

It can help to suggest a feeling that you think the student might be looking for: Do you want to feel (strong, confident, more calm, or accepted)?

You might also refer to the concept of total behavior, reminding students that they directly control their thoughts and feelings (the front wheels of the car) and, through choosing effective thoughts and actions, they can indirectly control their feelings and body state.

- What would you like to be able to do in terms of _____?
- What would you like to be able to say to yourself (thinking) when we solve this problem?
- If you achieved your want, what would you be able to do that you can't do now?
- How would you feel physically if you achieved your goal?

As a teacher, you also have wants and goals—such as protocols to be followed, students to be learning, rules to be followed, and so on. Before moving onto the second question, it's important that you state your wants as well. For example:

- I need to be able to teach.
- I need to be able to trust that the students are safe at all times.
- I need you to be here on time.
- I have the right to be treated with respect.

Question 2. What are you doing?

This component of PPC holds up the mirror to the student, asking him to look at his total behavior in terms of achieving his goals. Based on the premise that all behavior is purposeful, this set of questions looks at what the person is doing that is helping him achieve his goals or hurting his chances of success. It involves all four components of total behavior but focuses on what the student can most directly control: his thoughts and actions. After a thorough examination of what the student is currently doing (thinking, feeling), he will be able to make an evaluation of his behavior.

Here are some questions you can use to help hold up a mirror to what the student is doing.

- What are (were) you doing?
- If there were a video camera on you, what would it show?
- What are you doing to get what you want?
- What are you thinking in terms of achieving your goal?
- How are you feeling about your goal? (emotionally or physically)
- What have you done in the past to achieve a similar goal?
- What are you doing that is helping you achieve your want? What are you doing that is preventing it?
- What else are you doing?
- In this situation, who can you control? (This is useful if students blame others for their behavior.)

This line of questioning sometimes uncovers a conflicting want that is preventing the student from achieving his goal (such as wanting to socialize with peers rather than stay on task). When this happens, you may be able to help the student prioritize his wants (for example, by asking, "Which is more important to you—learning and doing well in class or socializing with your friends? Can you do both? Might there be a better time to socialize?") Or you can simply state, "Socializing during class is unacceptable. That's not what we agreed to in our Class Constitution. Let's figure out a way to replace that behavior with behavior that is going to help you achieve your goal."

Often, students will deny their behavior or try to deflect the teacher's attention to something or someone else. When that happens, avoid arguing with students. Sometimes I will surprise the student. I'll say something like, "That's funny. I saw you (or heard you) doing that. Maybe my eyes were playing tricks on me. Let's talk about what you can do that will help make sure I never have that same hallucination again." Or you can be very straightforward: "I don't want to argue with you. This is what I saw (or heard). Do you want to help solve this problem or just accept the consequence?"

Sometimes people admit their behavior but try to deflect your attention away from themselves: "Everybody else does it!" "Maria was talking to me first." "Mr. Z. lets us leave class early." "How come I'm the only one who you are talking to about this?" When that happens, you can help refocus the conversation in a few different ways. First, state, "I will talk to _____ at another time, but right now let's just focus on you." Or, "If Maria was talking and you didn't respond, would we be having this conversation? What can you do so that next time you don't get in trouble?" Or, "Maybe we need to have a faculty meeting to discuss this rule. But until it's changed, it's my responsibility to enforce it. I believe in fairness and consistency." Keep refocusing on what the student can directly control—his or her own thoughts, words, and actions.

Question 3. Is what you are doing going to get you what you want?

This is the evaluation. After the student and teacher have developed clear, compelling wants and completed an inventory of the student's behavior in terms of achieving her goals, it is essential to help the student evaluate her behavior.

When it becomes clear to the student that what she has been doing, saying, or thinking has not been helping her achieve her stated goals, she will feel a drive to change her behavior. In other words, she will be internally motivated to change. It is this internal motivation that is the key to sustained behavioral change.

Some questions that will help the student self-evaluate:

- Is what you're doing getting you what you want?

- Does what you are currently doing have a good chance of getting you what you want?

- How's it (the student's behavior) working?

- How much do you want _____? Is it worth it to you to change what you're doing?

- On a scale of 1 to 10, how important is it to achieve your goal? Would changing what you're doing (thinking, saying) help?

- If you were to give your behavior a grade in terms of achieving your want, what would you give it? What would you like to be able to give it?

Caution: This is a sensitive part of the process. If, during the "What are you doing?" part of the process, the student has already obviously made the evaluation that her behavior is not working, you can completely omit the evaluation questions. Asking students "How's that working for you?" after they have already determined that it is obviously not, may make them feel like they're being judged or criticized. In fact, be very aware of your tone of voice when asking evaluation questions. Avoid asking in a way that has the evaluation already built in ("How *that* working for you?"). For real behavioral change, it's important that the student *self*-evaluate.

Question 4. What's the plan?

Now it is time for the planning stage. For plans to be more likely to succeed, it's important that they demonstrate certain characteristics. An acronym to help you remember them is SMARTER.

A SMART plan is one that is **S**imple, **M**easurable, **A**ttainable, **R**esponsible, and that **T**eaches. For PPC, I like to add the additional letters -*er* to the end: **E**valuated and **R**epeated if necessary.

Simple. Behavioral change is hard. Starting with one simple step can lead to another. It isn't helpful for the student to consider all the self-discipline, effort, and hard work it might take to achieve his desired goal. That can be overwhelming and lead to the student giving up. Here are some examples of simple plans:

- A teacher aid agreeing to show up on time the next day.

- A student keeping his hands to himself all morning.

- A principal completing two observations that week.
- An aspiring marathoner downloading a running podcast.
- A student completing one homework assignment.

Once the student has succeeded in one small step, he will be much more motivated to continue that behavior and add to it.

Measurable. The plan is something that can be directly observed. It isn't something someone is *not* going to do, but rather what someone *is* going to do. That makes the plan measurable. In cases where people need to stop doing something, find a behavior they can use as a replacement, something that can be observed and counted.

Achievable. As the adage goes, "Nothing succeeds like success." It's critical that the first step in behavioral change be something the student can succeed at. In their enthusiasm, students sometimes make unrealistic plans. They may promise to do every homework assignment for the rest of the year. Your job is to break down the plan to one attainable step at a time that will get them closer to their long-term goal.

Responsible. This criterion of an effective plan has three parts:

- The plan itself must be responsible and socially responsible.
- It is the student's responsibility to come up with the plan.
- The only person who should be responsible for carrying out the plan is the student.

Time-Bound. At the end of a successful PPC, the student will be motivated to follow her plan. Therefore, that is when she should begin implementation. Otherwise, her motivation will soon dissipate. In the planning phase, try to achieve a commitment from students to follow-through on their plans immediately, within a day or two at the most. Otherwise, you will likely be back at the planning table.

Evaluated. It is important to follow-up with the student soon after implementation of the plan to help him evaluate its success. Look at the measurable information (the observed behavior) and evaluate whether the plan was successful or not. If it was successful, the student may plan an additional small step to improve his chances of achieving his long-term goals.

Repeated. This step may or may not be needed. If the student didn't follow through on her plan, the plan was unsuccessful, or more steps need to be taken to achieve the stated goal, then repeating PPC might be needed. The second and subsequent sessions are usually much shorter—reviewing or resetting the goals, evaluating current behavior, and creating another SMARTER plan.

To help your student make a plan, keep your questions fairly straightforward:

- What is one thing you could do today (or tomorrow) that will get you closer to your goal?
- What's your plan?
- What are your options? Which one is most likely to work for you? Which one are you more likely to follow through on?
- What can you replace (the unacceptable behavior) with?
- What are some things you can do differently?
- What is the first step?
- When? Where? How? (Be specific)

PPC

Four General Questions

What do you WANT?

What are you DOING?

Is what you are doing helping you get what you want?

Are you ready to make a PLAN?

PPC Examples

Elementary Example

On the way back from recess, Ms. Ismail overheard Savanna calling Miranda, another girl in the class, a "fat, ugly loser." Ms. Ismail decided to implement a PPC and kept Savanna back when the rest of the students went to music class. Ms. Ismail told Savanna that she overheard what Savanna said to Miranda.

At first, Savanna denied saying anything to Miranda. To set Savanna's mind at ease, Ms. Ismail said, "I'm not interested in punishing you or arguing with you. I know what I heard. What I want is for students in my class to get along. I'd like to work things out now, so it doesn't happen again."

When Savanna settled down, Ms. Ismail asked, "What is it that you wanted when you called Miranda a loser?" Savanna told her that Miranda and another friend had excluded her from jumping rope during recess. What Savanna said she wanted was for Miranda to feel as badly as Savanna did at that moment. Ms. Ismail pushed a bit harder, asking, "What is it you really want?" Soon Savanna expressed that she really just wanted friends.

When Ms. Ismail held up the mirror by asking, "Do you think calling Miranda a fat, ugly loser will help you be friends?" Savanna admitted that it wouldn't. Ms. Ismail helped Savanna make a plan to arrange a meeting with herself and Miranda at the end of the day. Savanna would apologize to Miranda and ask her if she could jump rope with her tomorrow. Ms. Ismail also helped Miranda make a "plan B" just in case Miranda said no: Take a deep breath, say, "Okay," and think, *If she doesn't want to be my friend, I'll find another.* But plan B wasn't necessary. Savanna and Miranda ended up getting along better for the rest of the year.

Secondary Example

Tye, a ninth grader, failed to hand in an important essay in English class. His teacher, Mr. Cummings, chose to use PPC and invited Tye to his room during his planning period when Tye was in study hall. Mr. Cummings set Tye at ease, having him sit next to his desk and letting him know that he wasn't in trouble. He told Tye that he noticed that his essay wasn't in his in-box, and he was concerned. He reminded Tye what he said on the first day of school: "I want all of you to be successful. I explained that I'd be here to help if you need it, but it's your job to meet me halfway and ask for help if you need it."

Tye replied that he "sucks" at writing and he didn't think he could ever write an essay that would get a passing grade. Mr. Cummings joked, "If

everyone were good at writing, I'd be out of a job." Then he asked, "What is it that you want out of English?" Tye said he'd be happy with a passing grade of 65. Instead of arguing with him or judging his low expectations for himself, Mr. Cummings asked, "Is not handing in a major essay going to help you get a 65 or hurt your chances?" Tye shrugged. Mr. Cummings delved a little deeper: "What is it that you want that's preventing you from writing this essay?" Tye said he didn't want to look stupid in front of his classmates and be embarrassed when he got his essay back with an F at the top.

Mr. Cummings flipped the student's "didn't want" into a want: "So, what you really want is to keep the respect of your peers?" Tye nodded. "If we can figure out a way for you to write that paper *and* keep the respect of your classmates, would you be interested in talking about that?" Tye said that he was. He made a plan to outline his essay that night and meet with Mr. Cummings the next day during study hall. It took Tye three revisions of his essay before his paper was acceptable, but he ended up receiving a B+ on it, and passing the year with a B- overall.

Adult Example

Corinne, a school food service worker, had frequently been coming in 10 minutes late, making it more difficult for her coworkers to serve and clean up breakfast for early arrivers. Michelle, her supervisor, decided to use PPC to address the problem, so after the lunch rush, she invited Corinne into her office. Corinne was immediately defensive: "I'm sorry, I know I was late again this morning. Please don't fire me. I'll be better from now on."

Michelle responded, "I don't want to fire you, Corinne. You're a conscientious worker. It just seems like you have a hard time getting here on time in the morning, which is a problem for me. But I believe that if there's a problem, then there must be a solution."

This set Corinne at ease. Michelle went on to ask, "How do you get along with the other members of the team?" Corinne said she really liked them. Now Michelle asked about Corinne's wants. "It seems like you all get along really well. Is that important to you?" Corinne admitted it was.

Then Michelle asked Corinne to self-evaluate: "If you continue to be 10 minutes late frequently, do you think your relationships with your coworkers will continue to be good?" Corinne was quiet, and then said no.

The conversation moved quickly from there. Michelle asked Corinne what she was currently doing that was making her late. Corinne admitted to hitting her snooze button three or four times every morning. When it came to planning, it was simple. Corinne moved her alarm clock across the room so she had to get out of bed. She was only late one more time that school year.

Using PPC with Younger Students

The PPC questioning process is very open-ended, and answering the questions requires more effort on the part of the student than on the teacher. For example, "How would your life be better if you achieved a passing grade in ELA?" requires a considerable amount of thought and conjecture. For younger students—and students with cognitive or emotional challenges—that level of analysis may be too difficult, especially if they feel stressed by the idea of being "in trouble." But you can still use the process with these students. Simply make the questions more closed and the answers more concrete in nature. Here are some examples:

- How would you like to feel about your language arts grade? What kind of grade would help you feel that way?

- Do you want to be a kind person? What kinds of things do kind people say or do? What kinds of things do they not say or do?

- Would it be better to get your work done now or during recess?

- You say you want to be good? What does that look like and sound like?

Planning is another aspect of PPC that looks different with younger children or those with limited cognitive or verbal communication skills. For older students and adults, the plan should come from the student. Younger students often struggle to come up with their own plan. It is often a "don't plan," such as "I won't blurt out during class anymore" or "I won't cut in line anymore." The teacher's role in working with these students is *not* to make the plan and force it on the student, but to offer a limited number of developmentally appropriate options and let the student choose. Once the student has heard some of the options, he may think of some on his own. Encourage that. The more ownership the student has in the plan, the more likely it is to succeed. Try not to judge his choices. If you have a concern about a student's choice, ask questions to help the student revise it.

Here are some examples of helping younger students plan:

- Some students I know have a special time set aside to do their homework. Some do their homework as soon as they get home. Others do it after dinner. Some students get up a half hour early in the morning to get homework done. Do any of those times sound good to you?

- When I'm angry, I sometimes have a hard time calming down. A few things that work for me are taking some deep breaths, writing in a journal, going to my "chill-out chair," or closing my eyes and picturing something I like to do. Do any of those ideas sound like something you could do?

- Do you want to clean out your desk now, right after lunch, or after school?

Using PPC to Analyze Success

I sometimes refer to PPC as a "plastic" process— it molds itself into many different situations. In addition to managing irresponsible behavior, PPC is a great process for ensuring continuous improvement. It might be used, for example:

By an academic department to analyze their success as a team and make a plan to be even more effective. As a leader, start off by asking team members to articulate their vision and mission as a team (What do you want?). Then ask the team to list current practices in terms of achieving the mission. (What are you doing?) The next step is crucial: Ask *evaluation* questions, such as: What practices are helping us achieve our goals? Are any holding us back? Are there gaps—areas we are ignoring? What does the data tell us? Based on that evaluation, the team would create a long-term *plan,* including short-term first steps.

By a teacher to help a class (a small group or an individual) analyze their success on a particular assessment or project. In this case, use the rubric or checklist (that the students have helped create) for that assessment as the *want*. Then lead the class (or cooperative group or student) through the checklist, having them look for specific areas where they satisfied the requirements. Next, ask the students to identify any areas of weakness. (What are you doing? Or, in this case, What did you do?) Based on that built-in evaluation, ask students to write in their agendas or learning journals what their *plan* is for the next assessment. Often, in the case of student success, their plans will include continuing to do many of the same things that helped them be successful this time and may also include some additional ideas.

By the school principal as part of a yearly professional review conference with individual teachers. As the school leader, you would sit down with teachers and discuss each item on the review (the *want*). Ask teachers for specific ways their behavior aligns with the evaluation rubric or checklist as well as areas they might improve. (What are you doing?) As the principal, you provide concurrent assessment, giving specific feedback of your observations. Based on your conversation, you and the teacher agree onan action *plan*.

By a school counselor to celebrate behavioral change and continue to help the student move forward. Use PPC as a follow-up to a previous behavior plan that the student followed. Ask the student what she said she wanted to achieve in the previous session (the *want*), then help her analyze what she's been *doing* that's been working. The *plan* will be to continue the effective behaviors and consider adding a new behavior to the plan, if needed.

If PPC is used *only* for dealing with behavioral problems, people will associate the process with "being in trouble," which may lead students to immediately shut down. But if PPC is used to analyze success as well as challenges, it will be perceived simply as a useful process for continuous improvement.

Frequently Asked Questions About PPC

How long does it take to complete PPC with a student?

As educators, time is always a concern. How long you need with a particular student can vary widely. It might take as little as three to five minutes with a highly compliant student. It could last an hour with a complicated issue. On average, however, you do not need more than 15 to 20 minutes to arrive at an effective plan, and another five minutes or so to check in and follow up with the student. While that is a considerable amount of time to spend conferencing with an individual student, it is well worth the time and effort when the positive behavioral change becomes real and sustained.

Who are good candidates for PPC?

Since time is in such short supply, it's important for teachers to choose their students wisely. It's a lot like hospital triage—many people could benefit from PPC. The two questions to ask, just as in triage, are: "Who needs it the most?" and "Who is most likely to benefit from it?"

Most educators agree the people who *need it the most* are those who are not performing well or who have frequent or chronic behavior problems. Those candidates are relatively easy to identify. It's not as easy to identify those who would *get the most benefit*—those who are most likely to be motivated toward positive change. I encourage novice teachers of PPC to choose students at first who are generally more affable and compliant. Then, having experienced success with them, gradually choose more difficult cases. Avoid working with highly resistant, belligerent, or uncommunicative students. With those students, continue to try to build a positive, trusting relationship and deal with their behavioral issues in the traditional way.

PPC is not infallible. It will work, but only if the student is willing to let it work. A joke I tell to make the point is:

Question: How many managers using PPC does it take to change a lightbulb?

Answer: Only one, but the bulb has to want to change.

So the bad news is that like any other human endeavor, PPC is fallible. But the good news is that while we can't *make* the lightbulb change, we do have a process that creates the optimum conditions under which the lightbulb will *want* to change.

What do I do if the student continues to deny or tell untruths, or is unresponsive?

While every behavioral management situation is unique, here are some useful guidelines for dealing with difficult students:

Remain calm. Don't take the student's lack of cooperation personally. Take a deep breath and stay in the front seat of your behavioral car.

Don't argue. Arguing with the student is a waste of energy and only serves to erode the relationship. Simply state the facts.

Offer another opportunity to take responsibility. Explain that you would like to work this out as a win-win, both of you getting what you want or need. But you will also need to explain that if you can't work it out this way, then you will simply administer the consequences. Then explain what those consequences will be in a nonthreatening, matter-of-fact way.

Administer fair, reasonable consequences. Again, express that if there is a next time, you'd prefer to work out the situation differently, but in this case, your only option is to dispense the consequences.

If you have reasonable doubt that the student is "guilty" of the infraction or you don't have sufficient documentation or credible witnesses, don't argue with the student. Instead, explain what the consequences would be if the behavior or act were to actually happen and perhaps use PPC to develop a plan to make sure it doesn't. This may not be perfect justice, but it gives the student a chance to change his behavior, provides clear expectations and consequences, and builds trust.

What if the student doesn't follow through on his or her plan?

People may end a session with the best intentions but still fail to complete their plan. When this happens, you have several options. One is to use PPC again, but this time focus only on revisiting benefits of achieving the desired result, explaining the consequences of continuing the current behavior, and nailing down the plan. This session will be much more brief and to the point.

Another option is simply to impose consequences. While not the ideal situation, imposing consequences teaches the person that you are fair, consistent, and mean what you say. It also teaches conformity to rules and expectations.

If the irresponsible behavior is not disrupting others, you may also choose to continue PPC over a long period of time. While you may not be able to find the time to use the whole process with students, a well-chosen question for them to think about may help initiate change. Privately and calmly tell them they don't have to answer, you just want them to think about questions like: "How important is it to you to (fill in the blank with the goal the student described in your first conference, such as get a passing grade)?" Or you can ask, "Is not doing your homework going to help you get a passing grade?" Or, "So what's your plan to pass the class?" Several times I've planted these seeds for change, and students have come in to make a plan and have followed through.

- - -

A student, Kai, was not performing at all. He attended class but was not reading, not writing, and failing quizzes and tests. He had a 17 average (out of 100) by the second week of October. I had what I felt was an exemplary PPC session with him, and he left the session enthusiastically with a SMART plan—but he did not follow it.

As a teacher of five English sections, a drama elective, a study hall, and lunch duty, I couldn't afford a lot more time with Kai. I had other students I needed to conference with. But as his teacher, I had a responsibility. As it happened, he was usually the last student to go out the door, so I had an opportunity to drop a PPC question a few times a week: "Kai, June 23—do you want to be on the stage graduating with your friends or sitting in the crowd?" "Kai, is what you're doing going to keep you on the football team?" "Kai, where do you want to be a year from now?" And *always*: "Kai, I'll be here when you are ready."

This particular "lightbulb" didn't choose to change until around the end of February. He came in with his girlfriend after school one day and said, "Mr. Erwin, I want to get outta this place. Can I still pass?" (When I heard those words, the ceiling opened up, a ray of sunshine came down, and I think I heard angels singing.) He had an entire semester to make up, but using simple plan after simple plan, he did it. And he graduated with a 74.

The last rule of the Process for Positive Change is, "Never give up on a person."

Restorative Discipline (RD): The Optimal Option

Restorative discipline (RD) is an effective approach to use when someone has hurt someone or something and is willing to make it right.[1] RD is an extension of PPC focused on adding an option to the planning component. It is based on the belief that when someone who has made a mistake and done something destructive or hurtful is given the option to take responsibility and make amends for his or her transgression, it will strengthen the offender and satisfy the target. It restores both the relationship and the classroom environment. It is meant only to be an option that is offered during the planning phase. Restorative discipline should never be forced.

Making It Right

For offending students (and their targets), taking personal responsibility in fixing the problem or making things right is a wonderful option. RD results in target satisfaction and offender accountability. It strengthens students, enhances the relationship between the teacher and the offending student, can lead to constructive dialogue between the offender and the offended, helps develop a more positive self-image for both parties, and it works. (See "Restorative Discipline: A Case Study" on page 178.)

[1] Gossen, D., 1996.

A *good* RD plan has the following characteristics:

- It provides satisfactory compensation to the target.
- It requires effort on the part of the offending student.
- It discourages future offenses.

An *excellent* RD plan also includes the following:

- It is relevant to the mistake or misbehavior, if possible.
- It is tied to a higher value or mission (for example, the touchstone values).
- It strengthens the offender, helping him see himself as someone who can fix mistakes instead of just suffering the consequences.

All successful RD sessions also have the following characteristics:

- The process is free of criticism, unhealthy guilt, and anger.
- There is no resentment or sense of overextending (or working harder than the student) on the part of the teacher.

The Offender's Plan

To make restorative discipline an option, during the planning segment of PPC, you simply ask, "Do you want to make this right?" If the answer is yes, ask, "What can you do to make it right?" The restorative plan might be apologizing to the person who was hurt in the same context in which the meanness occurred, helping the target with a subject he finds difficult, taking care of the person's cafeteria tray and trash after lunch, or any other simple act that would help make things right with the target.

It's important to let the offender come up with the plan for restitution. This puts the responsibility for making it right squarely on the offender's shoulders. If the student can't think of any way of making restitution, it's fine to provide suggestions. But if the student is simply waiting for someone else to fix the problem for him, you might dispense with restitution and instead dispense consequences.

It's never a good idea to force restitution. If you do, instead of strengthening the student and placing responsibility on him or her, it becomes

Restorative Discipline: A Case Study

One of the most successful examples of restitution I have personally experienced involved Mike, a high school senior. During study hall, he took my hall pass—a small ceramic model of Grendel (the monster from the *Beowulf* epic)—and went to the restroom. When he returned, I saw him wink to a buddy and then slam the fragile pass back on my desk, where it crumbled into a thousand little pieces. He shrugged his shoulders, said "Sorry," and started back to his desk. Not pleased, I took a deep breath, and invited him into the hallway for a brief counseling session. Here is how the conversation went:

Mike: I told you I was sorry for breaking your pass.

Mr. Erwin: I appreciate your apology, Mike. Unfortunately, I'm without a hall pass.

Mike: Can't you just use paper passes like other teachers?

Mr. Erwin: I guess I could, Mike, but I liked my Grendel pass. It's always available for students, and I don't have to stop in the middle of a lesson to write out a pass.

Mike: What are you gonna do, write me up?

Mr. Erwin: Writing you up doesn't do you or me any good. I'd rather work this out as a win-win. You don't get written up, and I get a hall pass.

Mike: How's that work?

Mr. Erwin: That's up to you. Are you willing to make it right?

Mike: I can't do ceramics, Mr. Erwin.

Mr. Erwin: That's okay. You don't have to figure it out right now. Today's Friday. Why don't you think about it over the weekend and let me know what you want to do on Monday.

Mike: Okay, Mr. E.

After our talk, I was not very optimistic that Mike would give a thought to me or Grendel over the weekend. I figured I was out a hall pass, and I couldn't really prove that Mike had done it on purpose (though I strongly suspected it). I was going to have to be satisfied with an apology. Instead, Mike was waiting for me when I arrived at school on Monday. He had a sheepish grin on his face and a brown paper bag under his arm. He reached in the bag, pulled out a small stuffed gorilla, and set it on my desk.

Mike: How's that?

Mr. Erwin: Perfect! It looks like Grendel, I have a hall pass, and no one will be able to break it. Thanks, Mike!

I wish I had a picture of the look on Mike's face when he walked out of my homeroom. He was so proud of himself for thinking of the gorilla and fixing the problem, he looked as if he'd burst. I never had a behavior problem with Mike again. In fact, Mike returned years later and brought up that incident. "Most teachers would have just yelled at me or written up a referral," he said, "but you gave me a chance to fix the problem. That's the way it oughta be."

I could have responded to Mike in many other ways—yelling, guilting, dispensing consequences, or publicly humiliating. But none of these would have resulted in Mike's taking personal responsibility, changing his behavior, improving his relationship with me, or empowering him to solve the problems that he created. Instead, they would have resulted in resistance, resentment, rebellion, or feelings of shame and guilt.

coercive and takes away all responsibility (and the good feelings that result from making things right).

RD often works well when you include the student who was the offender's target in the planning of the restitution. There are some pitfalls to this, however. For one, the target may not want to be in the same room as the offender. Afraid or embarrassed, he or she may not be in the emotional state to confront the offender. The other common pitfall is that targets—who may be humiliated or very deeply hurt—sometimes ask for too much for restitution. Involving the target in planning is a judgment call you have to make based on the students involved and what and where the incident occurred. It might be effective to meet separately with the target to discuss the restitution the offending student has suggested and try to gain the target's assent to the plan. A better time to bring the two students together might be after the restitution is made. (The Solving Circle on pages 179–180 provides a structure for that conference.)

More Examples of Restorative Discipline

The example on page 178 involves a high school student. Here is another example of an RD plan— one involving an elementary student.

Elementary Example

Chris, a second grader, had been entertaining his friends at lunch by playing with his food, and he often left a mess of spilled chocolate milk, thrown peas, or crushed cookies behind. His teacher, Ms. Gossen, led him through PPC, explaining the issue and setting him at ease by telling him she didn't become a teacher to punish kids. Still, she said, this current lunch behavior was unacceptable.

Using the concept of total behavior, she asked what he was thinking and feeling when he entertained his friends. He said he thought it was fun. She asked if he had thought about who had to clean up that mess. Then she asked, "When you think of that, how do you feel?" He said he felt "bad." She went on to begin planning RD by asking, "If you could fix the problem, would you feel better?" He said that he would.

"Since you made the cafeteria workers work harder," she said, "can you think of anything you could do to make their job easier?" He first agreed to stop playing with his food. Thinking a little longer, he asked if he could help pick up and empty trays after he finished his lunch. Ms. Gossen arranged it with the lunch monitors, and for one week, Chris helped out in the cafeteria. After that, the mess around his tray was minimal or nonexistent.

Some people criticize the RD process because nothing happens to the offender. I believe that nothing needs to happen *to* a person if something has happened *within*. Taking personal responsibility, developing and carrying out a plan—that takes a lot more effort than sitting in detention for an hour. And it strengthens the offender, satisfies the target, and restores the relationship.

The Solving Circle

The Solving Circle is a simple, practical conflict-resolution process created by William Glasser. It is a structured approach to the Process for Positive Change that can be used with students and staff to resolve conflicts and mediate disagreements. You can also teach the process so that your group (students or staff members) can resolve their own conflicts.

The Solving Circle is a six-step process, but unlike PPC, which can be fairly flexible, the Solving Circle is more formally structured. It begins with two students (as with the PPC, I am using that term to mean the recipients, or those who are engaged in the dispute) and a mediator sitting in a small circle. The mediator (teacher, counselor, assistant principal, peer mediator) starts by stating the following:

We are here today to improve this relationship. You don't have to be friends or even like each other, but for the benefit of you both and the whole class (department, team, school) you do have to get along. I'll be asking each of you some questions. Each person will have an equal amount of time to speak and be listened to. While one person is talking, there can be no interrupting. You will both be listened to. Our goal is to leave today with a plan for moving forward and not returning to the problem that led to this meeting.

Step 1. The Students Tell Their Side

Tell the students or adults you're counseling that they each have one minute to discuss what they see as the problem. Both people can use their time to complain about the other, blame her or him for the problem, say what they think the other person should be doing, or anything else. Each person is entitled to speak without interruption for a full minute. If the nonspeaking student interrupts, it is important to immediately say, "I'm sorry, you'll get your time. Right now, please listen."

Ask for a volunteer to go first or flip a coin.

Step 2. Who Can You Control?

After both people have had their minute of speaking, ask each person, "In this situation, who can you control?" After each person says, "Only myself," move on to Step 3. (A quick way to convince people of this truth is to explain that if they could control the other person, they wouldn't be in the Solving Circle right now).

Step 3. Find Something Good About the Other Person

Tell both parties, "Right now, you are not feeling very good about each other. Even so, I want each of you to tell me one good thing about the other person." This could be that the other person is good at math, really strong, funny, fun to play with, a good reader, a stylish dresser . . . anything! This sets the stage for improving the relationship.

Step 4. What Can You Do?

Tell both students to think of *one* thing they could do between now and tomorrow that would make this relationship a little better. This can be any little thing that will improve the situation. Here are some examples:

- I'll keep my hands and feet to myself during math class.
- I'll tell my friends that I was spreading a rumor.
- I'll sit on the other side of the table.

It's important that the students understand that this is something that only *they* can do, and it is not dependent on the other person doing anything first. It is simply something they will commit to in order to make things better. Thank the students for making that commitment and ask them to implement it within 24 hours. Schedule a follow-up meeting within two days.

Step 5. Follow Up

Usually, if the students have kept their commitments, by the next meeting the relationship is much improved. If it still needs improvement, repeat steps 2–5 and continue until it's no longer necessary. With kids, usually one meeting is enough. By the second meeting, things are smoothed out between them and no more mediation is necessary. For adults, two or three meetings will typically suffice.

Some teachers who use the Solving Circle in their classrooms have even drawn a literal solving circle on the floor in a part of the room. This area is designated for working things out. Others have a "peace rug" or a "connecting corner" for the same purpose. You might even consider adorning the area with a poster (see the thumbnail on page 181) to help mediators remember the process.

Just like with learning PPC, learning to use the Solving Circle—to take responsibility for our part of a relationship and to negotiate differences—has benefits for students and adults both in and out of school.

Final Thoughts

Even in schools with the ideal school climate, inevitably there will be times when behavior management is necessary due to any of a variety of reasons, including conflict, physical or relational aggression, misunderstandings, lack of impulse control, and stress- or anger-management issues. Traditional "common sense" behavior management strategies—things like rewards, isolation, punishment, and withdrawing affection—are more in line with animal training than with teaching or managing human beings. If we use what we know about human behavior instead, we will achieve more real, long-term behavioral change while simultaneously maintaining a sense of emotional safety and positive relationships—things that are essential to creating and sustaining a positive school climate.

That being said, the material in this book will reduce the need for behavior management strategies. Uniting the school community around a school touchstone, enhancing the sense of community with community meetings, prioritizing social-emotional skills, and helping everyone meet their Five Basic Human Needs inevitably lead to a more positive school climate—and the kind of community that people want to contribute their best to. What that can mean for your school, in concrete terms, is not only fewer discipline and behavior issues, but also less bullying, improved attendance, higher graduation rates, lower teacher and staff turnover, and higher student achievement. It also means that going to work feels good.

As we have all heard, a journey of a 1,000 miles begins with a single step. Improving school or classroom climate is a journey that can—and should—last years, not because it requires such a mammoth effort to change things, but because it involves a sustained effort over time. As current students move on from your school and new students come in, your work will continue—and it will continue to benefit students not only at school but in their personal and, eventually, their professional lives. It's like an extension of that 1,000-mile journey, one that is a pleasure to contemplate: your students living more fulfilled, capable, confident, successful lives, now and in the future.

The first step is up to you.

Printable Form

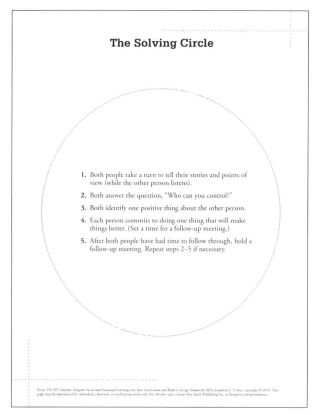

See digital content for full-size reproducible pages

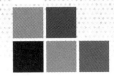

References and Resources

Adler, D. *A Picture Book of Paul Revere*. New York: Holiday House, 1997.

American Psychological Association. "Stress in America: Are Teens Adopting Adults' Stress Habits?" February 11, 2014. www.apa.org/news/press/releases/stress/2013/stress-report.pdf.

Anderson, L.H. *Thank You, Sarah: The Woman Who Saved Thanksgiving*. New York: Simon and Schuster, 2002.

Barile, J.P.; et al. "Teacher-Student Relationship Climate and School Outcomes: Implications for Educational Policy Initiatives." *Journal of Youth and Adolescence* 41(3): 256–267, March 2012.

Berger Kaye, C. *The Complete Guide to Service Learning*. Minneapolis: Free Spirit Publishing, 2010.

Binns, T.B. *The Bald Eagle*. Portsmouth, NH: Heinemann, 2001.

Booth, D. *The Dust Bowl*. Tonawanda, NY: Kids Can Press, 1996.

Bridges, R. *Through My Eyes*. New York: Scholastic, 1999.

Bright, R. *Love Monster and the Last Chocolate*. New York: Farrar, Strauss & Giroux, 2015.

Brokaw, T. *The Greatest Generation*. New York: Random House, 1998.

Brown, D.J. *Boys in the Boat (Young Readers Adaptation): The True Story of an American Team's Epic Journey to Win Gold at the 1936 Olympics*. New York: Viking, 2015.

Bryk, A.S., and Schneider, B. *Trust in Schools: A Core Resource for Improvement*. New York: Russell Sage Foundation, 2002.

Burns, R. "To a Mouse." In *Selected Poems*. New York: Penguin Books, 1993.

Cherry, L. *The Great Kapok Tree: A Tale of the Amazon Rainforest*. Orlando, FL: Harcourt, 1990.

Christian, S., and Tubesing, N.L. *Instant Icebreakers: 50 Powerful Catalysts for Group Interaction and High-Impact Learning*. Duluth, MN: Whole Person Associates, 1997.

Cohen, J., and Geist, V.K. "Research." National School Climate Center. January 2010. www.schoolclimate.org/climate/documents/policy/sc-brief-v1.pdf.

Collins. S. The Hunger Games Trilogy. New York: Scholastic, 2014.

Craigen, J., and Ward, C. *What's This Got to Do with Anything?* San Clemente, CA: Kagan Publishing, 2004.

Craighead George, J. *My Side of the Mountain*. New York: Dutton, 1959.

Creech, S. *Walk Two Moons*. New York: HarperCollins, 1994.

Curtis, C.P. *Bud, Not Buddy*. New York: Yearling, 1999.

da Costa Nunez, R. *Saily's Journey*. New York: Institute for Children, Poverty & Homelessness, 2002.

Dadey, D. *King of the Kooties*. New York: Walker Publishing Company, 1999.

Davis, S. and Nixon, C. *Youth Voice Project*. Spring 2010. njbullying.org/documents/YVPMarch2010.pdf.

Dickens, C. *A Christmas Carol*. New York: Global Classics, 2014.

Doll, J.J., et al. "Understanding Why Students Drop Out of High School, According to Their Own Reports: Are They Pushed or Pulled, or Do They Fall Out? A Comparative Analysis of Seven Nationally Representative Studies." *SAGE Open*. Nov. 2013. sgo.sagepub.com/content/3/4/2158244013503834.

Dryfoos, J.G. "The Prevalence of Problem Behaviors: Implications for Programs." In *Enhancing Children's Wellness: Healthy Children 2010* edited by Roger P. Weissberg et al. Thousand Oaks, CA: Sage Publications, 1997.

Durlak, J.A., et al. "The Impact of Enhancing Students' Social and Emotional Learning: A Meta-Analysis of School-Based Universal Interventions." *Child Development*, 82(1): 405–432, 2011.

Eaton, D.K., et al. "Youth Risk Behavior Surveillance—United States, 2007." *MMWR Surveillance Summaries*, 57(SS04), 1–131, 2008. www.cdc.gov/mmwr/preview/mmwrhtml/ss5704a1.htm

Eccles, J.S., et al. "Negative Effects of Traditional Middle Schools on Students' Motivation." *Elementary School Journal* 93(5): 553–574, 1993.

Erwin, J.C. *The Classroom of Choice: Giving Students What They Need and Getting What You Want.* Alexandria, VA: ASCD, 2004.

Erwin, J.C. *Inspiring the Best in Students.* Alexandria, VA: ASCD, 2010.

Fitzgerald, F.S. *The Great Gatsby.* New York: Scribner's, 1925.

Fritz, J. *You Want Women to Vote, Lizzie Stanton?* New York: Penguin Books, 1995.

Frost, R. *The Poetry of Robert Frost: The Collected Poems, Complete and Unabridged.* New York: Henry Holt and Co., 1969.

Frost, R. *Robert Frost's Poems.* New York: Simon & Schuster, 1971.

Glasser, W. *Choice Theory: A New Psychology of Personal Freedom.* New York: HarperCollins, 1998.

Glasser, W. *Counseling with Choice Theory.* New York: HarperCollins, 2000.

Glasser, W., and Glasser, C. *Getting Together and Staying Together: Solving the Mystery of Marriage.* New York: Harper Perennial, 2000.

Goodenow, C., and Grady, K.E. "The Relationship of School Belonging and Friends' Values to Academic Motivation Among Urban Adolescent Students." *Journal of Experimental Education* 62(1): 60–71, 1993.

Gossen, D. *Restitution: Restructuring School Discipline.* Chapel Hill, NC: New View Publications, 1996.

Graziano, C. "Public Education Faces a Crisis in Teacher Retention." *Edutopia.* Feb. 9, 2005. www.edutopia.org /new-teacher-burnout-retention.

Green, J. *The Fault in Our Stars.* New York: Penguin Books, 2012.

Harness, C. *The Amazing Impossible Erie Canal.* New York: Simon & Schuster, 1995.

Hassett, A., and Hassett, J. *Cat Up a Tree.* New York: Houghton Mifflin, 1998.

Hawes, A. "Jungle Gyms: The Evolution of Animal Play." *ZooGoer,* 25(1), 1996. matrix.msu.edu/hst/hst324/media /zoogoer.pdf.

Henton, M. *Adventure in the Classroom: Using Adventure to Strengthen Learning and Build a Community of Life-Long Learners.* Dubuque, IA: Kendall Hunt Publishing Co., 1996.

Herr, M. *Dispatches.* New York: Vintage Books, 1977.

Hesse, K. *Just Juice.* New York: Scholastic, 1998.

Hiaasen, C. *Flush.* New York: Yearling, 2005.

Hinton, S.E. *The Outsiders.* New York: Viking Press, 1967.

Hoose, P., and Hoose, H. *Hey, Little Ant.* Berkeley, CA: Tricycle Press, 1998.

Humphrey, S.M. *Dare to Dream: 25 Extraordinary Lives.* Amherst, NY: Prometheus Books, 2005.

Jensen, E. *Teaching with Poverty in Mind: What Being Poor Does to Kids' Brains and What Schools Can Do About It.* Alexandria, VA: ASCD, 2009.

Jensen, E. *Teaching with the Brain in Mind.* Alexandria, VA: ASCD, 1998.

Kagan, S., and Kagan, M. *Kagan Cooperative Learning.* San Clemente, CA: Kagan Publishing, 1994.

Kamma, A. *If You Were at the First Thanksgiving.* New York: Scholastic, 2001.

Kesey, K. *One Flew Over the Cuckoo's Nest.* New York: Penguin Books, 1962.

King, M.L. *I Have a Dream.* New York: Random House, 1991.

Knowles, J. *A Separate Peace.* New York: Scribner, 1987.

Kohn, A. *Punished by Rewards: The Trouble with Gold Stars, Incentive Plans, A's, Praise, and Other Bribes.* New York: Houghton Mifflin, 1993.

Koja, K. *Buddha Boy.* New York: Farrar, Straus & Giroux, 2003.

Krull, K. *Harvesting Hope: The Story of Cesar Chavez.* San Diego: Harcourt, 2003.

Lasky, K. *A Voice of Her Own: The Story of Phillis Wheatley, Slave Poet.* Somerville, MA: Candlewick Press, 2012.

Lawrence, J. *Harriet and the Promised Land.* New York: Aladdin Paperbacks, 1993.

Learning Standards for Science, Copyright 1996, New York State Education Department, used with permission. www.p12.nysed.gov/ciai/mst/pub/elecoresci.pdf.

Learning Standards for Social Studies, Copyright 1996, New York State Education Department, used with permission. www.p12.nysed.gov/ciai/socst/pub/sscore1.pdf.

Lee, H. *To Kill a Mockingbird.* New York: Grand Central Publishing, 1960.

Lee, J., and Shute, V.J. "Personal and Social-Contextual Factors in K–12 Academic Performance: An Integrative Perspective on Student Learning." *Educational Psychologist,* 45(3): 185–202, 2010.

Leedy, L. *How Humans Make Friends.* New York: Holiday House, 1996.

Lilly, M. *Quakers in Early America.* New York: Rourke Publishing, 2009.

London, J. *The Call of the Wild.* New York: Simon and Brown, 2012.

Loehr, P. "Intentionally Creating a Consistent School Culture Focused on Principles of High Achievement" research paper. Buffalo, NY: SUNY College at Buffalo Press, 2011.

MacGregor, M. *Building Everyday Leadership in All Kids.* Minneapolis, MN: Free Spirit Publishing, 2013.

MacGregor, M. *Building Everyday Leadership in All Teens.* Minneapolis, MN: Free Spirit Publishing, 2015.

MacNeil, A.J., et al. "The Effects of School Culture and Climate on Student Achievement." *International Journal of Leadership in Education* 12(1): 73–84, 2009.

Mattick, L. *Finding Winnie: The True Story of the World's Most Famous Bear.* New York: Little, Brown and Co., 2015.

McDonald. M. *Judy Moody Saves the World!* Somerville, MA: Candlewick Press, 2002.

McDonough, Y.Z. *The Life of Benjamin Franklin: An American Original.* New York: Henry Holt and Co., 2006.

McGovern, A. *. . . If You Sailed on the Mayflower in 1620.* New York: Scholastic, 1969.

Mikaelsen, B. *Touching Spirit Bear.* New York: HarperCollins, 2001.

Piper, W. *The Little Engine That Could.* New York: Platt & Munk Publishers, 1976.

Myers, W.D. *Malcolm X: A Fire Burning Brightly.* New York: Amistad, 2000.

O'Dell, S. *Island of the Blue Dolphins.* New York: Houghton Mifflin, 1988.

Palacio, R.J. *Wonder.* New York: Alfred A. Knopf, 2012.

Park, L.S. *A Long Walk to Water.* New York: Clarion Books, 2010.

Parker, D.C., et al. "Comparison of Correlates of Classroom Behavior Problems with and without a School-Wide Character Education Program." *Psychology in the Schools,* 47(8): 817–827, 2010.

Pink, D.H. *Drive: The Surprising Truth About What Motivates Us.* New York: Riverhead Books, 2009.

Pfister, M. *The Rainbow Fish.* New York: North-South Books, 1992.

Raphael, E. *Sacajawea: The Journey West.* New York: Scholastic, 1994.

Rappaport, D. *The Flight of Red Bird: The Life of Zitkala-Sa.* New York: Puffin Books, 1997.

Rawls, W. *Where the Red Fern Grows.* New York: Random House, 1961.

Robertson, J. *The Untold Civil War: Exploring the Human Side of War.* Washington, DC: National Geographic, 2011.

Rockwell, A. *They Called Her Molly Pitcher.* New York: Dragonfly Books, 2002.

Rohnke, K.E. *Silver Bullets: A Guide to Initiative Problems, Adventure Games, and Trust Activities.* Hamilton, MA: Project Adventure, 1984.

Rowling, J.K. *Harry Potter and the Sorcerer's Stone.* New York: Scholastic, 1997.

Santella, A. *Lewis and Clark.* New York: Scholastic, 2001.

Schmidt, A. *Hannah's Journey.* New York: Love Inspired Historicals, 2011.

Seuss, Dr. *The Lorax.* New York: Random House, 1971.

Shakespeare, W. *The Oxford Shakespeare: The Complete Works.* Oxford, England: Oxford University Press, 2005.

Silverstein, S. *The Giving Tree.* New York: HarperCollins, 1992.

Smith, B. *A Tree Grows in Brooklyn.* New York: HarperCollins, 1947.

Snodgrass, M.E. *Beating the Odds: A Teen Guide to 75 Superstars Who Overcame Adversity.* Westport, CT: Greenwood Press, 2008.

Spinelli, J. *The Library Card.* New York: Scholastic, 1997.

Steinbeck, J. *Of Mice and Men.* New York: Penguin Books, 1965.

Steinbeck, J. *The Grapes of Wrath.* New York: Penguin Books, 1967.

Szadokierski, I., et al. "Effectiveness of a Theoretically-Based Character Education Program." Unpublished research findings, 2010. Used with permission. www.smartcharacterchoices.com/pdfs/character educationeffectiveness-manuscript.pdf.

Taylor, R.D., et al. "Promoting Positive Youth Development Through School-Based Social and Emotional Learning Interventions: A Meta-Analysis of Follow-Up Effects." *Child Development,* 88(4): 1156–1171, 2017.

Terkel, S. *Working: People Talk About What They Do All Day and How They Feel About What They Do.* New York: The New Press, 1974.

Thapa, A., et al. "School Climate Research Summary." National School Climate Center. August 2012. www.school climate.org/climate/documents/policy/sc-brief-v3.pdf.

Twain, M. *The Adventures of Huckleberry Finn.* New York: Dover Publications, 1994.

Weissberg, R.P., et al. "Social and Emotional Learning: Past, Present, and Future." In *Handbook of Social and Emotional Learning* edited by Joseph A. Durlak et al. New York: Guilford Press, 2015.

Yousafzai, M. *I Am Malala.* New York: Little, Brown and Co., 2013.

Zemach, M. *The Little Red Hen: An Old Story.* New York: Farrar, Straus & Giroux, 1983.

Zinn, H. *A People's History of the United States.* New York: HarperCollins, 2003.

Index

About the Author

Jonathan C. Erwin, M.A., has been a professional musician, secondary English teacher, professional development specialist, college professor, and director of training and curriculum for a federally funded character education program. His previous books include *The Classroom of Choice* (ASCD, 2004) and *Inspiring the Best in Students* (ASCD, 2010). Jon is currently an independent educational consultant, a senior faculty member of the William Glasser Institute, and a trained HealthRHYTHMS facilitator. Jon's work focuses on providing research-based teaching, managing, counseling, and training approaches that appeal to intrinsic motivation and help children, adolescents, and adults develop physically, intellectually, emotionally, and socially. A martial arts enthusiast, Jon has earned a second degree black belt in karate and a first degree black belt in Tae Kwon Do. He lives in western New York.

"Emotional Intelligence in ELA and Social Studies:
Integrating Social-Emotional Learning into the
Curriculum in Ways That Satisfy State Standards,"
a free webinar with Jonathan C. Erwin, M.A.
Find it at **freespirit.com/webinar**.

Digital versions of all reproducible forms can be downloaded
at **freespirit.com/sel-forms**. Use password **care**.

Other Great Resources from Free Spirit

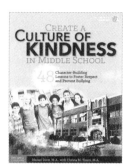

Create a Culture of Kindness in Middle School
48 Character-Building Lessons to Foster Respect and Prevent Bullying
by Naomi Drew, M.A., with Christa M. Tinari, M.A.

For middle school educators.
272 pp.; PB; 8½" x 11"; includes digital content.

No Kidding About Bullying
126 Ready-to-Use Activities to Help Kids Manage Anger, Resolve Conflicts, Build Empathy, and Get Along (Updated Edition)
by Naomi Drew, M.A.

For educators, grades 3–6.
304 pp.; PB; 8½" x 11"; includes digital content.

Boost Emotional Intelligence in Students
30 Flexible Research-Based Activities to Build EQ Skills (Grades 5–9)
by Maurice J. Elias, Ph.D., and Steven E. Tobias, Psy.D.

For teachers and counselors, grades 5–9.
192 pp.; PB; 8½" x 11"; includes digital content.

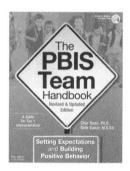

The PBIS Team Handbook
Setting Expectations and Building Positive Behavior (Revised and Updated Edition)
by Char Ryan, Ph.D., and Beth Baker, M.S.Ed.

For K–12 PBIS coaches and team members, administrators, and other school staff members.
216 pp.; PB; 8½" x 11"; includes digital content.

Free PLC/Book Study Guide
freespirit.com/PLC

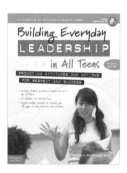

Building Everyday Leadership in All Teens
Promoting Attitudes and Actions for Respect and Success (Revised & Updated Edition)
by Mariam G. MacGregor, M.S.

For teachers and youth workers, grades 6–12.
240 pp.; PB; 8½" x 11"; includes digital content

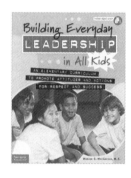

Building Everyday Leadership in All Kids
An Elementary Curriculum to Promote Attitudes and Actions for Respect and Success
by Mariam G. MacGregor, M.S.

For teachers, grades K–6.
176 pp.; PB; 8½" x 11"; includes digital content

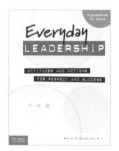

Everyday Leadership (Student Workbook)
Attitudes and Actions for Respect and Success
by Mariam G. MacGregor, M.S., foreword by Barry Z. Posner, Ph.D.

Can be used alone or with the curriculum guide *Building Everyday Leadership in All Teens.*
144 pp., PB, 7" x 9".

End Peer Cruelty, Build Empathy
The Proven 6Rs of Bullying Prevention That Create Inclusive, Safe, and Caring Schools
by Michele Borba, Ed.D.

For administrators, teachers, counselors, youth leaders, bullying prevention teams, and parents of children in grades K–8.
288 pp; PB; 7¼" x 9¼"; includes digital content.

Free PLC/Book Study Guide
freespirit.com/PLC

Interested in purchasing multiple quantities and receiving volume discounts?
Contact edsales@freespirit.com or call 1.800.735.7323 and ask for Education Sales.

Many Free Spirit authors are available for speaking engagements, workshops, and keynotes.
Contact speakers@freespirit.com or call 1.800.735.7323.

For pricing information, to place an order, or to request a free catalog, contact:

Free Spirit Publishing Inc. • 6325 Sandburg Road, Suite 100 • Minneapolis, MN 55427-3674
toll-free 800.735.7323 • local 612.338.2068 • fax 612.337.5050
help4kids@freespirit.com • freespirit.com